exploring

FLASH MX 2004

James L. Mohler

THOMSON

DELMAR LEARNING Australia Canada Mexico Singapore Spain United Kingdom United States

THOMSON

DELMAR LEARNING

Exploring Flash MX 2004

James L. Mohler

Vice President, Technology and Trades, BSU
Alar Elken

Editorial Director
Sandy Clark

Senior Acquisitions Editor
James Gish

Development Editor
Jaimie Wetzel

Marketing Director
Cyndi Eichelman

Channel Manager
Fair Huntoon

Marketing Coordinator
Mark Pierro

Production Director
Mary Ellen Black

Production Manager
Larry Main

Production Coordinator
Dawn Jacobson

Art/Design
Thomas Stover

Technology Project Manager
Kevin Smith

Editorial Assistant:
Marissa Maiella

Series Cover Design
Steven Brower

Cover Image
Operators Are Standing By, Oil on Canvas, @ David Arsenault

NOTICE TO THE READER

Publisher does not warrant or guarantee any of the products described herein or perform any independent analysis in connection with any of the product information contained herein. Publisher does not assume, and expressly disclaims, any obligation to obtain and include information other than that provided to it by the manufacturer.

The reader is expressly warned to consider and adopt all safety precautions that might be indicated by the activities herein and to avoid all potential hazards. By following the instructions contained herein, the reader willingly assumes all risks in connection with such instructions.

The publisher makes no representation or warranties of any kind, including but not limited to, the warranties of fitness for particular purpose or merchantability, nor are any such representations implied with respect to the material set forth herein, and the publisher takes no responsibility with respect to such material. The publisher shall not be liable for any special, consequential, or exemplary damages resulting, in whole or part, from the reader's use of, or reliance upon, this material.

contents

contents

preface

preface

INTENDED AUDIENCE

You might wonder why I'd set out to write yet another book on Flash, given the slew of books that already exists for Macromedia Flash. The primary purpose of this book is to provide a succinct text that covers the "need-to-know" information in a concise manner. Throughout this book you will find condensed information about the Flash software with a concentration of information that beginning web design students need to know. I don't delve into every detail or facet of the software, because often books that follow this path provide so many diatribes that students quickly loose interest. Rather, this text focuses on the critical features and functions and their use.

The primary audience for this book is the student at an educational institution with a two- or four-year focus. I realize that in most of these settings Flash may be just one small cog in an overall approach to web design and development. Thus, this book is intended to adequately provide enough content for a beginning course in web development.

FLASH AND EMERGING TRENDS

There is no doubt that Flash is here to stay—and that it has infiltrated almost every web developer's toolkit over the last couple of years. Although there still may be some negatives to using Flash, these are much fewer than when Flash first emerged. In addition, with proper education and training a designer can easily overcome the minor limitations and negative aspects that still haunt those of us who choose to use Flash.

As for trends related to Flash, the biggest is its growing complexity. Indeed, Macromedia has focused most of their time on extending the ActionScript language and trying to compete with higher-end visual programming tools. As such, the tool now offers a two-tier approach: a defined path for both designer and programmer. The tools to facilitate communication and operation between these two parts of the development equation will likely grow stronger in future versions.

Flash has really had little competition over its short lifetime. Adobe tried to compete in this arena, but the effort was unfortunately "too little, too late." Flash's foothold was too well established. However, one thing to keep an eye on is the upcoming Microsoft technology associated with Longhorn—as of the moment, dubbed Sparkle. Although no one can really see the effect Sparkle will have in this arena, it is certain that it will cause Flash to improve in a more rapid fashion. I am allowing myself some conjecture here, but students should nonetheless be made aware of the possibility of a true competitor to Flash emerging quite soon.

BACKGROUND OF THIS TEXT

As previously stated, this book is intended to provide a "need-to-know" approach to Flash. Whereas other books discuss every feature and function of the software, my approach here is to boil it all down to the most important points and place the emphasis there. Information found in this book is a compendium of my experience with Flash since about version 3 of the software. As well, this information is tempered through the eyes of someone with much classroom experience (about 10 years) and classical training in instructional design, as exhibited by my recognition among my peers and the degrees I hold.

I believe this book meets a need within the education market. Because most of us educators likely "make due" with a volume that is either overkill (which often leads many students to throw their hands up in the air, and believe they will never learn to use a tool) or too skimpy (which often yields the same frustration as the former, as well as questions along the lines of "Why did you make us buy this book?"), in this book I have attempted to hit the right balance, always asking myself the question, "Is this important at this stage for the student to know?" Only time will tell whether I have met my goal, but my aim in this book has remained constantly focused on that question.

TEXTBOOK ORGANIZATION

The first 10 chapters of this book focus on "asset building"; that is, designing, creating, and integrating all of the various pieces of base multimedia elements into Flash files. The next three chapters focus on animation—the heart of Flash's capabilities. Then the concluding two chapters focus on scripting and publishing. The following sections provide brief summaries of each chapter's focus and purpose.

Chapter 1: Overview and Tour

The opening chapter provides an introduction and tour of the Flash interface. The reader becomes familiar with the basic interface components and customizing the Flash GUI to their liking.

Chapter 2: Color

In Flash, primary to any creation is the definition of colors that can be used when drawing and animating. Thus, this chapter introduces the reader to the basics of color in Flash, including defining RGB color palettes, creation of individual color swatches, and the rudiments of how RGB and HLS color work.

Chapter 3: Selection and Drawing Tools

With an understanding of how to define colors, the reader moves on to learn about the variety of drawing tools within Flash. Because

Flash provides both natural drawing tools and typical Bezier tools, similarities and differences between these two modes of drawing are highlighted.

Chapter 4: Painting Tools

Although Flash is a vector environment similar to FreeHand or Illustrator, it nevertheless provides some tools that are typical of raster editors. Unlike other vector tools, Flash behaves as a hybrid environment integrating both vector- and raster-type tools for graphic creation. This chapter provides an overview of the painting tools available in Flash.

Chapter 5: Editing, Transformations, and Importing

There are times when a designer may find it easier to create graphic components in other programs and then import them into Flash—particularly if the designer has more experience with other programs. Similarly, assets may already exist in another form and rather than recreating them in Flash importing may be desired. This chapter combines the topics of editing and importing material in Flash.

Chapter 6: Text

An important part of any multimedia creation is working with text. This chapter discusses both the aesthetic and technical implications of using type within Flash. From the aesthetic viewpoint, the basics of typography in design are discussed. Concerning the technical implications, the chapter covers font usage and the various types of text elements that can be integrated in Flash.

Chapter 7: Bitmaps

Although Flash's primary focus is on vector graphics, it can utilize bitmap data just as easily. This chapter discusses the important issues related to preparing and importing bitmaps, while also discussing the limitations of using them in Flash.

Chapter 8: Sound

Sound can sometimes be a difficult element to integrate. This chapter provides a "learner friendly" overview of how to prepare and utilize sound in Flash. It discusses issues of timing and sequencing, as well as how to create files that are savvy to various bandwidth requirements.

Chapter 9: Video

Flash can integrate video into movies so that they may be more easily distributed over the Web. This chapter focuses on the fundamental concerns with video files and how they can be incorporated into Flash using the Video wizard.

Chapter 10: Symbols and Libraries

A key aspect of Flash movies is the use of reusable assets by way of something called symbols. This chapter opens with how symbols are created and used. Following an understanding of symbols, the reader must also understand libraries (collections of symbols within a Flash file) and how libraries can be used. This chapter delves into accessing a library and manipulating its symbols, as well as how libraries can share their symbols. Additionally, it covers how libraries themselves can be used across multiple movies via sharing.

Chapter 11: Keyframe Animation

Over time Flash has become known as the best way to distribute animations over the Web. Aside from its unique tweening capabilities, Flash permits the creation of traditional animation, sometimes called cel animation. As an introduction to creating animation in Flash, Chapter 11 provides the basics of animation creation by leading the reader through the creation of cel animation.

Chapter 12: Motion Tweening

Continuing the topic of animation, this chapter introduces the reader to motion tweening—the most commonly used type of animation in Flash. The reader learns how to animate position, size, orientation, and color effect using motion tweening.

Chapter 13: Shape Tweening

This final chapter on animation introduces shape tweening; that is, the lesser-used (compared with motion tweening) but important function of morphing of vector componentry from one shape, size, or color to another.

Chapter 14: ActionScript, Behaviors, and Interactivity

Chapter 14 provides in introduction to the use of actions to add interactivity to Flash movies. It covers the use of the Actions panel, as well as many of the basic things designers want to know how to do.

Chapter 15: Publishing Your Movies

The book concludes with an overview of various methods of publishing movies. This chapter discusses methods of distributing Flash web-ready SWF files, as well as the creation and use of projector files.

FEATURES

The following are salient features of the text and the book.

- Learning goals are clearly stated at the beginning of each chapter, and each chapter ends with a chapter summary that encapsulates the content of the chapter.

- The book has been written to meet the needs of design students and professionals for a visually oriented introduction to basic design principles and the functions and tools of Flash.

- Client projects involve tools and techniques a designer might encounter on the job to complete a project.

- A full-color insert provides stunning examples of design results that can be achieved using Flash.

- An In Review section is found at the end of each chapter to quiz a reader's understanding and retention of the material covered.

- Exploring On Your Own sections offer suggestions and sample lessons for further exploration and study of content covered in each chapter.

- A companion CD-ROM found at the back of the book contains free trial software.

HOW TO USE THIS TEXT

The sections that follow describe text elements found throughout the book and how they are intended to be used.

Charting Your Course and Goals

Each chapter begins with the sections *Charting Your Course* (a brief summary of the intent of the chapter) and *Goals* (a list of learning points). These sections describe the competencies the reader should achieve upon working through and understanding the chapter.

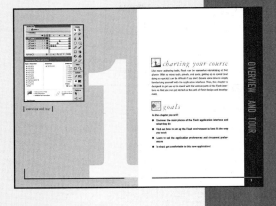

Don't Go There

Material with the heading *Don't Go There* appears throughout the text, highlighting common pitfalls and explaining ways to avoid them.

DON'T GO THERE

In the prior process, you will note that I had you create two swatches of the same color with varying alphas. This was purposeful. If you blend two different colors with two different alphas some pretty strange things can happen. Typically you end up with some haloing effects—where there are hints of one or the other color in the transparency. To avoid haloing, anytime you are creating a gradient that gradates Alpha, use the exact same RGB values in the two chips.

Try This

Boxed sections entitled *Try This* present tasks for the reader to experiment with. Following along with these will give the reader hands-on experience in working with Flash.

TRY THIS

Try creating various linear gradients and saving them as swatches. Try doing something real-world. For example, try creating a multicolor gradient that could be used to simulate the look of highly reflective metal (add a lot of sharp whites and blacks). Or, try to add a simulated horizon line (integrate some blue for a sky and brown for the gr

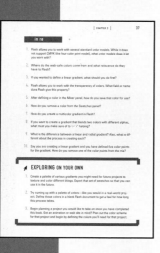

In Review and Exploring On Your Own

In Review and Exploring On Your Own are sections found at the end of each chapter. These allow the reader to assess his or her understanding of the chapter. The section "On Your Own" contains exercises that reinforce chapter material through further practical application.

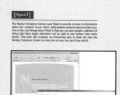

Adventures in Design

These two-page spreads contain client assignments showing readers how to approach a design project using the tools and design concepts taught in the book.

Color Insert

The color insert presents work that can be achieved when working with Macromedia Flash.

THE LEARNING PACKAGE

E.Resource

An instructor's guide on CD is available to assist instructors in planning and implementing their instructional programs. It includes sample syllabi for using this book in either an 11- or 15-week semester. It also provides answers to the end-of-chapter review questions, PowerPoint slides highlighting the main topics, and additional instructor resources. Order Number: 1401843921.

ABOUT THE AUTHOR

James L. Mohler is a Senior Research Scientist and Associate Professor at Purdue University. He has authored or coauthored over 20 texts, presented over 40 papers and workshops, written for 25 academic and trade publications, and taught over 15 different courses at Purdue, ranging in size from 22 to over 400 students. His teaching experience spans the entire range of post-secondary education, including undergraduate and graduate courses.

Currently James is working with the Information Technology group at Purdue, leading a group of highly talented artists and programmers who are building Purdue's next-generation web presence. He is also serving as the SIGGRAPH 2005 Conference Chair, where he will be assembling a diverse team of volunteers, contractors, and contributors that will be responsible for the largest computer graphics and interactive techniques conference in the world.

ACKNOWLEDGMENTS

I would like to especially thank the wonderful team at Delmar for all of their support on this book. The author is only a part of a much larger team, and thanks go to acquisitions editor Jim Gish, developmental editor Jaimie Wetzel, production editor Tom Stover, production coordinator Dawn Jacobson, and editorial assistant Marissa Maiella. Thanks also go to Carol Leyba for composition and Daril Bentley for copyediting. Finally, I would like to thank my wonderful wife Lisa, who has been patient and loving while I have spent endless hours in the office. Delmar Learning and the author would also like to thank the following reviewers for their valuable suggestions and expertise.

SHAWN BOECKMAN
Chair, Multimedia and Web Design Department
Art Institutes International Minnesota
Minneapolis, Minnesota

MARC HESS
Chair, Multimedia Department
Westchester Business Institute
White Plains, New York

DON MILLARD
Director, Academy of Electronic Media
Rensselaer Polytechnic Institute
Troy, New York

PETER SKORO
Visual Communication Department
Dakota County Technical College
Rosemount, Minnesota

QUESTIONS AND FEEDBACK

Delmar Learning and the author welcome your questions and feedback. If you have suggestions you think others would benefit from, please let us know and we will try to include them in the next edition. To send us your questions and/or feedback, you can contact the publisher at:

Delmar Learning
Executive Woods
5 Maxwell Drive
Clifton Park, NY 12065
Attn: Graphic Arts Team
800-998-7498

Or James Mohler at:
Purdue University
Purdue West Plaza, Suite D
1404 W. State Street
West Lafayette, IN 47907
jlmohler@purdue.edu

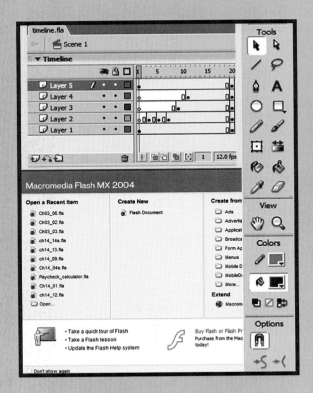

overview and tour

charting your course

Like many authoring tools, Flash can be somewhat intimidating at first glance. With so many tools, panels, and parts, getting up to speed (and doing so quickly) can be difficult if you don't devote some time to simply familiarizing yourself with the application interface. Thus, this chapter is designed to get you up to speed with the various parts of the Flash interface so that you can get started on the path of Flash design and development.

 goals

In this chapter you will:

- Discover the main pieces of the Flash application interface and what they do

- Find out how to set up the Flash environment to best fit the way you work

- Learn to set the application preferences and document preferences

- In short: get comfortable in this new application!

GETTING AROUND

Over the past couple of years, Macromedia has strived to make their applications look more and more alike—which is intended to make learning them easier due to their similarities. If you are familiar with other Macromedia applications you will probably be able to draw upon past experiences to help you with your work in Flash. However, if you don't have prior experience that is okay, too, as we will start from ground zero as we learn about Flash.

The Start Page

To make things easier for beginners, Macromedia has added a Start page to the Flash interface, as shown in figure 1-1. This page provides access to most of the things you might want to do when you first start the Flash application. It gives you access to the most recent documents you have worked with, lets you start new documents from the default setup or from a preexisting template, and it lets you select and access interactive items such as the Flash quick tour. If you click on the option beneath the Create New heading, labeled Flash Document, you are led to the Flash interface, where you actually begin to work with the application.

figure | 1-1

The Start page gives you quick access to options for starting your work session.

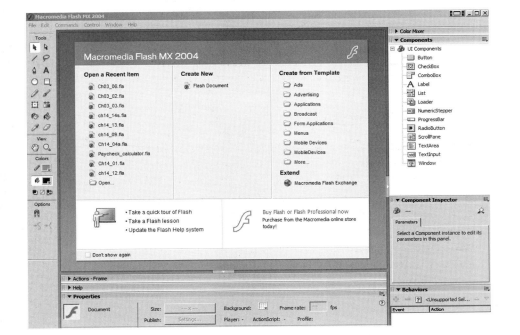

The Flash Interface

Figure 1-2 shows the basic Flash interface. Like all applications there are some things that are quite common (menus, window controls, and so on), yet there are four main pieces we should acknowledge, as they form the heart of the Flash user interface. These are the stage, the timeline, the toolbar, and the panels.

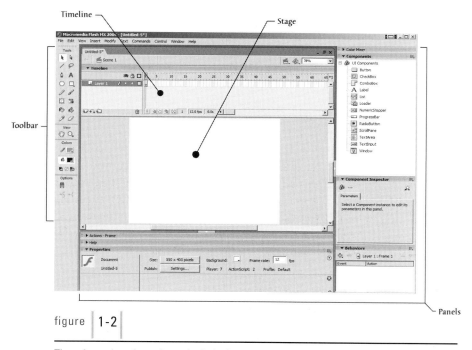

figure | 1-2

The primary interface pieces include the stage, timeline, toolbar, and panels.

All the World's a Stage...

As in real life, Flash's stage is where you define what your audience is going to see when they play your movies. You use the stage to define the screen positions for objects as they "enter and exit" the stage. Note that the "entering and exiting" can occur in more ways than can be counted. Objects can be made to move into position, fade into position, "cut" into position, and so forth. We'll get into more of these techniques in later chapters. The thing to realize is that when you create Flash movies you do your visual design activities on the stage.

Controlling Time

As you probably know, one of Flash's strengths is animation and thus some part of the interface must enable you to work with the element of time. And that is what the timeline allows you to do.

The timeline, shown in figure 1-3, is arranged as a progression of frames in which you define the content that will be displayed over time. The easy way to think of it is that the stage allows you to work with spatial information (what you see), whereas the timeline lets you work with temporal information (when you see it). When you create movies, you interchangeably work with the stage and timeline. You pick a point in time using the timeline and define the content that will be displayed at that time using the stage.

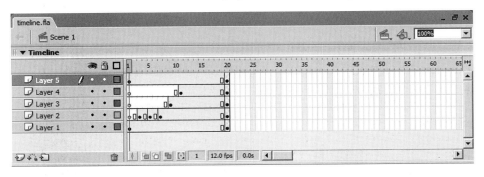

figure | 1-3

The timeline allows you to control when things appear on the stage.

At this point I should acknowledge that there is much more granularity to the timeline and the process of creating movies than just saying "pick a point in time and define your content." As we progress through subsequent chapters, we'll delve into the details more. For now, I just want you to understand the Gestalt view: the stage is used to control the spatial, whereas the timeline is used to control the temporal.

Tools

As you can likely guess, the toolbar (shown in figure 1-4) contains the graphic creation and editing tools Flash provides. Basically, all of the tools in the toolbar are for working with spatial content (i.e., graphical content) on the stage. There are specialized tools for working with the timeline, but they are not located in the toolbar; they are scattered in other locations, as you will see later.

Concerning the toolbar tools, if you have worked with other computer-based illustration or imaging packages you'll likely be able to decipher some of them using what you already know. But be forewarned that graphics in Flash don't exactly work like programs such as Illustrator, FreeHand, or Photoshop, even though similar tools exist in Flash's toolbar. Flash has some very unique features (or idiosyncrasies, depending on how you look at it). It behaves like a hybrid of an illustration and an imaging application. At this point we don't want to dive quite that deep yet, but we will deal with this issue later.

Panels, Panels, and More Panels

Undoubtedly Flash is a very robust package, allowing you to create almost anything you can imagine as it relates to multimedia. Quite honestly, its robustness is one of the reasons it is so popular. But to do all this, there are a lot of options and optional settings you can tinker and fiddle with. And because there are so many options for so many things in Flash, it is just plain impossible to fit them all into the Flash interface such that you can view them at the same time. That is what panels are all about.

Panels give you a way to selectively view certain sets of controls or features when and where you need them as you're working. If you're working on a graphic and need to align three or four objects, you open the Align panel and align your stuff, and can then close the panel. If you need to mix a color so that you can use it to paint with, you open the Mixer panel, create your color, and then close the Mixer. Thus, panels allow you to access certain features in the application, work with what you need to, and then close them to get them out of your way.

The Properties Panel

One of the most important panels (one you won't close very often, if at all) is the Properties panel. Figure 1-5 shows the Properties panel in its default "docked" position (more on docking in a moment). The Properties panel is used to view and set the characteristics of objects. Need to change the color or thickness of a line?

figure | 1-4 |

The toolbar provides tools for working with spatial content on the stage.

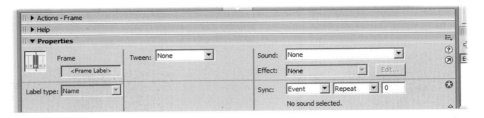

figure | 1-5 |

The Properties panel is used to view and set the values of object characteristics. It is also used with the timeline when creating animation.

Need to set the position of an object to a specific coordinate location on the stage? These two things and much more can be accomplished using the Properties panel. Note also that the Properties panel is not limited to spatial content only; it is also used in conjunction with the timeline when you work with animation. Additionally, the options displayed in the Properties panel change depending on what you have selected or what you are working with. There are some commonalities as you select different things, but the options shown are specific characteristics (most of which, if not all, can be dynamically changed). You will see this immediately as we move into Chapter 3.

Docked Versus Undocked

Realizing that everybody likes to customize their workspace, Macromedia has provided a means for you to dock and undock your panels (as well as the toolbar and timeline). Docking and undocking simply implies whether a panel is physically attached to the workspace (docked) or is floating somewhere on the desktop (undocked). Earlier I said that you couldn't view everything all at once, but that is only a half truth. If you have multiple monitors, you can very nearly view everything (all panels and such) simultaneously by undocking panels and placing them in a monitor all on their own. Even though you can do this, you likely won't, but the fact that you can is nice!

Figure 1-6 shows the basic idea of docking and undocking panels. By default, panels that you open are displayed in the right-hand side of the application interface (see figure 1-2). However, you can click-drag the panel so that it "floats" in front of the rest of the interface if you want. You can also expand, contract, and re-dock

items just by moving a panel back to the docking area to the right
of the application workspace.

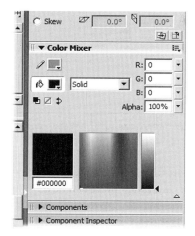

(a) Docked

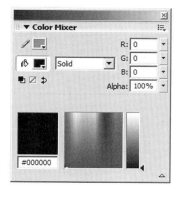

(b) Undocked

figure | 1-6

Panels can be undocked from their default location
and moved anywhere on the screen (a). When
undocked they float (b) and can be collapsed (c).

(c) Undocked, collapsed

The trick to all of this docking and undocking is grabbing the right
spot on the panel when you want to undock a panel. If you don't
grab the right spot, it will collapse instead of detach. To detach a
panel you must grab the small dotted area to the left of the arrow
(see figure 1-6a).

Predefined Panel Sets

One question you may be asking is, "What happens if you detach
all the panels and want to go back to the original docked panel con-
figuration?" Good question. If you access the Window | Panel Sets
menu option you will find that you can return to the default panel
configuration with a click or two. You can also save your own panel
arrangements. For example, you could set up different arrangements for certain screen resolutions. And of course, depending on
whether you are a designer or programmer you may have an affin-
ity for certain sets of panels. Thus, you can save your panel
arrangements based on those characteristics too.

> ## ▶ TRY THIS
>
> Before moving on, open the Flash application and tinker with the panels for a bit. Try undocking and redocking the panels to get a feel for how this process works. Also, take a peek at the Window | Panel Sets menu options to see the available options. Try creating some custom arrangement of open panels and then save it. Once you get more familiar with the different panels, as well as how Flash works, you may want to return to working with panel sets to create your own custom configuration.

DON'T GO THERE

Another thing to note about floating panels is that multiple panels can be combined into one floating window. You can mix and match which panels appear together, and so on. However, I find it much easier to work with each panel as its own window rather than combining them. If you combine panels, you'll find that in many cases the panels get too tall to fit on the screen when they are all expanded, and thus you spend more time expanding and collapsing them than actually doing work. I suggest just leaving each window floating on its own—particularly if you have a multiple monitor configuration.

PREFERENCES AND DOCUMENT SETTINGS

Now that you have a feel for the overall composition of the interface, let's talk a moment about setting up the application preferences. There are two sets of preferences that are noteworthy: general application preferences (settings that once defined will exist each time you start Flash) and document preferences (settings that are specific to a particular movie or file you are working with). Let's first examine the former.

Application Preferences

The Preferences dialog box provides tabbed access to five main groupings of options and is accessed via Edit | Preferences. Suffice it to say there is not much to say about some of them, as they are pretty self-explanatory. As well, the Flash Help menu (accessed via Help | Using Flash) details the nitty-gritty about all of them. If you want to get really specific and know what each does, I suggest visiting the Help file. However, I do wish to acknowledge some of the important ones:

The General tab is shown in figure 1-7.

- *Undo levels:* The default number of Undos that can be consecutively performed is 100, which is usually more than enough. But the maximum is 300.

- *Selection options:* The *Shift select* checkbox is pretty important. If it is selected, Flash will behave like FreeHand in that you will have to hold down the Shift key to select multiple graphic objects on the stage. If this checkbox is deselected, Flash will behave like Illustrator, where you hold the Shift key to select a single object. So, if you are familiar with one or the other, choose appropriately. If you are familiar with neither, leave this checkbox selected.

- *On launch:* This determines how Flash starts up. With most applications, you generally start with a new, blank document already opened, but with Flash you have a few options. Flash offers a nifty tool called the Start page, which is basically a warm-and-fuzzy screen that lets you select from a wider range of starting options. You can also open the last document you were working on, if you prefer.

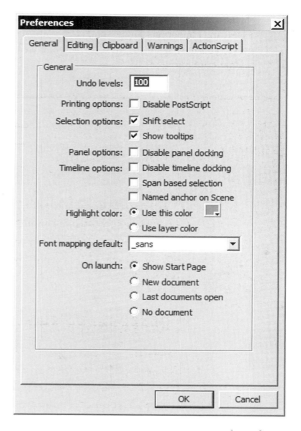

figure | 1-7

Be aware of *Undo levels* and *Selection options* within the Preferences | General tab.

The Clipboard tab is shown in figure 1-8.

All of the settings in the Clipboard tab are related to copying and pasting into Flash. Macromedia has established these settings to help you control the file size of content coming into Flash via the clipboard. The thing to know is that if you are pasting into Flash from

figure | 1-8 |

Settings in the Clipboard tab limit the amount of data that can be inserted via copy and paste.

some other application Flash may prompt you and say something like, "Cannot paste because of file size limits." This is due to the settings in the Clipboard tab. If you increase the *Size limit*, you can paste just about anything into Flash. However, your Flash file size will increase as a result.

There are three tabs in the Preferences dialog box we won't talk about at this point. These include the Editing, Warnings, and ActionScript tabs. Later in this book I will point out preferences you should be aware of in these tabs on an as-needed basis.

"Document" Preferences

In addition to the general application preferences, we should also acknowledge the document preferences (actually called document properties). These preferences are specific to each movie file you create and allow you to control things such as the stage size and so forth. Figure 1-9 shows the Document Properties dialog box, which is accessed via the Modify | Document menu option.

The settings in the Document Properties dialog box are pretty important, so rather than referring you to the Help file, let's take a moment to point out what each of these settings does.

● *Dimensions:* This setting defines the size of the stage. Note that you can set the stage up to match the printer, the content on the stage, as well as the default (550 pixels by 400 pixels) using the Match buttons in the dialog box. In general, the stage size can be as small as 1 pixel by 1 pixel, to as large as 2,880 pixels square.

Document Properties

Dimensions: [36.65 px] (width) x [369.85 px] (height)

Match: [Printer]   [Contents]   [Default]

Background color: [▾]

Frame rate: [12]   fps

Ruler units: [Pixels   ▾]

[Make Default]   [OK]   [Cancel]

- *Background color:* This little interactive control allows you to select a specific background color from a palette of defined colors. In Flash, you must define or create a color and save it before you can use it, which will be discussed in Chapter 2.

- *Frame rate:* This setting controls the rate of playback of the Flash movie. The default is 12. Understanding frame rate in Flash is a little tricky because of the way Flash movies are processed by the computer. More on this in Chapter 11.

- *Ruler units:* This defines the default units for measurement. The default is pixels, which is appropriate for most scenarios in which you are designing for screen. If you happen to design a Flash movie specifically for print, you may want to revert to inches or points.

Keyboard and Toolbar Customization

Although we need not spend a tremendous amount of time discussing these next two issues, I at least want to mention them so that you are aware of them. First, like other Macromedia applications Flash allows you to customize the keyboard shortcuts associated with most, if not all, of the menu commands in Flash. If you are used to other applications and don't care for Flash's keyboard shortcut combinations (or if you are like me and have small hands that make some combinations difficult), you can change them using Edit | Keyboard Shortcuts. The dialog box that ensues (shown in figure 1-10) allows you to make Flash's keyboard shortcuts mimic any number of other applications. You can also create your own customized keyboard combinations.

figure | 1-10 |

You can customize
Flash's keyboard
shortcuts using Edit
| Keyboard
Shortcuts.

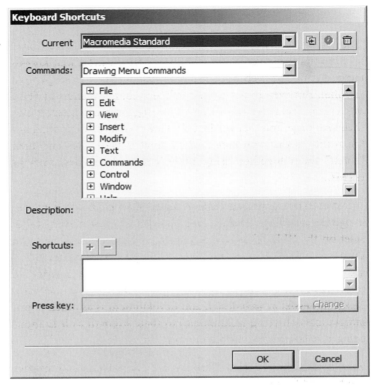

In addition to customizing the keyboard, you can customize the
tools and their arrangement in the toolbar. To access this capabili-
ty you use the Edit | Customize Tools Panel menu option. This
brings up a dialog box that allows you to redefine the arrangement
of the tools. Now, given that you are just getting started with Flash,
I wouldn't recommend doing this just yet—otherwise, when I refer
to specific tools later on in the book what you see may not match
what you see in the book. For now, just realize that you can customize this if you wish.

THE HOLISTIC VIEW

To conclude this chapter we need to discuss a few global issues
related to Flash development. I am a big picture person—having a
holistic view helps me decipher the details and ultimately makes
learning whatever, easier. The following sections will deal with
some miscellaneous "big picture" items that I think will make subsequent chapters easier to understand.

Don't Limit Your Thinking

One of the first things to acknowledge about Flash is that there are several ways to deliver content with it. By far the most well-known method is via the Web, but Flash is actually broader in scope than just that. But even in the context of the Web, newcomers to Flash often think that they will just create one big Flash file, insert it into their web page, and that will be that. However, more often than not the reality is that you create many smaller Flash files and then "stitch" them together using other web technologies, such as HTML.

You should not approach Flash as an be-all/end-all web solution, altogether avoiding other technologies. Flash is just like any other asset on the Web—that is, it is akin to a raster image in that you should use Flash as a dynamic asset within your web creations. You should look for ways to chunk Flash files into other technologies, rather than trying to build the entire proverbial world inside Flash. Being successful at web design and development is as much about integration and using technologies to their strength as it is about being a master of any one technology.

Now, apart from the Web, Flash has a place as well. Flash movies can be used for interactive multimedia presentations delivered on CD or via other means. It can also be used to develop applications (that is, software designed to do work, rather than just communicate information). I am also aware of institutions that are now using Flash in lieu of PowerPoint due to small files and the wealth of capabilities that can be included. In short, don't limit your thinking about the applicability of Flash, nor think of Flash as a total solution in any scenario. Always consider the range and scope, with Flash being a part of the solution.

File Formats

Another issue we should discuss is file formats. There are three basic file formats you will immediately see when you work with Flash. These include the FLA (native Flash file), SWF (compressed, web-ready Flash file) and the EXE (executable). The native Flash file (FLA) is the file you create, open, save, and so on inside the Flash application. To be able to utilize FLA files you must have Flash. It goes without saying that FLA files are not what you want to distribute to the world. These are your uncompressed working project files

important

that, although you may share them with a development group contain all the blood, sweat, and tears you've put into a project.

On the other hand, the files you will distribute to your audience will either be SWF or EXE files. Both can be generated out of Flash, but which you choose to use will depend on your project's purpose and your delivery mechanism.

SWF Files

If you are placing Flash content inside web pages you will use the SWF format. SWF originally stood for Shockwave Flash File, but now (ahem…) Macromedia says it means Small Web File. Anyway, these files are compressed and often protected—protected meaning you cannot open them back into Flash. Although we'll likely talk a little about these as we go along, creation of these will be discussed in Chapter 15 when we talk about publishing to the Web.

What makes SWF files special is that the user must have a player application available to be able to view the file. The player can be in the form of a true application (the Flash player is installed when you install Flash, but it can also be downloaded from Macromedia's site and installed apart from purchasing the Flash application) or as part of the browser. When an SWF file is part of a web page, the player is in the form of a browser plug-in or component the user must install.

EXE (Projector) Files

If you are creating projects that will be distributed via CD, DVD, or sneakernet (other storage media), EXE files may be your chosen flavor of file. Basically, EXE files in Flash are SWF files that have special code added to them so that a player application is not necessary. In other words, the EXE file is the SWF and the player code wrapped together in one file. Note that these files are often called projector files. And, regardless of which platform you are developing on (Mac or PC) you can create projector files for both platforms on either Mac or PC. Again, Chapter 15 will delve into the creation of these files.

NOTE: I realize that some of you may want the scoop on all this right now. For logical flow I have reserved the topic of publishing till the last chapter. However, if you want the skinny on SWF and EXE files right now, you can visit Chapter 15 for a preview or you can access the Flash Help file (see the topic Publishing).

Working with Files

The final noteworthy topic for this chapter deals with playing Flash movies. In this text we won't get into movie playback issues until we get to Chapter 11, when we deal with animation, but I realize that you may start accessing various web sites to look at sample files real soon. Thus, discussion of movie playback seems appropriate.

In most cases, when you open a Flash FLA file into the Flash application, the easiest way to play the movie back is to use the Control | Test Movie menu option. At this point I won't acknowledge all the issues surrounding what this does, but it is the Test Movie option that will allow you to see all of the movie's content as intended by the movie's creator.

The primary issue of note when using the Control | Test Movie option is that the FLA file must be on a writable computer drive. If the FLA is being opened off of a CD or other fixed media, Test Movie will give you an error. In these cases, copy the FLA file (and in some instances there may be multiple pieces you will need to copy) to your hard drive or other writable storage media and Test Movie will work properly.

SUMMARY

In this chapter we've started down the road of getting familiar with Flash. Although it might have been tempting to skip over this introductory material, you now have a holistic view of the Flash application interface. As you move on keep in mind the difference in function of the stage and timeline, which is where many newcomers to Flash get hung up. Also, keep in mind the main Preference and Document settings we discussed. As you're working you may find you'll want to tweak or change some of these settings, depending on how you work.

in review

1. The toolbar tools are specifically designed to work in conjunction with which part of the Flash environment?

2. What is the stage and what kind of stuff do you do with it?

3. What is the timeline and what can you control with it?

4. How do you undock a panel?

5. Where are panels typically docked?

6. What does the Properties panel let you do?

7. Where can you set the physical size of the stage?

8. If you are trying to paste something into Flash and you get a file size error, what should you do?

9. What is the difference between FLA, SWF, and EXE files?

10. How do you get a movie to play back and what is the limit of using it?

✦ EXPLORING ON YOUR OWN

NOTE: For several of the following items, you need to access the Flash Start page. Make sure you have the On Launch preference set to Show Start Page (Edit | Preferences | General tab). Then close all open document windows (select File | Close until all open windows are closed). The Start page will pop up once all documents are closed.

1. Access the Flash Start page and click on the *Take a quick tour of Flash* option to extend what you have read in this chapter.

2. Access the Flash Start page and click on the *Take a Flash lesson* option. This will open the list of Lessons in the Help window. Select the *Getting Started with Flash* lesson and read through it.

3. Examine the Help file information pertaining to system and document preferences.

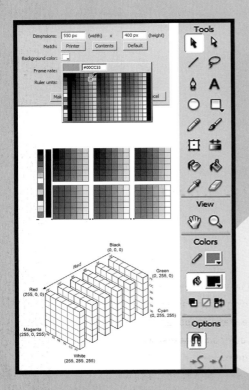

| color |

charting your course

Prior to diving right into the tools for drawing, painting, and editing, let's first deal with color and how it works in Flash. Defining and saving color is foundational to anything you wish to do in Flash.

Typically when you start a project design you'll begin with basic concept sketches and at some point arrive at establishing the color palette for whatever it is you are designing. Whether it is a static image, an animation, or an entire site, you begin by defining the color scheme that will be used. Projects that don't begin with the definition of color ahead of time typically suffer from poor visual results at the end— ranging from simply an odd color that sticks out like a sore thumb or a truly nasty design with colors all across the board. By making color decisions from the start (and vehemently sticking to them), you can avoid color problems at the end.

As a tool, Flash follows this basic design principle, in that you begin (prior to ever creating anything) your project by defining the colors you'll use. In Flash, before you can use a color you must define and save it—much like the traditional artist who dabs the paints he or she will begin with on the mixing palette. Once defined, these colors can then be used for the background of the stage, entities you create, and so on. With this in mind, let's get to it!

 goals

In this chapter you will:

● **Find out how RGB color works**

● **Learn about mixing color for screen output**

- **Discover how you create solid colors and gradients in Flash**
- **Find out how to create fully or partially transparent colors**
- **Learn to save, delete, and edit saved colors in the Swatches panel**
- **Realize how to use colors and gradients you have defined**

AN RGB COLOR PRIMER

One of the hurdles that every digital designer must overcome is how to work with digital color. To be quite frank, RGB color is just plain weird. The key to understanding it is simply acknowledging that (1) the primary colors you work with are different from those of traditional art (but functionally work the same way), and (2) RGB is a numerically based color system (as opposed to visually based).

The first of these two keys explains part of RGB's awkwardness. In traditional art, you typically deal with red, yellow, and blue as your primary colors. From that basic set, all other colors are created (note that we could also include black, white, and browns, as artists typically use these colors to "cheat" a little). Nevertheless, by skillfully combining various amounts of red, yellow, and blue an artist can literally create any color. While some are more difficult to get than others (purple, for example), all color can be created from various combinations of the primary colors.

With RGB, the same is basically true. By adding various amounts and combinations of red, green, and blue we can arrive at any color. However, the primary issue is that with RGB we are adding light to an already black screen, rather than adding pigment to a white page. While we need not get into the intricacies of physics to address the differences of reflection versus projection, understand that working with RGB color is essentially the same as working with RYB in traditional art—at least from the artist's perspective.

Where RGB gets really different is when you address the issue of it being numerically based. In art, we deal with amounts of pigment, but not to the extent of specifically measuring it. On the computer, however, we must be exact. So we deal with specific ranges of red, green, and blue. In RGB, the range is 0 to 255, and by varying those amounts for each of the values, we end up with a different resulting color.

The RGB Color Cube

At this point it seems prudent to take a look at the RGB color cube. As you look at figure 2-1, remember that the primary colors are red, green, and blue. By default, black and white also exist: when there is no red, green, or blue present, it is black. When we have added all the red, green, and blue that we can add, we have white.

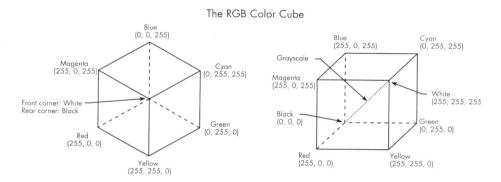

Now, granted one of the other peculiarities of the RGB color space is the fact that it makes a cube. This usually throws people off, but don't be intimidated by it. It is really just a different way of working with color: you are doing the same thing as you do in the traditional art sense, but are instead working within the confines of what the computer can handle. As you get more used to dealing with digital color, RGB will become more familiar (possibly even "user-friendly").

figure | 2-1

The RGB color cube.

The Web-safe Cube

Another thing we should acknowledge is something called web-safe colors. If you have been around or have used the Web for very long at all you have likely heard of them. These are basically special colors you can use to help alleviate color problems on the Web. While their significance is decreasing, Flash's default colors are the standard 216 web-safe colors. Figure 2-2 shows you where these colors come from. Essentially, the web-safe colors are specific "slices" through the RGB color model. Later you will see how Flash's default swatch colors sync with figure 2-2. Just realize that there is logic to the decision on what is a web-safe color and what is not.

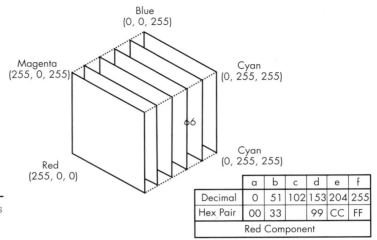

figure 2-2

The web-safe colors
are specific slices
through the RGB
color cube.

Hexadecimal Color

No digital color primer for the Web would be complete without mention of hexadecimal color. In figure 2-2 you saw some hexadecimal information in the image (where it shows decimal and hexadecimal equivalents). Hexadecimal color is simply a special means of representing the numerical value for the red, green, and blue components.

Earlier I mentioned that each of the RGB component colors varies from 0 to 255. For the computer to more easily understand these numbers they are converted to hexadecimal values (that is, base 16 rather than base 10 representations). So, instead of a red value of 255 you end up with a red value of FF—weird huh? Basically, counting in hexadecimal goes something like 0 to 9 and then A to F.

So what does it all mean, you ask? Well, when you define color in a web page, all a browser can understand as it relates to color specifications is hexadecimal numbers. While we need not get into the nitty-gritty of it, just realize that there may be times when you will need to get hexadecimal color specifications in and out of Flash. You'll see how to do this later.

NOTE: If you would like to learn more about hexadecimal color or web-safe color, I suggest you do a quick search at Google. There are a tremendous number of resources out there that detail every facet of it.

HSB Colors

A final issue I should mention is that in addition to the RGB color cube you may also see references to the HSB (hue, saturation, and brightness) model. This means of specifying color is typically easier to deal with than the RGB method. Flash actually lets you use either. With the HSB color system, you work like you normally would with traditional art colors; that is, you work with hues, saturation (purity of color), and brightness (value or lightness/darkness of a color). Figure 2-3 shows the HSB color model so that you have a conceptual grasp of it.

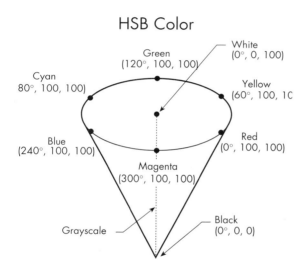

HSB Color

Green
(120°, 100, 100)

White
(0°, 0, 100)

Cyan
80°, 100, 100)

Yellow
(60°, 100, 1C

Blue
(240°, 100, 100)

Red
(0°, 100, 100)

Magenta
(300°, 100, 100)

Grayscale

Black
(0°, 0, 0)

figure | 2-3 |

The HSB color space provides an alternative means of establishing digital color.

MIXING COLORS

Now that we have some of the rudimentary stuff out of the way, let's press on into Flash. My goal is to tie the stuff you read in the introductory pages of this chapter to some "real-world" things in Flash as we go along. So, if the opening pages sounded like Greek, they should make sense once you complete this chapter.

To begin the process of establishing color in Flash you use the Mixer panel. Figure 2-4 shows the Mixer panel and labels the main parts of it. Take a moment and familiarize yourself with it. Then I'll explain how you create colors and gradients within it.

figure | 2-4 |

The Mixer panel is where you create color in Flash.

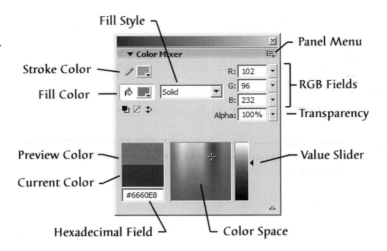

Fill Style

Panel Menu

Stroke Color

Fill Color

RGB Fields

Transparency

Preview Color

Value Slider

Current Color

#6660E8

Hexadecimal Field

Color Space

Defining Colors and Gradients

In the Mixer panel there are several different types of "colors" you can create. You can create solid colors that can be used as fill, line, or background colors. Solid colors are also the basis for creating the second type of saved color, called gradients, which can be used for fills. Gradients can include linear or radial gradients, as you will see shortly. And, there is a third type of color, called a bitmap color, where you can assign a bitmap as a fill. However, discussion of this will be reserved for Chapter 7. Let's get started with creating solid colors.

Creating Solid Colors

There are basically two ways to define a solid color in the Mixer panel: entering numerical values of a color specification into the appropriate fields or using the interactive controls. If you know an exact RGB color specification (such as 204, 53, 35) you can enter it directly in the RGB fields (see figure 2-4). Or you can directly enter a hexadecimal value into the Hexadecimal field. You can also enter HSB values by selecting the HSB option from the Mixer panel's menu. This changes the RGB fields to HSB, where you can then enter the appropriate values.

However, more often than not you may want to use a more intuitive approach to selecting color using the interactive controls (color space and value slider). To create a solid color using the interactive controls:

1. Access the Color Mixer using the Window | Design Panel | Color Mixer option.

2. Set the Fill Style drop-down menu to Solid.

3. Click-drag within the Color Space area to set the color cross-hairs in the general vicinity of the color band you want. Note that you will not see the preview color change just yet.

✱ IMPORTANT

4. Now click-drag the small black triangle to the right of the value slider up to an appropriate location. The default starting location of the value slider is at zero when you first access the Mixer panel. In the previous step that was why the preview color chip did not change color when you clicked it. Once you have adjusted the value slider, the preview color should now be something other than black.

5. Continue to adjust the location of the color cross-hairs and the value slider until you find the color you want.

6. When you have the color you want, access the Panel menu and select Add Swatch. This saves the color for later use. We'll look at accessing the swatches a little later.

▶ TRY THIS

Now that you understand how to define a solid color, try creating a few more to get the hang of how it works.

Creating Linear Gradients

Both linear and radial gradients are based on solid colors; that is, you have to create some solid colors before you can create linear or radial gradients. To create a linear gradient, you access the Mixer panel and set the Fill Style drop-down menu to Linear. When you do this, the controls in the Mixer panel change, as shown in figure 2-5.

figure | 2-5 |

With the Fill Style drop-down set to Linear, you are provided extra interactive controls.

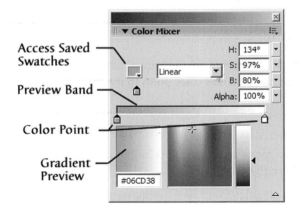

Access Saved Swatches

Preview Band

Color Point

Gradient Preview

Now to define a linear gradient:

1. Make sure the Fill Style drop-down is set to Linear.

2. Click on the leftmost color point to make it active, which changes the color associated with it. When a color point is active, the triangle above the color point is black. Inactive color points are gray, and you can only select one color point at a time.

IMPORTANT ✱

3. Now access the currently saved color swatches (see figure 2-5) by single clicking. Single clicking the color chip reveals all currently saved color swatches. Note that there is a bunch of predefined swatches. If you saved your own swatches when you created solid colors, they will be at the bottom of the list.

4. Click on one of the colors. This sets the currently active color point to the color you have selected.

5. Click on the rightmost color point and set its color by accessing the color swatches and choosing a color. You now have a linear gradient that blends the two colors you have selected.

6. Select Add Swatch from the Mixer panel menu so that you can use it later.

Now that you have the basics under your belt, realize you can create multicolor gradients just as easily. To create a multicolor gradient:

1. Access the Mixer panel and set the Fill Style drop-down to Linear.

2. Set the leftmost and rightmost color points to define the leftmost and rightmost colors in the blend.

3. Next, click somewhere in the center of the preview band. Doing so will add a new color point to the gradient.

4. Click-drag the new color point to somewhere within the color band.

NOTE: You can remove unintended color points by click-dragging them away from the color band.

5. Make the new color point you just added the active color point.

6. Set its color by accessing the saved swatches and choosing a color.

7. Add more color points as desired by clicking elsewhere in the color band. Again, get rid of unintentional color points by click-dragging them away from the color band.

8. Select Add Swatch from the Mixer panel menu when you are done.

*— IMPORTANT

A couple of final notes you should realize: you can click-drag any of the color points in the color band, including the leftmost and rightmost points. Also, as you create linear gradients you will notice that the gradient only goes "one-way." To create gradients that go in different directions, you do something called "transforming" (rotating, scaling, moving) the fill after it has been used on the stage. You'll learn about that in another chapter. For now, just focus on defining fills and saving them as swatches.

▶ **TRY THIS**

Try creating various linear gradients and saving them as swatches. Try doing something real-world. For example, try creating a multicolor gradient that could be used to simulate the look of highly reflective metal (add a lot of sharp whites and blacks). Or, try to add a simulated horizon line (integrate some blue for a sky and brown for the ground).

Creating Radial Gradients

Creating radial gradients is not so much different than creating linear gradients. Essentially, the gradient occurs around a radius rather than in a rectangular fashion. As far as defining the gradient, use the same technique as with linear gradients; only select Radial in the Fill Style drop-down instead of Linear.

> ### ▶ TRY THIS
>
> Experiment with creating radial gradients and see what different types of effects you can come up with.

NOTE: Keep in mind that the bitmap fill style will be discussed in Chapter 7.

Working with Transparency (Alpha)

Now let's add one unique capability to your tool bag—that is, the ability to control transparency. Beneath the RGB fields in the Mixer panel is an Alpha field. This field lets you control the opacity/transparency of the colors you create. With transparency settings you can do all sorts of things—particularly when you layer filled objects over the top of one another. Let's take a look at how you control the Alpha property of colors.

Creating Transparent Colors

Alpha is just like the numerical setting associated with any one of the component colors. So, just as you can establish the amount of red, green, or blue in a color, so too can you control the opacity. To create a color with a transparency value:

1. Access the Mixer panel, set the Fill Style to Solid, and define a solid color.

2. Next, change the value in the Alpha field to 50 (which is 50 percent). When you do this you will notice a grid that is revealed behind the preview color. This grid indicates that the color has an Alpha (transparency) setting.

3. Once you have assigned the Alpha you want, select Add Swatch from the Mixer panel menu.

Now at this point, transparency may not mean a whole lot. But suffice it to say it is important and you will see the application of it later as we start drawing, painting, and creating animation. An alpha setting basically lets you have objects that are partially (or totally) see-through, letting things beneath them show up. Later we'll see some cool things you can do with animation and transparency.

NOTE: Typically when people learn about transparency and colors the first question they ask is whether you can set the background of the stage to a transparent color. Indeed you can, but it is not by creating a transparent color and setting it to the background. Rather, setting the background of a Flash movie to transparent is a function of HTML coding—and one caveat is that it only works in Internet Explorer. When we get to Chapter 15 we will broach this issue.

TRY THIS

Try creating several different colors that have various transparency settings.

Creating Gradients with Transparency

Now you are likely saying to yourself, "If you can create transparent solid colors, it must mean you can also create transparent gradients." If you are saying that, indeed you are correct! And, just as gradients are based on their defined solid colors, so too is the transparency in gradients based on the transparency of the solid colors that compose them. To create a linear gradient that blends from a solid color to completely transparent:

1. Begin by defining a solid color you want to use in your gradient. Once you have defined the solid color, save it as a swatch.

2. Next, create a second solid color with the same RGB parameters but with the Alpha field set to zero. Then save it as a swatch.

3. Now, change the Fill Style drop-down to Gradient so that you can create a gradient from the two prior colors you defined (one has 100-percent Alpha, the other has 0-percent Alpha).

4. Click on the left-most color point and access the color swatches via the color chip in the upper part of the panel. Select the 100-percent Alpha color you created in step 1.

5. Click on the rightmost color point and set it to the 0-percent Alpha color you created in step 2.

6. Save the newly defined gradient as a swatch.

!DON'T GO THERE

In the prior process, you will note that I had you create two swatches of the same color with varying alphas. This was purposeful. If you blend two different colors with two different alphas some pretty strange things can happen. Typically you end up with some haloing effects—where there are hints of one or the other color in the transparency. To avoid haloing, anytime you are creating a gradient that gradates Alpha, use the exact same RGB values in the two chips.

SAVING AND USING COLORS

Up to this point we've been defining colors and saving them away, not really being too concerned about where they are being saved. Now it is time to see where they actually go—namely, the Swatches panel. One important note about swatches is to realize that they are saved with the movie file. So, swatches you define in one movie are not automatically transferred to the next movie (although you can do that by exporting and importing them). Each new Flash document starts from the base of 216 web-safe colors shown in figure 2-6. Then you can add your own colors, as previously described.

As shown in figure 2-6, the upper part of the panel includes all of the predefined solid colors, while the lower portion displays the predefined gradients. As you select Add Swatch from the Mixer panel, your own custom solid colors and gradients are added to the collection of colors in the Swatches panel.

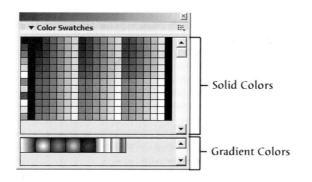

figure | 2-6 |

The Swatches panel holds the colors that are saved from the Mixer.

Examining the Swatches Panel

At the beginning of this Chapter I acknowledged that the default swatches in the Swatches panel are the 216 web-safe colors (plus the 16 base interface colors that are displayed down the left-hand side of the solid colors section). Take a look at figure 2-7. This figure shows the relationship between the web-safe color cube mentioned at the beginning of this chapter, and the default color swatches in Flash. Note that the swatches are basically the slices through the color cube. This will help you decipher what is going on and will make selecting color easier.

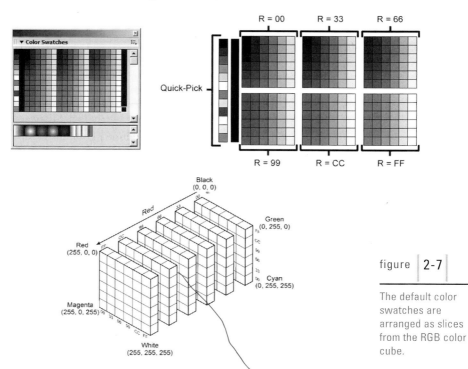

figure | 2-7 |

The default color swatches are arranged as slices from the RGB color cube.

Adding, Removing, and Using Swatches

Already you have learned one way to add colors to the swatches by using the Mixer panel's menu. If you have the Mixer and the Swatches panels open at the same time, you can add the current color in the Mixer to the Swatches by moving the cursor over an open space in the Swatches panel and clicking. You'll see that when you move the cursor over an open space in the Swatches panel that the cursor changes to a paint bucket, indicating that you can add the Mixer color to the Swatches panel. Removing swatches from the panel is easy. To remove a swatch:

1. Open the Swatches panel.

2. Hold down the Ctrl (PC) or Command (Mac) key and move the cursor over a swatch. You will see that the cursor changes to a pair of scissors.

3. Click and the swatch will be permanently removed from the Swatches panel.

One final note about the Swatches panel is that it is helpful to leave it open as you work. If you drag the cursor over existing swatches in the panel, the cursor changes to an eyedropper. Clicking will make the color currently under the cursor the current color in the Mixer (as well as for the currently selected tool—more on that later).

Working with Swatches

Let's finish up this section on the Swatches panel by simply acknowledging some of the hidden treasures that can be found in the Swatches panel menu. These options include:

- *Duplicate Swatch:* This lets you duplicate an already existing color swatch. This is helpful if you need to create a transparent version of an already existing color.

- *Add or Replace Colors:* Adding or replacing colors lets you import colors from external files, including those from preexisting Flash color sets (CLR files), Photoshop color tables (ACT files), as well as standard GIF images.

- *Load Default Colors:* Basically, resets the Swatches to the original set that exists when you start a new document.

- *Save Colors:* Lets you export the colors you have created as a Flash color set file (CLR).

- *Clear Colors:* This deletes all swatches except black and white.

- *Web 216/Sort by Color:* These two options allow you to sort the colors in the panel by their default Web 216 arrangement or by their actual hue.

USING COLORS

Now that you have taken a gander at mixing and saving colors, let's take a moment to acknowledge all the ways you can use them (briefly, mind you). As you progress through the rest of this book, you'll get more than an inoculation of using colors.

The Background Color

Already you saw even in the Mixer panel itself how the color Swatches panel "feeds its colors" to all other parts of Flash. Recall in the Mixer when you were looking at defining gradients, the small color chip that when clicked on expanded to show all the swatches currently defined in Flash. You will see this over and over.

For example, if you select Modify | Document you are presented with the movie properties, as shown in figure 2-8. When you click on the color chip located there, the chip expands to let you select from all the swatches currently defined in the movie.

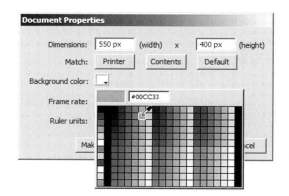

figure | 2-8

The Swatches panel feeds its colors to all other places where you need to define color, including the Document Properties window.

So, to change the background color of the Flash movie to some color you want, you:

1. Mix that color in the Mixer panel.

2. Save that color as a Swatch, at which point it becomes available in the Swatches panel.

3. Then you access Modify | Document Properties to set the background color.

Tool Colors and the Properties Panel

In addition to the selection of color for the background you will find that all of the drawing and painting tools provide similar access to the color swatches. As we move into the next chapter you will see this first hand as you start working with the Line, Pencil, Oval, and Rectangle tools. Hopefully it is evident at this point why I have devoted an entire chapter to talking about color definition in Flash. As you move into subsequent chapters it should make getting up and running much easier.

SUMMARY

In this chapter you have looked at how to work with color in Flash. The two key items you should understand are how the Mixer and the Swatches panels work, independently as well as in conjunction with each other.

The basic strategy, as in the general design process, is to establish the color palette for the project you are working on prior to actually starting the work. Flash forces this issue, making you define your colors with the Mixer and then save them to the Swatches for use. Essentially all the tools in Flash, as well as the Document Properties dialog box and the Properties panel, require that your colors be defined as swatches. While some may not like this approach, using this to your advantage will help you avoid color fandango when you reach the end of your project.

1. Flash allows you to work with several standard color models. While it does not support CMYK (the four-color print model), what color models does it let you work with?

2. Where do the web-safe colors come from and what relevance do they have to Flash?

3. If you wanted to define a linear gradient, what should you do first?

4. Flash allows you to work with the transparency of colors. What field or name does Flash give this property?

5. After defining a color in the Mixer panel, how do you save that color for use?

6. How do you remove a color from the Swatches panel?

7. How do you create a multicolor gradient in Flash?

8. If you want to create a gradient that blends two colors with different alphas, what must you make sure of to avoid haloing?

9. What is the difference between a linear and radial gradient? Also, what is different about the process in creating each?

10. Say you are creating a linear gradient and you have defined five color points for the gradient. How do you remove one of the color points from the mix?

⟡ EXPLORING ON YOUR OWN

1. Create a palette of various gradients you might need for future projects to texture and color different things. Export that set of swatches so that you can use it in the future.

2. Try coming up with a palette of colors—like you would in a real-world project. Define those colors in a blank Flash document to get a feel for how long this process takes.

3. Begin planning a project you would like to take on once you have completed this book. Got an animation or web site in mind? Plan out the color scheme for that project and begin by defining the colors you'll need for that project.

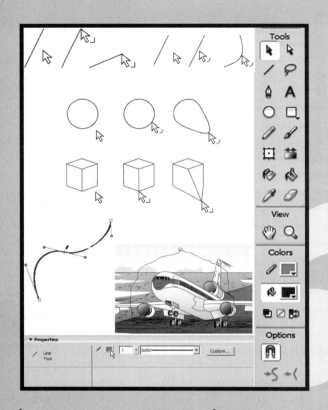

selection and drawing tools

 *charting your course*

In the last chapter you got up to speed with defining and saving colors in Flash. It's not rocket science, but it is important in the context of content creation. In this chapter you'll move on and start creating objects using the drawing tools in Flash. I have purposely devoted chapters to different aspects of the content creation process. There is a chapter on drawing, a chapter on painting, and a chapter on manipulation (editing). The reason for this is the unique way in which Flash works.

As you start creating digital content in Flash, you will find some peculiarities as compared to other "traditional" graphics software. Flash is really unlike any other graphics creation engine—which is good and bad. It is good because it is a refreshing approach and allows a little more creative freedom than some other tools. The bad part is that you kind of have to throw prior assumptions out the door. Regardless of which way you want to look at it (I prefer the optimistic viewpoint) there is much to learn. Let's get started.

 *goals*

In this chapter you will:

- Understand the purposes of the various tools (and groupings of tools) in the toolbar

- Discover how Flash's view and selection tools work

- Find out how to use the natural and Bezier drawing tools

FLASH'S DRAWING ENVIRONMENT

Before we jump right in and start drawing, let's take a minute to get the grasp of the entire picture as it relates to tools in Flash. While all the tools are thrown together in the toolbar, it will likely be helpful to briefly acknowledge what the tools are and what they do. Then we'll dive into the details in this and the next two chapters.

The Available Tools

figure | 3-1 |

The toolbar includes tools that fall into one of six categories.

All the tools in the toolbar fall into one of six categories, based on purpose. The following sections give you the quick skinny on them; this and subsequent chapters will delve into more detail on them. Figure 3-1 shows the toolbar with the various categories of tools acknowledged.

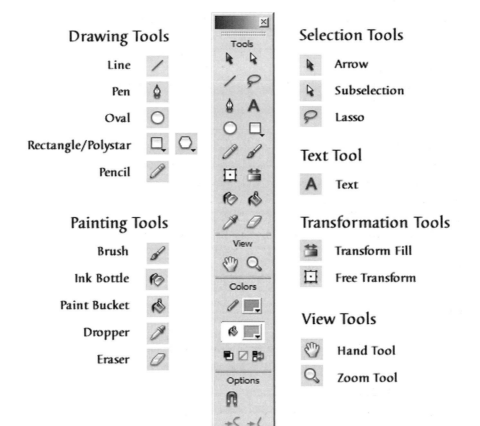

Drawing Tools

Line

Pen

Oval

Rectangle/Polystar

Pencil

Painting Tools

Brush

Ink Bottle

Paint Bucket

Dropper

Eraser

Selection Tools

Arrow

Subselection

Lasso

Text Tool

Text

Transformation Tools

Transform Fill

Free Transform

View Tools

Hand Tool

Zoom Tool

View Tools

There are two tools that are for controlling the view state of the work area: the Zoom tool and the Hand tool (for panning). Not much else can be said here except that there are also several view control menu options in the View menu.

Selection Tools

Selection tools are designed to choose or select objects on the stage so that you can do something to them. Picking an individual object lets you change its properties, while selecting several objects allows you to do something to all of them at the same time, such as scaling or moving them. There are three selection tools: the Arrow tool, the Subselection tool, and the Lasso tool.

Drawing Tools

The drawing tools include the Line, Pen, Oval, Rectangle, Polystar, and Pencil tools. These tools are designed for you to create line entities, as well as shapes that can be filled. With Flash, you will learn that you can also work with traditional Bezier points (such as with the Pen tool) or use what Macromedia terms the "natural drawing" approach.

Painting Tools

The Paint tools, which is one of the oddities of Flash (you don't typically think of "painting" in a vector tool) include the Brush, Ink Bottle, Paint Bucket, Dropper, and Eraser. You're probably thinking, "These sound like tools I might find in Photoshop or PhotoPaint." Indeed, Flash's drawing environment is like a combination of Photoshop and Illustrator or PhotoPaint and FreeHand. More on this in the next chapter!

Text Tool

Yep, you guessed it: there is only one tool for text creation, even though there are multiple types of text entities that can be created.

Transformation Tools

The transformation tools include a tool for freely transforming (moving, scaling, rotating, and skewing) objects on the stage, as well as a tool for manipulating the fill style position, orientation, and scale. In the last chapter I mentioned that to change the direction of a gradient you, transform it. We'll look at this more closely in Chapter 5.

ZOOMING AND VIEWING

One of the first things to learn in Flash is how to quickly zoom and pan as you are working. Flash provides a Zoom tool and a Hand (pan) tool that you can select to zoom and pan. However, there are shortcut keys that make zooming and panning quicker. Table 3-1 shows the keyboard combinations for zooming and panning.

One of the critical things in doing any work on the computer is efficiency. Learn to use the zooming and panning keyboard combinations, rather than constantly running to the Zoom or Hand tool in the toolbar.

Table 3-1: Keyboard Shortcuts for Zooming and Panning

Function	PC	Mac
Zoom In	Ctrl + spacebar	Command + spacebar
Zoom Out	Ctrl + Alt + spacebar	Command + option + spacebar
Pan	Spacebar	Spacebar

When you use the keyboard combinations for zooming, you can either single click (which will zoom in or out around the place you clicked) or click-drag (which will draw a rectangle to which the zoom level will be set).

In addition to the keyboard shortcuts shown in Table 3-1, you should also be aware of the ones listed in Table 3-2. The shortcuts in Table 3-2 will help you quick zoom to the exact point you want and may save you time.

Table 3-2: Additional Shortcuts for Zooming

Function	PC	Mac
Zoom In	Ctrl + =	Command + =
Zoom Out	Ctrl + -	Command + -
100% (show at 1:1 ratio)	Ctrl + 1	Command + 1
Show Frame (zoom to entire stage)	Ctrl + 2	Command + 2
Show All (zoom to content on stage)	Ctrl + 3	Command + 3

TRY THIS

Start Flash and begin a new document. Try the various zooming and panning shortcuts mentioned in the previous section. When you first start using the short-cuts, it may feel awkward at first. But force yourself to become accustomed to using them—they will save you a lot of time!

View Menu Options

While we are talking about view settings, it would be good to also acknowledge the settings in the View menu. We need not discuss all of them—a quick gander at the menu and you'll see several related to zooming and panning. But what I would like to draw your attention to are the Preview modes and the settings in the bottom of the menu. First consider the latter of those two.

In the bottom of the View menu you see several "drawing assistance" items. These include:

- *Rulers:* This displays rulers around the stage. They are also important if you want to be able to use guides (to add a guide to the stage you click-drag the guide from the ruler). Rulers off —no guides!

- *Grids:* While I don't usually use the grid feature, it is worth mentioning (I use guides instead). When you establish your layout grids for screen designs, grids or guides can be used.

- *Guides:* These are one of the most helpful things. Guides are basically little "blue-lines" (actually they are green by default, but they function like blue-line markup in traditional art and illustration), you can use to visually align things on the screen.

- *Snapping:* Another very useful feature. This controls "what snaps to what" when you are drawing. You can snap to grids, guides, pixels, and objects. You can also use something called "snap align" to help better align objects to other objects on the stage.

The second noteworthy item is the Preview Mode menu option. Frequently you may have some very complex drawing elements on the screen—complex in that it really pushes your computer when the screen needs to be refreshed (which is most noticeable when you pan or zoom). If you get a bunch of stuff on screen and your computer slows down, you can change the Preview Mode setting to speed up redrawing of the screen. Basically, the preview modes are a progression of visual quality on the screen—with Outline being the fastest to redraw and the poorest visually and Full being the best (with everything perfectly drawn, filled, and antialiased).

figure | 3-2 |

The Preview Modes provide different screen quality settings so that you can speed up the redraw time as you are working.

Figure 3-2 shows the visual results of each Preview Mode setting on a section of the image. The settings have the following effect:

- *Outline* displays everything as the basic line entities that compose the artwork.

- *Fast* displays both lines and fills in their defined colors, but doesn't antialias (blur the edges of) them.

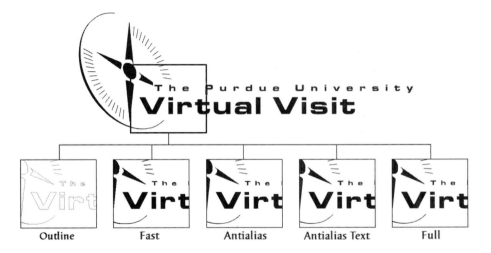

Outline   Fast   Antialias   Antialias Text   Full

- *Antialias* blurs the edges of fills, lines, and arcs, but ignores the edges of text.

- *Antialias text* blurs the edges of fills, lines, and arcs, as well as text.

- *Full* blurs everything on the stage.

SELECTION TOOLS

One of the important things to understand in Flash is how you select objects on the stage. Flash provides three different modes of selecting objects, which are represented by the three different selection tools.

Arrow Tool

The simplest (and most flexible) tool for selections is the Arrow tool. This tool is a "natural drawing tool" that lets you pick objects on the stage, as well as manipulate them. The basics of selecting objects go something like this:

- To select a single object, click on it and Flash will display a dotted pattern over the object, indicating that it's selected.

- To select multiple objects, hold the Shift key while selecting multiple objects. Once something is selected, you can then transform (move, scale, or rotate) or delete it. You'll read about transformations in Chapter 5.

- If you click-drag across a series of objects, the bounding box created by the drag will select only those portions of the object contained within the box. More on this when we discuss the Lasso tool.

NOTE: If you want Flash to automatically select multiple objects without having to hold the Shift key down, access the Edit | Preferences | General tab and deselect the Shift Select checkbox.

Another thing you can do with the Arrow tool is perform basic transformations on points and curves. Although there is a chapter devoted to editing, it seems prudent to mention this capability here (more so that you don't get confused by how it behaves).

When an object (line or arc) is not selected and you move the cursor close to a point on an object, you have the ability to transform the object. Move close to an endpoint and you can move the endpoint by click-dragging. Move close to the center of a line or near an arc and you can bend or bow the arc. Figure 3-3 shows this basic idea. The main thing to keep in mind here is that this "editing" feature only works when the object is *not* selected. If the object is selected, you cannot "edit" it.

figure | 3-3 |

The Arrow tool allows you to use "natural" editing on objects.

Moving an Endpoint

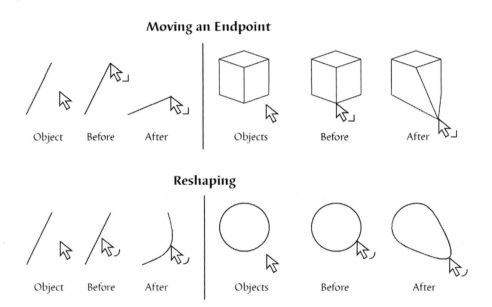

Reshaping

Subselection Tool

If you have any prior experience with tools such as Illustrator or FreeHand, what you can do with the Arrow tool is likely new to you. You may be thinking, "So, can Flash behave like vector tools I am used to—that is, can you work with the points that compose a vector element?" Answer—YES!

The Subselection tool is designed for just that. If you select the Subselection tool and then click on an entity, Flash will show you the points that make up the vector object, as shown in figure 3-4. Unfilled points denote unselected points, while filled points denote selected points. And, when a point on a curve is selected, handles appear that allow you to toggle and twist the Bezier curve.

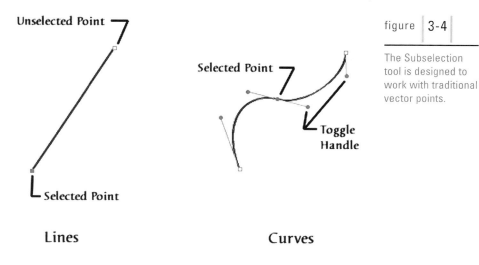

figure 3-4

The Subselection tool is designed to work with traditional vector points.

Lines   Curves

Lasso Tool

The last selection tool is the Lasso tool, and while I don't use it a whole lot it is worth mentioning. Unlike other environments, vector elements in Flash can be partially, as well as totally, selected. Thus, the Lasso tool allows you to select a portion of an object (or objects) by drawing a closed polygon. Any part of a line, arc, or fill that falls inside the selection area will be selected. Figure 3-5a shows the Lasso tool in use. Once the area defined by the Lasso is closed (when you connect the end to the beginning), the portions of everything inside will be selected. This is very similar to the tool of the same name in Photoshop.

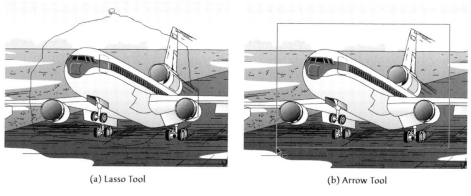

(a) Lasso Tool   (b) Arrow Tool

figure 3-5

The Lasso tool (a) and the Arrow tool (b) can be used to select a portion of an object.

Figure 3-5b shows a similar thing with the Arrow tool, which we brushed over in that section. If you click-drag across objects with the Arrow tool, a rectangular selection is defined. Like the Lasso tool, any portion of an object that falls inside the area will be selected.

NATURAL DRAWING TOOLS

One of the niftiest features of Flash is how it's drawing tools work. The natural drawing tools are a real departure from what is typical of vector drawing tools. If you have ever used Illustrator or FreeHand, likely you have been frustrated by having to connect lines, using tools such as a knife to cut something, as well as making sure a polygon is closed before you can fill it. If you've shared in some of these frustrations (as well as others), the natural drawing tools should be a refreshing change to what you are used to.

Line Tool

As you can probably guess, when you select the Line tool it lets you draw straight line segments on the stage—click-drag and voilà, you have a line. But note that when you select the Line tool the Properties panel displays several options that you can adjust concerning the line you are about to draw, as shown in figure 3-6. Regardless of the tool you select from the toolbar, the Properties panel will always show you optional settings for the tool you have selected. With the Line tool, you can set the line color, line thickness, and line style. Note that you can also set the line color, by accessing the Stroke color in the Colors section of the toolbar.

figure | 3-6 |

When you select a tool, the Properties panel displays the optional settings for the tool, which affect the entity that is drawn.

TRY THIS

Give the Line tool a whirl. Try drawing lines with different colors, styles, and thicknesses.

In figure 3-6, you see a button called Custom, which lets you define custom line styles. Be careful how many custom line styles you define—they can add considerable amount of data to your resulting file. Try to stick to the "predefined" line styles if possible.

Pencil Tool

Whereas the Line tool lets you draw line segments, the Pencil tool allows you to do free-form drawing. The Pencil tool can be kind of awkward to use—but it's more natural when you have a stylus as opposed to a mouse.

Nevertheless, the important thing to note is the optional setting that appears at the bottom of the toolbar in the Options section (who knows why Macromedia put it there instead of in the Properties panel). This optional setting lets you define how the free-form line you draw will be interpreted. The default option is Straighten, which forces your free-form line to straight line segments. The Smooth option converts your line to a flowing set of arcs, while Ink leaves the line as you have drawn it.

> ### ▶ TRY THIS
>
> Try using the Pencil tool with the different option settings. Can you see the difference between the Straighten, Smooth, and Ink settings? What are they?

Oval Tool

Like tools of the same name in other packages, the Oval tool can be used to draw ellipses and circles that are filled or unfilled. When you choose the Oval tool, you need to set both the Stroke and Fill colors. To create an Oval without a fill, you must select the No Fill button, shown in figure 3-7.

A couple things to note about the Oval tool:

- To create a circle, hold the Shift key while creating the oval.

- By default, the Oval tool draws with the cursor on the outside of the oval. To draw from the center of the oval, hold the Alt (PC) or Command (Mac) key to draw from the center.

figure | 3-7

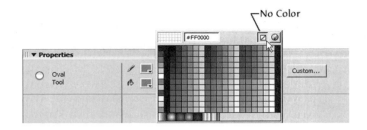

To create an oval
with no fill, choose
the No Fill button in
the swatches pop-
up window.

● When you create a filled oval, the fill is not attached to the oval—as it is in programs such as Illustrator or FreeHand. This means you can click-drag the fill away from the bounding elliptical line. We'll talk more about this in Chapter 5.

TRY THIS

Use the Oval tool to draw a bunch of filled and unfilled circles and ellipses to get the hang of how it works. Try using the Alt or Command key to see the difference this key makes when drawing. Also, try selecting and moving the fill in an oval—different, huh?

Try this: create an oval with a fill. Select the Arrow tool and double click on the fill. What happens? When you double click on a fill, Flash selects not only the fill but the line that surrounds the oval.

Rectangle Tool

The Rectangle tool functions essentially the same as the Oval tool except, well, it creates rectangles instead. Like the Oval tool you can create filled or unfilled rectangles. As well:

● To create a square, hold down the Shift key while creating the rectangle.

● Hold the Alt (PC) or Command (Mac) key to draw the rectangle from the center.

● When you create a rectangle, the lines that compose the rectangle are actually four distinct lines, rather than joined into one entity.

● Like ovals, fills in rectangles can be dragged away from their surrounding lines.

> ▶ **TRY THIS**
>
> Draw a number of rectangles, with and without fills. Try drawing one or two with the Alt or Command key pressed. Also, try double clicking on a fill that still has its four lines around it. Notice that when you do this the fill and all four lines are automatically selected.

Polystar Tool

The Polystar tool is a new tool in Flash 2004. It basically lets you create various polygons and stars. To access it, click and hold on the Rectangle tool (this will reveal the Polystar tool).

Once the Polystar tool is selected, you will see an Options button in the Properties panel. If you click this button a pop-up window will appear that will let you set the various parameters for the Polystar entity.

> ▶ **TRY THIS**
>
> The Polystar is a pretty cool tool and can be a time saver when you need to draw polygons or stars. Give this tool a little workout and see what you can create with it. Make sure you try to draw at least one polygon and one star to see how they work.

BEZIER DRAWING TOOLS

While most would likely be content with the tools previously described, some of you are likely itching for more control over your vector elements. The last tool we have yet to describe in this chapter is designed for just that—getting at the points that actually compose vector artwork. Earlier you saw the Subselection tool and how it could be used to access the points that compose existing line work. The Pen tool complements the Subselection tool by allowing you to draw lines and arcs in a point-based way.

Pen Tool

When you select the Pen tool, you'll see the familiar options appear in the Properties panel—no need to rehash that. What is important with the Pen tool is *how* you create lines and arcs.

To use the Pen tool, begin by either single clicking on the stage (which creates a non-Bezier-based point) or click-dragging (to create a Bezier point). If you create a Bezier point, how far you click-drag will determine the distance of the toggle handle from the actual point (the larger that distance, the bigger, or more dramatic, the curve).

 **DON'T** GO THERE

One of the keys to being really successful with using the Pen tool to draw curved elements is to use as few points as possible. The more points you have, the harder it is to control the curves.

▶ **TRY THIS**

While it may be awkward if you have never used such a tool, try getting up to speed with the Pen tool. Begin by just creating straight line segments that are interconnected (this is pretty easy). Once you get the hang of that, try creating a series of interconnected curves. Getting used to using the Pen tool is sort of like learning to do illustration with templates such as a "French curve." Once you do it a little while, it becomes more natural.

SUMMARY

In this chapter you have reviewed the basic groups of tools that appear in the toolbar, as well as delved into the view, selection, and drawing tools. Already you have begun to see some of the interesting things Flash can do and some of the ways in which it is differentiated from other tools. For example, in this chapter you have seen that Flash allows the traditional approach to vector graphics (use of point-based editing) as well as its unique natural drawing capabilities. In the next chapter you will examine the painting tools. And then, Chapter 5 will bring it all together by discussing editing.

1. What's the difference between the Arrow and Subselection tools?

2. What are transformation tools?

3. What are the shortcut keys for zooming? For panning?

4. What does Outline Preview Mode do? What is the advantage of using it?

5. To be able to use guides in Flash, what must be turned on?

6. How can you tell if an object is selected in Flash?

7. What does the Lasso tool do?

8. Where do the optional settings for tools appear? Careful, this is a trick question. Make sure you consider all tools!

9. What's one unique thing about fill elements in Flash (as compared to other tools)?

10. What's the most important thing to keep in mind when using the Pen tool?

↗ EXPLORING ON YOUR OWN

1. Using the tools you learned about in this chapter, create some content on the stage and try the different Preview Mode options in the View menu. Can you see the difference visually?

2. Use the various drawing tools to create a bunch of objects on the stage. Make sure you include elements with lines, as well as some entities that have fills. Now use the Lasso and Arrow tools to select a portion of those objects. Make sure you try different settings for the Lasso tool—that is, its default "free-form" mode as well as Polygon mode.

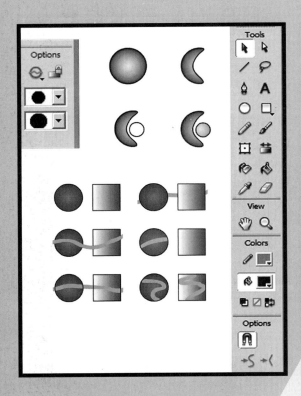

painting tools

charting your course

In prior chapters I have acknowledged the uniqueness of Flash as a graphics creation tool. Between this chapter and the next you will start to see more specific examples of what I mean by this. In short, the simple fact that Flash has "painting tools" should raise some questions in your mind—particularly if you have worked with other vector tools.

Packages such as Illustrator and FreeHand do not have a paint bucket, eraser, and the like; rather, these are typical of bitmap tools. However, while the existence of these tools may seem odd at first, you will find that it is a refreshing approach to the creation of vector content and it gives you quite a bit of flexibility as you create the graphic elements for your Flash movies. With that said, let's get busy.

 goals

In this chapter you will:

- Learn about the "painting" tools in Flash
- Discover how to use the Ink Bottle to change the characteristics of lines
- Find out about the Dropper tool and how it can be used to select already existing line or fill characteristics
- Use the Eraser tool to edit vector content in a really unique way

BRUSH TOOL

figure | 4-1 |

Several of the options for the Brush appear in the toolbar.

The Brush tool provides the ability to paint with various colors, brush sizes, and shapes akin to tools of the same name in raster programs such as Photoshop or PhotoPaint. Once you select the Brush tool, you choose a Fill color, a brush size, and shape (all of which are in the toolbar, as shown in figure 4-1). Once these options are set, you then can begin drawing on the stage.

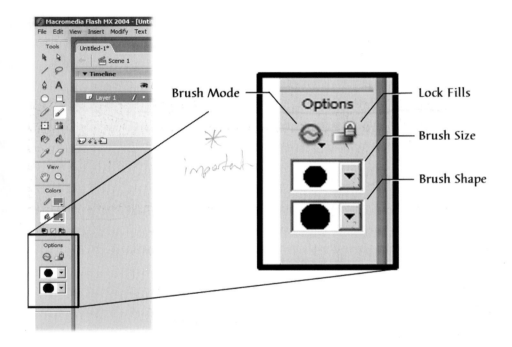

The thing to keep in mind about the Brush tool is that the entities you create with it are vector elements. In reality, Brush entities are closed polygons with no borderline. Where the Pencil, Line, and Pen tools create a line with a thickness, the Brush tool creates closed, smooth polygons that have no borders. An easy way to see this is to draw a line with the Pencil (and give it a beefy thickness) and then draw a similar Brush stroke. Then set the View | Preview Mode to Outlines. Then you can see the base-level vector componentry that composes the created elements, as shown in figure 4-2.

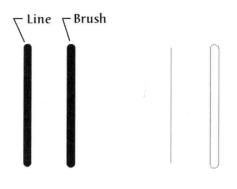

figure | 4-2

The difference between a fat line and a brush stroke can be seen when you view it in Outline Preview mode.

TRY THIS

Try your hand with the Brush tool to see how it works. Draw various brush strokes with different colors, brush sizes, and styles.

Smoothing

When you select the Brush tool, one option you should notice is the Smoothing option that appears in the Properties panel. This setting allows you to control how smoothly the brush stroke is drawn (a higher setting creates more flowing edges; a lower setting creates a rougher edge).

Painting Modes

One of the cool things you can do with the Brush is change what is painted when you use the Brush. When you select the Brush tool, the Brush Mode button appears in the Options section of the toolbar (again, who knows why things like this don't appear in the Properties panel). This lets you set what is painted when you use the tool. Figure 4-3 shows the effects of the different options.

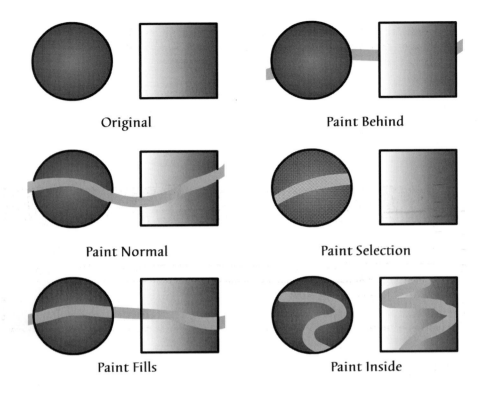

Original   Paint Behind

Paint Normal   Paint Selection

Paint Fills   Paint Inside

figure | 4-3 |

The Brush Modes let
you select what is
painted with the
Brush.

As shown in figure 4-3, Brush Modes determine whether the Brush paints over the top of stuff or not. The following list describes what the different modes do:

- *Paint Normal:* This simply causes the brush stroke to paint over the top of everything—lines and fills. In essence, this deletes anything that would be behind the stroke you create.

- *Paint Fills:* This option paints over the top of fills, but not lines. Basically, the brush stroke is "broken" where it crosses lines.

- *Paint Behind:* This mode causes the brush stroke to be drawn behind other entities.

- *Paint Selection:* This allows you to paint in a specific area. You select a fill and then the brush stroke only appears within the selected fill (or fills—you can select multiple fills and paint across them).

● *Paint Inside:* Although this setting may seem odd, it is designed for "constrained" painting. Paint Inside constrains the brush stroke inside the fill in which you start painting.

NOTE: We are going to skip the Lock Fills option as it relates to the Brush and Paint Bucket and return to it when you learn about the Dropper tool. Trying to explain it apart from the Dropper won't make a lot of sense.

▶ TRY THIS

Create a filled oval and a filled rectangle on the stage, similar to what is shown in figure 4-3. Try the various Paint Modes to see how they work. Make sure you try your hand at painting within a specific selection (this is pretty cool, and can be a big time saver).

PAINT BUCKET

At first glance, the purpose of the Paint Bucket tool is likely pretty obvious: you use it to fill large areas with solid or gradient colors. However, there is one noteworthy thing to mention about the Paint Bucket: to fill areas with color, you do not have to ensure that the area is closed. To assign fills in most vector environments, you have to be "anally retentive" about whether an area is closed or not. What a pain! In Flash, however, you can assign fills (or more aptly, fill areas) whether they are closed or not.

When you select the Paint Bucket, you will find the Gap Size button that appears in the bottom of the toolbar, near the Lock Fills button. With this little button you select the size of gap you want Flash to ignore. The default is Close Small Gaps, and this makes Flash ignore infinitesimally small gaps that might exist within otherwise apparently closed polygons (which is a godsend, by the way). You can choose other settings to make Flash ignore larger and larger gaps. Now there is a threshold: about 3 pixels is what the largest gap setting will fill. But all in all, this feature is relatively handy.

▶ **TRY THIS**

Well, the Paint Bucket is not all that exciting by itself, is it? But give it try anyway. Make sure you try messing around with filling polygons that have gaps in them.

INK BOTTLE

While some may argue that the Ink Bottle is really a drawing tool, not a painting tool (I waffle back and forth on this), the Ink Bottle allows you to change the color, style, or thickness of existing lines. If you select the Ink Bottle, the Properties panel will show you settings reminiscent of what you saw with the Line, Pencil, and Pen tools. Basically, select the attributes you want the existing line to have and click on a line on the stage. Voilà! The line now has the new attributes.

! DON'T GO THERE

As I issued in the prior chapter, make sure you don't use too many custom line styles in your Flash movies. Custom line styles can make your files much larger than necessary. I typically stick with Flash's standard line styles.

One thing to note about the Ink Bottle, however, is that if you have a bunch of lines that intersect one another, each click of the Ink Bottle will only change one line segment at a time. Thus, if line A is intersected by lines B and C (which themselves do not intersect), and you want to change the style of line A, you'll have to click three times—once on each segment of line A. And that's as close as we'll get to talking math in this book! But we will talk about a faster way to do this in Chapter 5 when I break out the quick tips and tricks for editing.

▶ **TRY THIS**

Create a bunch of lines on the screen using the Line tool—some that intersect and some that don't. Now use the Ink Bottle to change the characteristics of the lines. Oooh! Aaah!

DROPPER

The Dropper tool (ahem) is like the tool of the same name in bitmap programs: it lets you quickly sample fill colors (solids or gradients) from objects you have already created on the stage. If you select the Dropper, place the cursor over an existing fill on the stage and then click on the fill. When you drag the Dropper tool over a fill, a small paint bucket will appear as part of the cursor. Once you have clicked a fill on the stage, the Dropper will set the current color to the color of the fill you clicked on. Then Flash will automatically switch the current tool to the Paint Bucket (so you can start painting with the color you picked up with the Dropper).

Yet, the Dropper is not just for work with fills; it also permits you to "pick up" line characteristics from already existing lines. This is particularly useful. For example, if you have a line that already has the thickness, color, and style you want, use the Dropper to quickly pick up those attributes. When you drag the Dropper over a line, the cursor will show a small pencil as part of the cursor. This is how you tell whether you are about to sample line attributes or fill attributes. With the Dropper over a line, click and you will pick up the characteristics of that line. Like using the Dropper on fills, when you click on a line with the Dropper, the Ink Bottle will be immediately selected—so you can then change other lines to the characteristics sampled by the Dropper.

▶ TRY THIS

Let's take a closer look at the Dropper. Start a new Flash document and create some lines with various characteristics (thicknesses, styles, and so on). As well, create some ovals or rectangles that have fills. Select the Dropper and drag it over a fill and a line. See the difference between the two cursors? Now pick a fill color and transfer it from one object to another. Do the same thing with some of your lines.

Lock Fills

As we have talked about other tools that also include the Lock Fills option (Brush and Paint Bucket), I have reserved talking about it until now. The Lock Fills option basically lets you continue the color or gradient of a fill into a new blank area. Lock Fills becomes very useful when you are rendering (adding color to) artwork. The best way for me to explain it is to provide an applied example.

TRY THIS

Let's see what the Lock Fills option does. Begin by creating an oval with a gradient, as shown in figure 4-4a. Then use the Arrow tool to deform the oval, as shown in figure 4-4b. Create a second oval (with no fill) near the deformed oval (figure 4-4c). Use the Dropper tool to sample the fill in the deformed oval. Once you click on the fill with the Dropper, the Paint Bucket is automatically selected. More importantly, the Lock Fills option is automatically selected. With the Paint Bucket selected, click in the oval you created that had no fill (figure 4-4d). Notice that because the Lock Fill option was selected the fill from the deformed oval was continued into the second oval.

figure | 4-4 |

A little exercise to investigate the effect of the Lock Fills option.

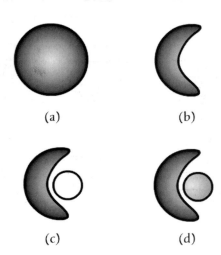

(a) (b)

(c) (d)

ERASER

To conclude our discussion of the painting tools, we end with the Eraser tool. Like the Brush tool, the Eraser provides different modes that affect how the tool behaves. In short, the Eraser tool lets you delete or erase portions of lines and fills. What makes it interesting are the different modes you can set.

Eraser Modes

When you select the Eraser tool, the Eraser Modes button appears in the Options section of the toolbar. Like the Brush, the Eraser lets you control whether you delete lines or fills (or both), as well as to constrain the erasure within selections. Figure 4-5 shows the various options.

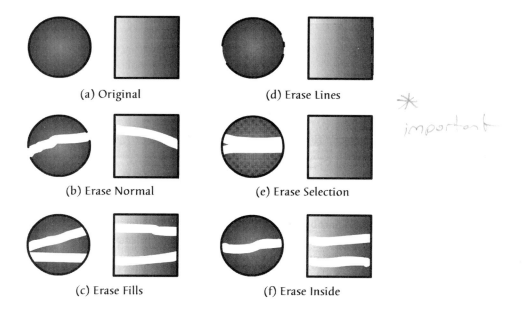

(a) Original   (d) Erase Lines

(b) Erase Normal   (e) Erase Selection

(c) Erase Fills   (f) Erase Inside

figure | 4-5

The Eraser modes allow you to control what is erased.

SUMMARY

In this chapter you have taken a look at the various painting tools available in Flash. As you can see, Flash permits a wide range of flexibility as it relates to creating graphic components. To conclude our discussion of working with vector graphics in Flash, the next chapter will deal with issues surrounding editing in Flash as well as importing and exporting graphical content.

in review

1. What's the difference between the Paint Bucket and the Ink Bottle tool?

2. How can you tell if the Dropper is going to sample a fill or line?

3. What tool is selected after you use the Dropper on a line? On a fill? *Ink Bottle*

4. What does Lock Fill do?

5. If you are having trouble getting the Paint Bucket to fill an apparently closed area—that is, you click and it doesn't do anything—what should you adjust or change?

6. What's the difference between a stroke created by the Brush tool and a thick line created by the Line tool?

7. What does the Smoothing setting do for the Brush tool?

8. How do you control what the Brush tool paints over? What are the different options and what do they do?

9. How do you control how the Eraser behaves? What are the options and what do they do?

✦ EXPLORING ON YOUR OWN

1. Now that you know how to work the drawing and painting tools, try your hand at creating a piece of artwork in Flash. Start with some basic line work and then render the piece.

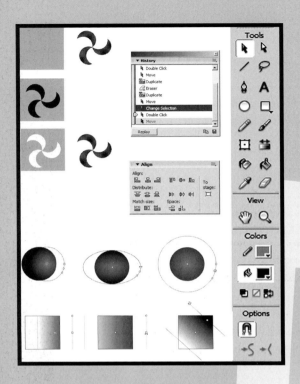

| editing, transformations, and importing |

charting your course

In the last couple of chapters you have been getting up to speed on the various drawing and painting tools in Flash. Hopefully you can now clearly see some of the really unique aspects of Flash—given both its illustration and painting qualities. Again, this is why so many designers and developers love it, because it gives everyone an option as to how they wish to work. In this chapter, we'll come full circle by dealing with editing issues, transformations, and importing and exporting vector content.

 goals

In this chapter you will:

- **Learn about stage and overlay objects**

- **Find out about concepts such as grouping, layering, and scenes**

- **Acknowledge some of the peculiarities of how stage objects behave**

- **Learn about some of the special editing features for stage objects**

- **Discover the editing features for overlay objects**

- **Know how to use the transformation tools in Flash**

- **Understand how to import and export content**

CONCEPTS

Now that we've laid some groundwork, let's discuss some basic concepts you should understand. Whether you are new to computer graphics or not, the concepts presented in the following section are critical to really understanding how to efficiently and effectively use Flash. And, since many of the concepts are more global in nature—that is, you will find similar themes in other packages—you can even transfer some of what you learn here to other software programs.

Environment Hierarchy

Often software books skip over conceptual things. This really bugs me. Inevitably such books skirt conceptual issues, telling you every detail but never addressing it in a way that explains *why* something works the way it does. So, you'll have to excuse the professor in me for a moment. I wish to explain something that will help you understand why some of the peculiarities of Flash exist.

Stage Objects

Up to this point in the book you have been working with the "lowest level" elements that exist in Flash—that is, lines, arcs, and fills, which are defined by points. Whether you choose to work directly with points or not depends on which drawing tool you choose. The Arrow tool does not work with points; the Subselection tool does. The Pen tool does work with points, while the Line and Pencil tools do not. Effectively, this is what is meant by natural drawing (not working with points), or the traditional Bezier approach.

Points or no points, these types of elements (which we will call "stage objects") behave a certain way—that is, they can interact with one another, as you began to see in the last chapter. For example, if two lines lie over the top of one another, they automatically "break" each other at the intersection. We'll look more closely at such peculiarities later in this chapter.

Overlay Objects

Now, there is a second "level" of elements that behave differently than stage objects, and I refer to them as "overlay objects." I chose that term because you can overlay them on top of one another and they don't affect one another. In essence, overlay objects and stage objects behave in two different ways. Overlay objects include objects that are grouped, as well as text entities, (which will be discussed in Chapter 6), bitmaps (Chapter 7) and symbols (Chapter 9). Let's first deal with the concept of grouping.

Grouping

The concept of grouping is common to many graphics packages. It is basically where you tell the software that you want to treat all of the entities as a set of objects you can manipulate. The most common reason to group things is so that you can transform (move, scale, rotate, or skew) them, but you can do a variety of other things with them too (more on that later). To group objects, you select them on the stage and then choose Edit | Group.

Symbols, Bitmaps, and Text

Because there is a chapter devoted to each of these items, I only want to acknowledge them here as part of the Flash hierarchy. Symbols, bitmaps, and text elements are all overlay objects. Symbols are special reusable elements that for the most part function like groups. What makes them different from groups is that they are only stored once in your files. Bitmaps and text are self-explanatory at this point. We'll get into the nitty-gritty in their respective chapters.

Layering

In addition to the concept of stage and overlay objects, we should also mention two other structural things that exist in Flash files. The first is layers. Layers give you a way of organizing your files spatially—that is, the ability to layer the stage front to back with various levels of art elements. Layering is a concept that is a carry-over from traditional production art. In this sense, artists would typically mount different parts of artwork on transparent sheets and then combine the sheets over the top of one another to create a single image, as shown in figure 5-1.

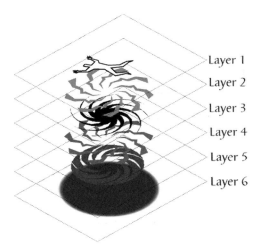

Layer 1
Layer 2
Layer 3
Layer 4
Layer 5
Layer 6

(a) Conceptual View   (b) Actual View

figure | **5-1** |

The concept of layering is a carryover from traditional art.

This is conceptually the same thing that happens in Flash. Flash's timeline lets you create different layers (which are transparent) until you put something on them. Up to this point, we have only been working on the default, one-layer document. As we move into later chapters we will deal with layers more.

NOTE: When you get to the chapters about animation, we'll take some time to focus on layers—how you create them, how you can manipulate them, and so on. For now, just realize that Flash provides layering capability.

Scenes

The second structural component in Flash is called scenes. Scenes allow you organize your content temporally (or, over time). Scenes are the topmost organizational structure in a Flash file, aside from the movie file itself. With scenes, you can break your movie into logical temporal structures that mimic scene segments in a play or movie (that is where the concept is derived from). Again, I only want to acknowledge this facility here so that you can get the holistic view of the Flash environment. We'll deal with scenes when we start talking about animation.

The Holistic View

Okay, we have covered what may have appeared to be a mish-mash of various items. Let's tie it all together:

- The Flash document hierarchy is composed of stage objects, overlay objects, layers, and scenes.

- Stage objects include base elements: lines, arcs, and fills.

- Overlay objects include text, bitmaps, groups, and symbols.

Given these statements, examine figure 5-2. It graphically shows what the prior sections have discussed, and it gives you a mental picture of the Flash hierarchy as it relates to stage and overlay objects. Note that text objects and bitmap objects are overlay objects by default (however, you can break them down so that they become stage objects). To convert stage objects to overlay objects, you can either group them or convert them to symbols. The latter is preferable.

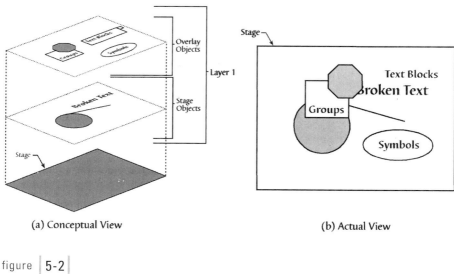

(a) Conceptual View   (b) Actual View

figure 5-2

Stage versus overlay objects.

Now, aside from stage and overlay objects, figure 5-3 shows the hierarchy of Flash movies. Layers are organizational structures for separating the depth of spatial content in the environment. Scenes are organizational structures for separating content temporally. Movie files (documents) are composed of scenes (temporal segments). Each scene is composed of layers (spatial segments).

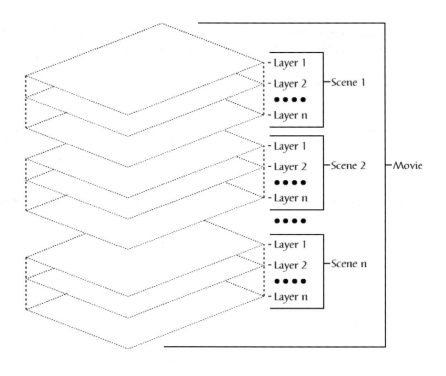

figure | 5-3

The Flash environment hierarchy.

Stage Object Peculiarities

In prior chapters I have acknowledged a few of the peculiarities of the Flash environment. Already you have seen that lines automatically clip one another and that double clicking various elements automatically selects adjacent objects. Let's finish this by examining fill clipping and interaction and shape recognition.

Fill Clipping and Interaction

Ungrouped fills behave in a very specific way. Already you have probably noticed that when you create filled ovals and rectangles, the fill can be separated from the bounding lines. You should also realize that when fills are moved over the top of other objects and deselected, they delete whatever is behind them.

TRY THIS

Create two filled rectangles on the stage that do not overlap. Use the Arrow tool to select one of the filled rectangles. To quickly select the fill and its lines, double click on the fill. Move the filled rectangle over the top of the other filled rectangle and deselect. When you deselect, parts of the background rectangle are deleted by the foreground rectangle. To keep this type of deletion from occurring, you must either place the objects (rectangles and their fills) on separate layers, or group each rectangle.

In addition to what I call the "deletion effect" that you saw in the prior task, fills in Flash also interact with one another. Basically, the interaction that occurs is a Boolean operation—that is, a Boolean union or subtraction. When two fills are the same color and they are overlapped and deselected, they merge together into one entity (Boolean union), as shown in figure 5-4.

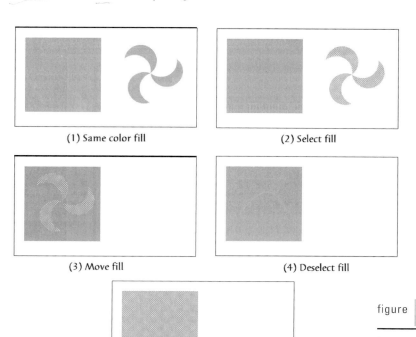

(1) Same color fill   (2) Select fill

(3) Move fill   (4) Deselect fill

(5) Fills are merged

figure | 5-4

Fills that are the same color merge together when overlapped and deselected.

If two fills are different colors and they are overlapped and dese-lected, they subtract from one another, as shown in figure 5-5. Keep in mind that the way you overcome the merging and sub-tracting properties of fills (as well as the slice-and-dice property of lines) is to use groups or layers.

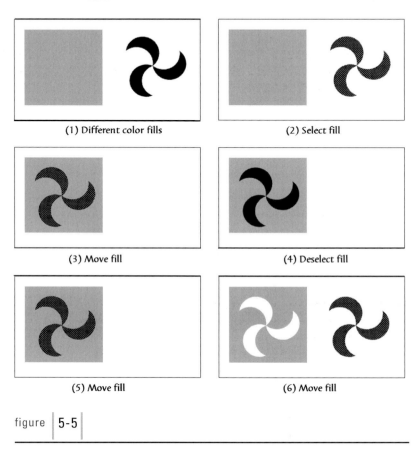

(1) Different color fills	(2) Select fill
(3) Move fill	(4) Deselect fill
(5) Move fill	(6) Move fill

figure | 5-5 |

Fills that are different colors subtract from one another when overlapped and select-ed.

TRY THIS

Experiment with the unioning and subtracting properties of fills. Try grouping the elements to see what effect it has on this property.

Shape Recognition

A final noteworthy feature is something called shape recognition. Flash can recognize basic shapes you create. Draw some lines in the rough form of a triangle and a square, and choose Modify | Shape | Straighten. Flash will try to transform your rough drawing into the respective shape, as shown in figure 5-6. Doesn't always work perfectly, but is a handy tool.

Similarly, you can have Flash "smooth out" things you have drawn with the Pen. If you choose the Modify | Shape | Smooth option, Flash will transform a rough or jaggy curve to a more natural, flowing one.

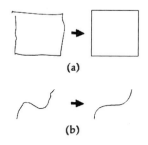

(a)

(b)

figure | **5-6**

Straighten can recognize basic shapes from rough lines (a), while smooth can be used to create more flowing arcs (b).

Editing Stage Objects

In addition to shape recognition, Flash provides four other editing commands you should be aware of. All of these are located in the Modify | Shape submenu. These are:

- *Optimize:* This command will try to simplify the vector elements that compose a graphic element. You can control the amount of smoothing. When you are working with a lot of graphical components, you'd be surprised how much you can shrink a file by using the Optimize command to simplify your drawings.

- *Convert Lines to Fills:* Pretty self-explanatory, but one word of caution on this capability. Converting a lot of lines to fills will make your file size increase (there is no way around this). Thus, use this option only when you absolutely need to.

- *Expand Fill:* This little tool either expands or insets a fill by a certain number of pixels.

- *Soften Fill Edges:* Like converting lines to fills, you have to be careful with the Soften Fill Edge option because it can dramatically increase file size. This option creates "blurred edges" on a fill. The blur is composed of multiple fills that blend from the fill color to transparent.

> ▶ **TRY THIS**
>
> Get a better understanding of the stage object editing commands. Create some fills and try the Expand Fill and Soften Fill Edges commands. Try converting some lines to fills, too.

Overlay Editing

In our discussion of stage versus overlay objects I mentioned that overlay objects behave differently from stage objects. One of the most notable things is that overlay objects don't merge, subtract, or cut each other. But overlay objects can also be used to do a couple other things, as described in the following sections.

Arranging Elements

Already you have seen that layers can be used to organize things in the depth dimension. However, you can also arrange the depth of things within a layer—except that you can only do so with overlay objects. Stage objects have only one depth (that is why they merge, delete, subtract, and cut each other). If you access the Modify | Arrange submenu, you will find the common z-order (depth arrangement) commands.

> ▶ **TRY THIS**
>
> When you have multiple overlay objects in a layer, try using the menu options in the Arrange submenu. Try clicking on a stage object and accessing the menu. Note that the options are grayed out and cannot be used.

Locking and Aligning

A common feature of most graphics packages is the ability to lock elements as well as align (or distribute) a series of elements. One difference you will notice in Flash (as compared to other packages) is that once an overlay object is locked, it cannot be selected. To lock an element, select it and use Modify | Arrange | Lock. To unlock any and all elements (note that you cannot unlock elements individually), use Modify | Arrange | Unlock All.

Just as the Arrange commands cannot be used on stage objects, so too the locking and aligning tools cannot be used on them.

DON'T GO THERE!

To align or distribute elements in Flash, you use the Align panel, shown in figure 5-7. In addition to being able to align and distribute objects to one another, you can also use the stage as an alignment reference. Another neat feature is the ability to match the size of elements to one another. The *Match size* options (in the bottom of the panel) let you force all elements to be the same size (vertically or horizontally).

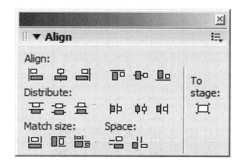

figure | 5-7

The Align panel can be used to align or distribute multiple overlay objects on the stage.

Breaking Objects

A final command I should mention is the Break Apart command. The Break Apart command can be used to convert an overlay object back to its stage-level elements. However, the Break Apart command does some different things, depending on what you use it on:

● On groups, generally Break Apart does the same thing as ungroup. If you have nested groups—in other words you have a group A grouped inside group B—selecting Break Apart once leaves group A intact. Using Break Apart twice will break both groups.

- On symbols, Break Apart will split the symbol into stage objects. However, like groups, if you have nested symbols, Break Apart will progressively break things apart (more on this in Chapter 9).

- On text entities, Break Apart will convert the text element into respective fill elements (more in Chapter 6).

- On bitmaps, Break Apart allows you to use the bitmap as a fill or it permits you to slice and dice the image into pieces (more in Chapter 7).

!DON'T GO THERE

When using the Break Apart command, you have to be careful. If you break nested groups or nested symbols apart, the stage-level interaction between elements (unioning, subtracting, and cutting) that occurs can do some strange things. Just be conscientious when using Break Apart to make sure something doesn't go awry.

HISTORY PANEL

One very important addition to the latest release of Flash is the History panel, shown in figure 5-8. This feature allows you to back-step through the changes that have been made in a movie so that you can selectively decide how far back you want to go. Think of it as a visual way to see what you have done in the environment (a visual "undo," if you will). The small arrow on the left side of the bar shows the current "location" in the processes you have executed. To step backward through what you have done, click-drag the small arrow. Note that you can step backward and forward in the history, replay a particular step and save it, and copy a series of steps.

figure | 5-8 |

The new History panel gives you a lot of flexibility when you are working.

TRY THIS

Open a new Flash document and create some basic entities on the screen using the drawing and painting tools. Open the History panel and try manipulating the arrow that controls where you are in the steps you have performed. Try replaying a few of the steps to see how it works.

TRANSFORMATIONS

Now we'll move onto one of the most interesting parts of the Flash environment: performing transformations on objects. Transformations are simply moving, rotating, scaling, or skewing objects. Flash gives you a lot of flexibility and there several ways to do transformations.

Although Flash provides some special tools for working with transformations, the most rudimentary (moving) can be accomplished using the Arrow tool. There is one thing you should note about the Arrow tool, however. If you hold the Ctrl (PC) or Command (Mac) key when click-dragging an object, Flash will duplicate the object rather than move the original. When Flash is duplicating something, a small white plus sign appears as part of the cursor. With that said, let's look at some of the different ways you can perform transformations, and on which objects you can perform them.

Info and Properties Panels

While it may not need mentioning, I do want to draw your attention to these two panels and the fact that you can use them to absolutely position objects on the screen. Both panels provide the ability to insert specific height and width information, as well as specific screen locations for objects. While you have already encountered the Properties panel, figure 5-9 shows the Info panel.

▼ Info

W: 242.4   X: 157.3
H: 278.5   Y: 52.5

R: 153
G: 255   + X: 353.7
B: 255   Y: 287.4
A: 100%

figure | 5-9 |

The Info panel can be used to set the size and location of objects.

Free Transform Tool

One of the best tools in Flash is its Free Transform tool. This is an "all-in-one" type of tool that can be used to perform any transformation. Figure 5-10 shows the cursor states that appear when you drag near a selected element with the Free Transform tool.

figure | 5-10 |

The Free Transform tool is an "all-in-one" tool allowing any transformation.

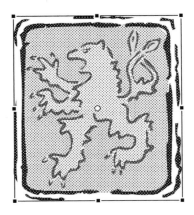

	Move
	Rotate
	Vertically Skew
	Horizontally Skew
	Proportionally Scale
	Horizontally Scale
	Vertically Scale

The transformation that is performed is based on where the cursor is located:

*important

- If you drag near a corner, you can proportionally scale or rotate.

- If you drag near a midpoint, you can disproportionally scale (scale along a horizontal or vertical only) or skew.

- If you drag over the selected element, you can move it.

▶ **TRY THIS**

Try using the Free Transform tool on some objects of your choosing. Make sure you try each of the different types (move, rotate, proportional and disproportional scale, and skew).

If you tried the prior task, you likely noticed that the transformations are all based around the center of the object you selected. If you refer back to figure 5-10, notice in the center of the selected element (center of the griffin) there is a filled, white circle. This circle is the origin point for the transformation. And, as you could likely guess, it can be relocated by click-dragging it. This makes it possible to transform around any point in the image. The origin for the transformation can also be moved outside the image (basically, it can be located anywhere). However, the location is not saved (if you deselect and start again, the origin reverts to the center of the selection).

> ## TRY THIS
>
> Try using the Free Transform tool again, only this time change the origin point for the transformation to see the effect it has.

Transform Panel and Transform Submenu

In addition to using the Free Transform tool, there are two other ways to perform transformations. The first is the use of the Transform panel. With it, you can enter numerical values for scaling, rotation, and skew. Access the Transform panel by selecting Window | Design Panels | Transform.

The Modify | Transform submenu provides a tertiary means of performing transforms. This allows you to select a specific transform you want to use. A couple of additional items exist here, too, including clockwise and counterclockwise rotations of 90 degrees and the typical Flip Horizontal and Flip Vertical menu options.

SPECIAL TRANSFORMATIONS

In addition to the normal transformations, Flash provides two special transformation tools that are designed to work on stage-level objects. These two capabilities will not do anything to overlay objects.

Transform Fill Tool

The Transform Fill tool allows you to change the way a gradient appears inside a fill. When we talked about creating fills in Chapter 2, I told you not to worry about changing the size, orientation, or position of a fill. Now we will return to that issue.

When you create an object with a linear or radial gradient fill, the fill is created in a default location and orientation. If you select the Transform Fill tool in the toolbar and click on the fill, small handles will appear around the fill, as shown in figure 5-11. As you move near these handles you are able to rotate, scale, or move the gradient within the fill. The Transform Fill tool works somewhat like the Free Transform tool: which handle you move the cursor near determines which transformation you can perform on the fill.

figure | **5-11**

Which handle you drag near determines the transformation.

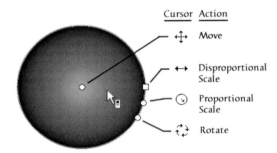

The Transform Fill tool permits you to perform all types of transformations on the fill, as shown in figure 5-12. You can also perform multiple transformations; that is, you can apply a scale, rotation, and move all at the same time.

figure | **5-12**

The basic transformations that can be made to linear and radial fills.

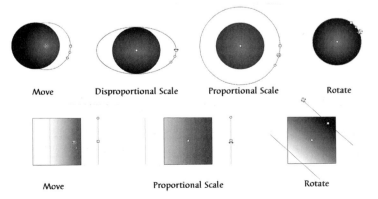

Envelope and Distort

Two final transformation features I should acknowledge are the Envelope and Distort options for the Free Transform tool. Again, these two items work on stage objects only. To use them, select a set of stage objects and choose the Free Transform tool. When you do this, the Distort and Envelope options will appear at the bottom of the toolbar. Distort allows you to perform free-form angular manipulations on a selection set, as shown in figure 5-13a. The Envelope option allows you to bend or bow the midpoints or corner points (small handles appear, akin to the Bezier control points found when using the Pen or Subselection tool). Move the handles to deform the selection (see figure 5-13b).

Original

(a) Distort

(b) Envelope

figure | 5-13

The effect of the Free Transform tool's Distort (a) and Envelope (b) options.

IMPORTING AND EXPORTING ARTWORK

When you are importing vector artwork into Flash, FreeHand is quite simply the best tool to use. Special features exist in both Flash and FreeHand that allow them to share each other's data quite readily. Nevertheless, Flash supports a wide variety of formats for both importing and exporting. Here are some quick tips concerning some specific file formats:

- The EPS format, while it does work very well on the Macintosh, is quite tricky on the PC. There are various flavors of the format on the PC and all too often an EPS file from one program will be unreadable by another.

- Like EPS, PICT works really well on the Mac, but is unpredictable (at best) on the PC. If you're in a Mac-only shop, use it.

- The WMF format is a very popular format on the PC. However, it does not retain arcs and circles. Try using the EMF format instead. It retains arcs and circles and works extremely well in the Microsoft Office products.

- If you are working with other people who use a variety of platforms—particularly UNIX—CGM is a common format. Works well when UNIX is in the mix, but otherwise is not all that useful.

- When exporting to another vector program (including FreeHand), the AI format (Adobe Illustrator) is the best to use. It is robust and widely supported—even in FreeHand.

- When exporting an image for general use, the EMF format is preferred on the PC. Again, it is quite robust and widely supported.

SUMMARY

In this chapter you have examined quite a few things—from editing objects to importing and exporting content. While you may have found some of the conceptual discussions dry, they are important. As I have taught newcomers to Flash, more often than not, when something goes haywire it is due to not understanding the way Flash works. In the next chapter, we'll step over into dealing with text and the myriad things you can do with it in Flash.

1. Name the different types of stage objects.

2.. Name the different types of overlay objects.

3. What are the unique characteristics of stage objects? Of overlay objects?

4. How do you spatially arrange content in Flash; that is, what facility does Flash give you for spatially ordering the depth in your movies?

5. How do you temporally arrange content in Flash; that is, what facility does Flash give you for temporally ordering your content?

6. What happens if you overlap two fills that are the same color? What if they are different colors?

7. What operation can you perform on stage objects that will reduce your file size?

8. What does the Break Apart command do?

9. What operations does the Free Transform tool allow you to do? What about the Transform Fill tool?

10. What are the two special transformations that exist for stage objects?

↗ EXPLORING ON YOUR OWN

1. Plan and create a complex drawing using the drawing, painting, and editing techniques you have learned. Try creating an organic and a non-organic graphic to see the positives and negatives of the Flash environment.

2. Try importing and exporting graphics between Flash and some of your other favorite tools. Are there particular file formats that work better?

ADVENTURES IN DESIGN

BUILDING CONTENT GRAPHICS

While this text focuses on Flash, often you will work between tools to create your designs—particularly as it relates to what I would call "content graphics" in your Flash movies. What are content graphics? you ask. Basically what I mean by this are the graphics that become part of the information you are presenting within your Flash movies. Indeed, even though a lot of your time will be spent in Flash, using Flash doesn't negate the use of other tools, such as Adobe Illustrator or Macromedia Freehand. The extent to which you will use these other tools in combination with Flash will be based on your experience.

You can build everything you need in Flash—but if you have experience with these other tools, you may find it handy to import starting artwork from other vector programs and then colorize and finish up the artwork in Flash. An example I created in just this fashion is the graphic (which I eventually animated) shown in figure A-1.

Figure A-1. The Cyber Outpost image.

Professional Project Example

The Cyber Outpost image was created for a web site that was intended to be a "stopping place" for information about web design. I started by creating a quick concept sketch, as shown in figure A-2. While I realize most digital designers want to jump right to digital tools and begin working, I recommend beginning with good-old paper and pencil because you can quickly jot down ideas and play with a design without having to deal with the hassles inherent in doing it on the computer. I venture to say pencil and paper will always be quicker for stuff like this.

Figure A-2. A basic concept sketch for the Cyber Outpost image.

Once the pencil sketch was done, I actually started the basic line work for the image in Freehand, as shown in figure A-3. I find that because of my familiarity with Freehand I can more quickly create mechanical things in it —as opposed to starting in Flash. Now, you'll have to choose what is best for you. This is just my preference. Ultimately, choose whatever is most convenient and fastest for you.

Figure A-3. Creating the basic line drawing of the image in Freehand.

There is no one right or wrong way—it is an issue of efficiency.

Once the basic line work was done, I imported it into Flash and began colorizing it. I typically like to do the gradient work and colorization in Flash, because importing images from other packages with gradients and fills already intact can sometimes lead to some strange results in Flash. Plus, I like Flash's fill and gradient capabilities much more than those available in Freehand or Illustrator.

Your Turn

Now, come up with your own idea for a basic graphic image you can create. Imagine you are being hired to design a web site that is going to be an information repository of some sort. Maybe it is focused on some medical topic, scientific topic, or really any topic you can think of. Then, devise some sort of catchy graphic that can be used to represent the site, similar to the Cyber Outpost image representing a repository of information about developing content for the Web.

Self Project Guidelines

1. Once you have a focus for the project (that is, what kind of informa-

tion will be in your repository), brainstorm ideas that can be used to represent the site in a graphic. I find it often helps to doodle with different concepts on paper. You can also use the Web to help sprout ideas.

2. After creating several doodles, consider which might be the best to bring to life. Consider all aspects when choosing "the one." Will most of your audience associate this graphic with the content being portrayed in the site? Does the choice provide flexibility in use (that is, could you animate it if you decided to; can it be used as a logo of sorts)?

3. The next step is to create a digital representation of your idea in a more solid form. There are two ways to do this: (1) Recreate the sketch in Flash or some other package to get the basic line work in place; or (2) scan in your sketch (if it is pretty solid) and then trace over it to create a vector line work version of it.

4. When it's complete, now get the line work into Flash and start using the drawing, painting, and editing tools to colorize it. When choosing your colors, remember to begin with some color scheme in mind. But understand there is nothing wrong with creating a couple of different versions (with different color and stuff) and then choosing the one you like best. More often than not, this is the approach I use. The first creation often does not become the final creation!

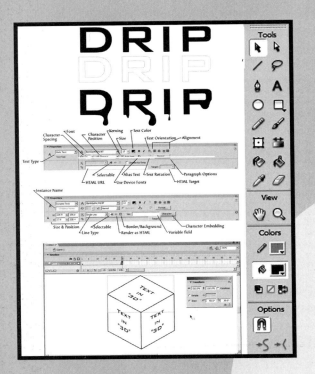

| text |

charting your course

While a lot of what you will create in Flash will be graphical, text components are equally important. As you have likely learned in coursework or simply through experience, text elements—and particularly the characteristics of those text elements—can drastically affect your designs. In this chapter you'll take a look at how you can control the various attributes (font family, style, size, and so on) of text elements. You will also learn about the three major types of text entities Flash provides. Each type is designed for a specific purpose.

 *goals*

In this chapter you will:

● **Understand the basics of typography and learn valuable tips about using text in design**

● **Find out how the Text tool works**

● **Discover the three types of text entities in Flash MX 2004**

● **Know the difference between text blocks and text labels**

● **Find out about font mapping**

TYPOGRAPHY PRIMER

While we need not detail every aspect of typographic design, there are a few items that it would be helpful to acknowledge as it relates to the study of typography. Likely you've had (or will have) courses that focus on the study of type and all of its intricacies. All we need here is a quick primer to acknowledge some specific terminology.

Attributes

When dealing with typography, there are generally two sets of terms. One set deals with the *legibility* of type (being able to distinguish the different letters that compose a font), while the other set deals with the *readability* (ability to distinguish groups of words). While many use these terms synonymously, there is actually a difference between them. The following terms are common to typographic design and are ones you should be familiar with:

● *Font, font face, or font family:* Describes particular groupings of fonts that have a different look or style. The two major categories of fonts are serif (fonts with "feet and tails") and sans serif (without "feet and tails").

● *Size* and *weight:* Size describes the overall height of the text, typically measured in points or picas. Weight describes the thickness or lightness of the strokes that comprise the font face.

● *Posture:* Describes the orientation of the text. Making something italic changes the type posture.

● *Treatment:* Describes embellishments to a font to improve legibility and readability. This could include changing the letter spacing (spacing between characters), which is sometimes called tracking, or by changing the kerning. Kerning is the spacing between specific combinations of characters. By adjusting the spacing (kerning), you improve readability.

In addition to the terminology related to type, there are also terms associated with blocks of text. These include:

● *Alignment:* Describes how multiple lines of text (that compose a paragraph) are arranged relative to one another. Paragraphs can be left-, right-, or center-aligned. They can also be justified, where lines of text are made flush on both left and right sides. To justify paragraphs software increases letter spacing and/or word spacing.

- *Line spacing:* The amount of space between adjacent lines of text in a paragraph; also called leading.

As you begin looking at the Properties panel and how it can be used to set the characteristics of text entities, these terms will be related to the controls you will see.

Typographic Tips

While many do not realize it, there is a lot of time and effort that has been spent on performing research related to typography and its use. Entire careers can be spent examining how best to represent a message with type so that it is optimally readable and legible. Although space does not permit lengthy discourse on this, the following are some simple "rules-of-thumb" you can use to be more successful. The overarching thing to keep in mind when using text in your movies is that the utmost importance is legibility and readability:

- In choosing a type face for your text, make sure the type does not overpower the text; that is, the font face should compliment what is being said, not distract from it.

- Use color for emphasis, rather than italicizing or bolding elements.

- In general, use sans serif fonts for large text items and serif fonts for paragraphs of text. While there are cases where you might depart from this, when serif fonts are large they get "noisy." Similarly, when sans serif fonts are shown in paragraph form (or at a small size) they become cumbersome on the eyes and hard to read.

- Don't overuse fonts. Choose one or two fonts and stick with them throughout an entire project. Also, don't use several similar font faces. If there is not enough contrast between font faces, it can be counterproductive.

- Paragraphs should have between 35 and 65 characters. Less than 35 appear broken, while more than 65 may cause the reader to "double" (reread lines).

- DO NOT SET ANYTHING IN ALL CAPS. While it may get attention, it is much harder to read.

- Do not center-align paragraphs, ever!

- Always consider your audience and what the text is being used for when defining your text entities (as it relates to font selection and size).

- Generally, paragraphs should be 10 to 12 points, while headings should range from 14 to 30 points. Anything smaller than 8 points on screen is nearly unreadable to most people.

- Line spacing should generally be 1 to 2 point sizes larger than the font point size.

- Proofread! Proofread! Proofread! Although most software (including Flash) provide a spell-checker, no spell-checker is as intelligent as a human.

As we move on and start looking at the Text tool in Flash, remember that the rules listed in this chapter are "rules of thumb," not absolutes. Design is about creativity and not being limited to a hard-and-fast set of guidelines. The longer you do design work, the more you will realize that there are appropriate times to break rules. But *in general*, the rules presented in this section will help you become a better designer.

THE TEXT TOOL

Flash basically provides a single tool for working with text. If you have used other packages, you will find the basic formatting controls very familiar. However, text in Flash can do several things not found in other packages.

Types of Text Entities

Flash provide three different types of text entities, and you can fluidly change a text element from one type to another. The three types are:

- *Static:* This type of text entity is used when you want to create a text entity whose content will not change during the course of a movie. Static text objects can be used for labels (such as a label for a text field), headings, or for paragraphs of text. There are two types of static text objects, labels and blocks, and the difference between them will be discussed momentarily.

● *Dynamic:* This type of text object is used when you want to display to the end user text that is based on some data source, such as a variable or property in the movie.

● *Input:* This kind of text element is used when you want the user to be able to enter data, such as in a Flash-based form.

Knowing that there are different types of text objects, let's move on and take a look at the properties associated with the Text tool.

Tool Properties

When you select the Text tool, the Properties panel displays many options, as shown in figure 6-1. Depending on which text type is shown in the drop-down menu to the left of the Properties panel, the various Text tool properties will change. Figure 6-1 shows the properties for static text.

Figure 6-1 shows a lot of settings you have at your disposal. These options include:

● *Text Type drop-down list:* Determines what type of text object you are going to create.

● *Font drop-down list:* Sets the font face that will be used for the text object.

● *Character Spacing field:* Controls the character spacing.

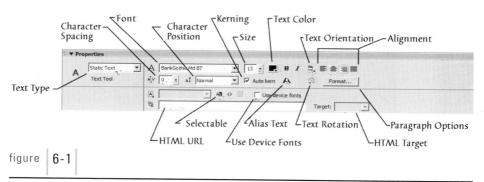

figure | 6-1 |

The properties associated with the Text tool when creating a static text entity.

- *Character Position drop-down list:* Creates subscript and super-script text.

- *Font Size field:* Controls the size of the text within the text object.

- *Auto Kern checkbox:* Turns kerning on and off.

- *Text (fill) Color control:* Defines the color of the text.

- *Bold and Italic buttons:* Allow you to style text as bold or italic.

- *Text Direction and Rotation buttons:* These two options work together. They permit you to change the definition of how text "flows" within the field, which is specifically designed for repre-senting Asian text in Flash.

- *Alias Text:* Allows you to turn off antialiasing on a text entity.

- *Alignment button:* Controls the alignment of the entire block of text.

- *Format (paragraph properties) button:* Provides indent, line spacing, and left and right margin settings.

The options in the bottom of figure 6-1 are "special" formatting properties, not necessarily related to "how the text looks." These include the following:

- *Selectable button:* Makes the text in the object selectable by the end user at runtime. By default, Static Text is not selectable.

- *Use Device Fonts checkbox:* Allows you to tell Flash not to embed the font associated with the text object in the resulting web-ready Flash file.

- *URL Link and Target fields:* Allow you to specify that the entire text object be treated as a hyperlink. When assigning a URL to a text object, you can also specify an HTML target for the link to be loaded into.

LABELS AND BLOCKS

When you create a static text element, how you create it determines whether it is what Flash calls a label or a block. If you single click on the stage and enter your text, a text label is created. When you

do this, a small circle appears in the upper right-hand corner of the
text object-bounding box, as shown in figure 6-2a.

This is an example of a label

(a)

This is an example of a text
block

(b)

figure 6-2

With static text, you
can create (a) text
labels or (b) text
blocks.

If you click-drag with the Text tool (to create an area for the text
entry) and then enter your text, a text block is created. When you
do this, the text object displays a small square in the upper right-
hand corner of the object on the stage, as shown in figure 6-2b.

"What's the difference between a text label and a text block?" you
may ask. As far as manipulating, formatting, and so on, there is little difference. In both cases you can make the object a multiline
text object. For text labels you must press the Enter key, whereas
text blocks automatically wrap when you reach the right-hand
bound of the text object. The real difference relates to accessibility
and how the Flash player acknowledges the object.

In the first case, a text label, Flash will assume that something
needing a label will follow (or be in close proximity to) the object,
such as an input text object. If a non-visual browser is being used
to view the Flash movie, the Flash player will automatically "read"
the content of the label for the end user. Text blocks, on the other
hand, function as independent elements and are not tied to anything else in the environment. If you are designing web sites and
striving to accommodate web accessibility guidelines, as well as
ADA requirements, you should be cognizant of this difference.

One of the things to note about both types of static text objects is
that you can use the handle on the right-hand side to change the
width of the text object. If you click-drag the handle it will size, but
when you size a text label in this way it is "converted" to a text
block. This is visible in that the handle changes from a circle to a
square. If you want to "size" a text label and have it remain as a text
label, you must use the Text tool to manually enter carriage returns
in the text (using the Enter key).

DYNAMIC TEXT

Dynamic (as well as Input) text entities give you quite a few capabilities. In both cases, you generally connect the text field to either a variable or property through ActionScript coding in Flash. While we are not going to get into the nitty-gritty of ActionScript just yet, we will at least acknowledge how you can use Dynamic and Input text entities to connect to code.

figure | 6-3

Selecting Dynamic from the Text Type drop-down provides additional text options.

First, examine figure 6-3. It shows the various properties that are available when you select Dynamic from the Text Type drop-down menu in the Properties panel.

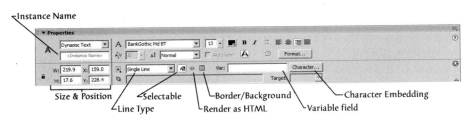

The additional options (shown in figure 6-3) are:

● *Size and Position fields:* Allow you to view and change the width, height, and position of the Dynamic text object.

● *Instance Name field:* This is the name of the text object.

● *Line Type drop-down list:* Defines how many lines of text can be in the object.

● *Selectable button:* Determines if the text can be selected by the end user at runtime.

● *Render as HTML button:* Defines whether the content in the Text field should be interpreted as HTML code.

- *Show Border button:* Controls the border and background for the field.

- *Var field:* The name of the variable or property associated with the text object.

- *Character button:* Allows you to specify whether or not font outlines for the field are embedded.

While many of these characteristics are important, the most important are the Instance Name and Var fields (they are how you make the field dynamic). There are two approaches. If you use Instance Name, you write ActionScript code that continually updates the text entity by referring to its name. The alternative is to assign the text entity a variable name (then you use ActionScript to update the variable). Whenever the variable is updated, so is the field. Later in this book we'll work with dynamic text fields. For now, just understand what they are.

INPUT TEXT

The third type of text entity is the Input text field. Input fields are differentiated in that the user is able to enter data, and as movie author you are able to capture and do something with that data. The properties for Input text fields are basically the same as those for Dynamic text objects, and because you need to know some ActionScript to be able to use them we will reserve further discussion for Chapter 14.

USING HTML

One of the cool things about text elements in Flash is that they can support a limited number of HTML tags when set to Dynamic Text or Input Text. From the developer's perspective, this means you can create text elements in which specific elements are used as hyperlinks. It also means that you can use the rudimentary HTML formatting capabilities in the text elements in your movie.

Flash supports the following basic HTML tags:

- *<A>* (anchor): Adds hyperlinks to words or phrases in a text object

- *<P>* (paragraph): Defines a paragraph block

- *<B>* (bold): Bolds selected text

- *<I>* (italic): Italicizes the text

- *<FONT COLOR>*: Changes the color of the text

- *<FONT FACE>*: Changes the typeface used in the text

- *<FONT SIZE>*: Changes the font size of the tagged text

One caveat is that if you use the anchor tag in a text object you will need to also use the *<FONT COLOR>* and *<U>* tags. The link does not automatically display as a different color and is not underlined because it is in a web browser. You must manually set these parameters using all three tags together.

Also realize that you must close your tags. When you code HTML by hand, you can get away with not closing the *</p>* tag. However, the rule Flash follows is stringent: you must close all tags.

EDITING AND MODIFICATION

Editing text entities is pretty straightforward. If you have used any computer-based tool that includes text you'll find Flash works in a natural way. But, to make sure we are all on the same page, a few quick snippets about text editing seem prudent.

Editing Text Entities

To change the text within an existing text object, you single click on it. To change the properties of an entire text object, select the object on the stage and use the Properties panel to change overall characteristics. To change the attributes of a word or phrase within a text object, select the Text tool and click on the text object. Then, click-drag across the word or phrase you wish to change to select it, and then use the Properties panel to change the formatting or style of the selection. Note that you can have text within a single text object in which certain words or phrases are larger or styled differently.

Transforming Text Entities

Another thing you should realize about text objects is that you can use the Free Transform tools (all except the Distort and Envelope options) and the Transform panel on them. This lets you create text entities that look like they are in a 3D orientation, as shown in figure 6-4.

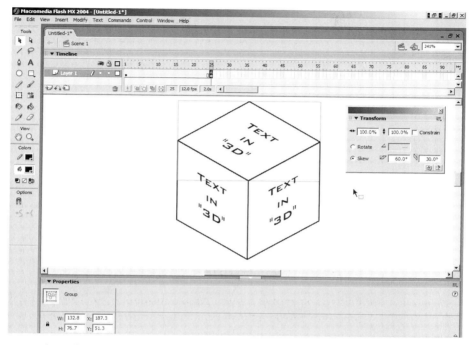

figure | **6-4**

The transformation tools can be used on text objects.

Using Break Apart

A final note concerns breaking text apart. Typically you will want to leave your text objects as "true" text objects—such that you can go back and edit the text, formatting, or other properties. However, there may be times when you will want to break the text apart so that you can add some artistic flair for a specific purpose. For example, imagine you wanted to create some text that said "DRIP" and then you actually wanted to manipulate the text so it looked like it was dripping. To do this, you would use Modify I Break Apart.

When you use Break Apart on text, the text is first decomposed into separate text blocks for each letter. When you use Break Apart a second time (in sequence), the text is decomposed into its fill elements. So, essentially you must use Break Apart twice on the text entity to break it into fill elements. As shown in figure 6-5, while the text may "look" the same, if you change the Preview Mode to Outline you see that the text is broken down into separate fills. Then you can modify the text with the drawing or painting tools to add whatever effect you want.

figure | 6-5 |

Broken text is decomposed into fill elements that can then be manipulated.

(a) Broken Text

(b) Outline Mode

(c) Stylized Text

FONT MAPPING

Web-ready Flash files typically include all information necessary to properly render fonts in your movie at runtime (this is one of its big pluses). Flash can utilize most computer fonts, including Type 1 PostScript, TrueType, and (on the Macintosh) bitmap. Each font embedded in a Flash SWF file increases the file size slightly. Generally, the amount of data added to a Flash file is less than 30 KB, but it depends on the "ornateness" of the font.

Ultimately, Flash gives you control over whether or not to embed a font in the resulting SWF file. The default is to include all required fonts, but you can tell Flash not to include a font description if you like. Recall that one of the properties for static text was the Use Device Font checkbox. With dynamic and input text there was a button called Character. These are how you tell Flash not to include a particular font description, or to include only certain aspects of the font description (in the case of the Character button).

When you select Use Device Font, or No Characters (for dynamic or input text), you are in essence assuming that the end user has the particular font on her machine. "What happens if she doesn't?" you ask. When the user does not have a font, Flash will automatically make a choice using font substitution. Sometimes the choice is good, but most of the time the choice is inadequate and your screen designs will look poor as a result.

The immediate thought is likely, "Why would I ever choose not to embed a font?" The reality is that there are advantages to not embedding fonts — the primary being smaller file sizes. Another is the fact that at sizes smaller than 10 points device fonts are displayed more cleanly.

Nevertheless, there are many scenarios in which it might be advantageous to not embed fonts, but the primary question when deciding this is: "Do you absolutely control the playback machine?" If so, do not embed fonts (and you'll save some bytes in the size of your file). If not, embed fonts. There is nothing more embarrassing than a font that goes awry in a presentation, making text unreadable or, worse, totally ruining a very aesthetically pleasant design.

Default Device Fonts

Flash provides three default device font options in the Font menu: _sans, _sans serif, and _typewriter. Typically, _sans is Arial on Windows, and Helvetica on Macintosh. The _serif setting is usually Times New Roman on Windows, and Times on Macintosh. The _typewriter setting is typically some derivative of Courier on either platform. Of course, all of this also depends on whether or not the user has made any custom configuration changes to her operating system.

Because so often people are developing for the Web, seldom is there a real need to use the default device fonts. The only exception is when you want the text in your movie to "shift" on one platform or another, or from machine to machine.

There are differences not only among font families, such as Arial versus Helvetica, but even visually significant differences between versions of the same font on different platforms. For example, Helvetica on the Macintosh is about 2 point sizes smaller than Helvetica on the PC. If you have a paragraph that has 10 lines, it may shrink as much as 100 pixels from one platform to another. In short, unless you know for sure that you will absolutely control the end playback machine—and more importantly, the fonts on that machine—device fonts in any scenario cannot be recommended by this author.

Fonts That Cannot Be Embedded

A final note in this section regards the fact that not all fonts on a machine are usable by Flash. A quick way to tell if Flash has a problem with a font is to assign it to an object and see if Flash antialiases it (set View | Preview Mode | Antialias Text). If the font appears jaggy on the screen, it means the font is not being properly interpreted by Flash and will not be properly embedded in a resulting SWF file.

Substituting Fonts

One of the nicest things in Flash MX 2004 is its font mapping capability. First, note that font mapping has to do with the sharing of native Flash files (FLAs), not font issues within web-ready SWF files. It is common for a group of developers or designers to share an FLA file (or set of FLA files) during development. However, often from designer to designer, or from designer to coder, the fonts each has may not be consistent across machines.

In Flash MX 2004, when you open a file that calls for fonts you do not have on your machine, you have the option of temporarily "reassigning" the font to something you have on your machine. You do this through the Font Mapping utility (Edit | Font Mapping). The nice thing about this feature is that it is "temporary." This allows a firm to freely pass files from designer to designer, or to anyone else for that matter, without having to worry about everybody having the same fonts.

SUMMARY

In this chapter we have examined most of the things you need to know about text in Flash. We will return to Dynamic and Input text entities later. As you start integrating text into your movies, keep in mind the "rules of thumb" presented in this chapter. They will help you. The next chapter is the last of the "asset" chapters. In it, you'll learn about bitmaps and how they can be used in Flash.

1. What is the difference between readability and legibility?

2. What is the difference between leading and kerning?

3. What is justification?

4. Name three specific "rules of thumb" for text.

5. There are two types of static text entities. What are they and how are they different from each other?

6. What is the difference between a Dynamic text element and an Input text element?

7. When working with Dynamic or Input text objects, what are the two fields you use to make them function (that is, be dynamic)?

8. What transformations can you apply to text objects?

9. Why would you want to break text apart?

10. How do you make Flash embed fonts so you don't need them at runtime (this could be viewed as a trick question)? How do you make it so Flash does not embed fonts? If Flash doesn't embed fonts, where do fonts come from during playback?

⬈ EXPLORING ON YOUR OWN

1. Try intermixing fonts into some of your designs. Try creating various design effects using text.

2. Choose an action word, such as *running, dripping,* or *flying.* Then break apart the text and make the work look like it is doing the action word.

3. Create a form in Flash to collect some data you would like to find out from users of a particular site.

| bitmaps |

7

charting your course

Throughout the prior chapters I've no doubt touted Flash's vector capability. Indeed, the fact that Flash deals so wonderfully with vector content is the primary reason it has caught on so well. And the fact that it is vector is what makes its files so small.

However, in this chapter we'll take a look at putting bitmaps into Flash. While Flash excels with vector content, it handles bitmap content no differently than other programs. Flash files with bitmaps in them get just as big (file size-wise) as other program files. Now, while I don't wish to be absurd and say never use bitmaps, I will say that you must conscientiously use them—and only use them when you can't do something another way.

 *goals*

In this chapter you will:

- **Learn about the primary characteristics of bitmap graphics**
- **Find out how to prepare graphics for use in Flash**
- **Learn to import bitmaps into Flash**
- **Discover how bitmaps can be used in Flash**

BITMAP CHARACTERISTICS

If you have ever tried to print out a bitmap you are likely familiar with the negative aspects of them. They have fixed visual quality, the files are beefy, and often they can choke whatever program you're using them in or whatever printer you're printing from.

Yet bitmaps, once you understand how they work, are really quite friendly. The trick is to understand two particular technical points: visual clarity and color fidelity (i.e., resolution and bit depth). Additionally, there are a couple other fine points worth mentioning. Yet, let's first begin with a quick review of their visual characteristics.

Visual Characteristics

Bitmaps, unlike vector elements, are composed of small dots, as shown in figure 7-1. The analogy I always use is that bitmaps are like pointillism, or stippled artwork. Where vector artwork is composed of lines, a line in a bitmap is composed of a series of hundreds of dots touching one another. Where a vector image is composed of maybe a hundred vector elements (lines, arcs, circles, and so on), a bitmap of the same image may be composed of tens of thousands of dots (pixels).

figure | 7-1 |

Bitmap images are composed of dots, or picture elements (pixels for short).

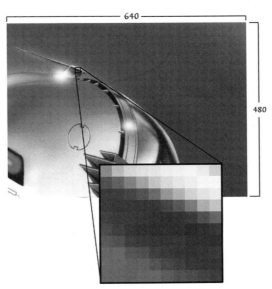

10 pixels by 10 pixels

Using this analogy, it is usually quite evident why a bitmap would be bigger in file size than a vector image. Think of it, a bitmap you create—depending on how much visual quality you need for a given output device—may have as many as 307,200 pixels (at least that is the case for a "small" image at 640 pixels by 480 pixels). And this doesn't take into consideration color fidelity (bit depth) either! If you are talking a bitmap for print, it is very easy to have pixel ranges from 1,000,000 to 5,000,000, generally speaking. Thus, when you go to print such images or even take its smaller counter-part and put it on the Web it's no wonder it prints so slow, brings the computer to a crawl, or makes the browser load so slowly. It's akin to rush hour on the freeway between San Diego and Los Angeles!

Nevertheless, even though file size is one of the biggest issues when dealing with bitmaps, there are some advantages to them as well. Bitmaps are the only way to get truly photographic content repre-sented in your work—well, except for painstakingly recreating photorealistic images by hand. So, ultimately your choice in whether or not to include bitmaps is whether you need photoreal-istic imagery to communicate whatever it is you are trying to say.

Technical Characteristics

While the space in this book doesn't permit a lengthy explanation, I would be remiss if I did not acknowledge the technical character-istics of bitmaps. Even though this will be brief, it is an area that really demands more investigation. There are numerous resources on the Web that can give you detail ad infinitum. Here, I'll focus on the brief version just so you know what the issues are.

Visual Clarity

Already I have acknowledged the issue of visual clarity. In techni-cal terms what this refers to is resolution—the number of pixels per a given area. Figure 7-2 shows an example of an image at vari-ous resolutions. When resolution is not high enough, the image looks grainy. When the resolution is too high, the file is overly large. The key as it relates to resolution is to realize that on screen all you need is 72 pixels per inch. Anything more is just wasted data—which wastes the user's time and makes your creation bigger than it needs to be.

300 DPI   150 DPI   72 DPI

figure | 7-2

Examples of different visual clarities (resolutions).

Color Fidelity

To this point I really haven't explained what color fidelity is. In short, color fidelity is the representativeness of the colors in the image. In addition to there being "a lot" of pixels in an image, each pixel has a range of color it can be. This range is established by something called bit depth, which is directly related to the nitty-gritty of bits and bytes in the computer.

All you really need to know here is that there are two basic bit depths you deal with on the Web: 8-bit and 24-bit. When I say "8-bit" that means that each pixel in an image can be represented by any one of 256 colors. When I say "24-bit" it means that each pixels in an image can be represented by any one of 16.7 million colors. Suffice it to say that 24-bit looks better. And, unless you are designing for specific audiences (such as K-12 and some specific international audiences) more often than not you will be dealing with 24-bit bitmaps. Figure 7-3, although shown in grayscale, shows the rough difference between the two.

figure | 7-3

The difference between 24-bit and 8-bit images.

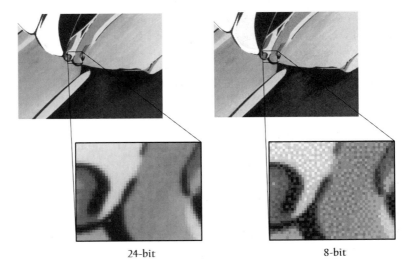

24-bit   8-bit

File Size and Compression

With bitmaps, the biggest negative is file size, which is directly related to image clarity and color fidelity. To combat the file size issue, compression schemes are typically applied to raster images. While there are technical differences between compression algorithms, in general, bitmaps are compressed based on the number of redundant colors in the file. The more redundancy, the more the file can be compressed.

As it relates to bitmaps, there are two general types of compression schemes you should be aware of: lossless and lossy. As their names imply, lossless loses no data (the decompressed file is exactly the same as the original uncompressed file) and lossy does lose data (the decompressed file is not exactly the same as the original compressed file). Where data is lost in lossy forms is in color accuracy (some colors may shift on transit) and in image clarity (some resolution is lost). Lossy compression is used in JPG images, while lossless is used in formats such as GIF and PNG. We'll look at this a little more closely when I show you where you set compression options in Flash.

Extra Data

A final aspect about bitmaps is the issue of "extra data" (called alpha data) that can exist in a file. When graphics folks hear the term "alpha" they usually think "transparency"—which is generally right. However, alpha data can actually be any extra data associated with a bitmap. Yet, with the bitmaps you import into Flash the only alpha data Flash can understand is transparency data. In essence, in addition to each pixel having a color fidelity (bit depth) it has extra data that describes whether or not it is transparent. This becomes an issue when you deal with GIF files, which can maintain their transparency when you import them into Flash.

IMPORTING BITMAPS

Importing and using bitmaps in Flash is, for the most part, a straightforward process. Once in Flash, bitmaps can behave like other assets in Flash, but you can also do some pretty unique things with them. However, the most important thing is to prepare your graphics prior to importing them. Mainly this means setting the correct resolution prior to importing (you do not want to scale bitmaps up or down in Flash) and ensuring that the images are the proper color depth (and that they use the proper color model).

Preparing Bitmaps

There are any number of packages you can use to prepare your raster images for use in Flash. Anything from the top-end, expensive packages (such as Photoshop) all the way down to shareware tools will more than likely allow you to set the resolution and color depth.

Setting Resolution

As it relates to resolution, you want to know the specific size you will want your bitmap images once they are in Flash. You want to absolutely minimize the amount of scaling you have to do in Flash, because there are some negatives to scaling bitmaps in Flash. You can get a rough idea of the size you need by using the Rectangle tool to measure the area where the bitmap will be (use the Properties panel or the Info panel to determine the pixel size needed). The optimum is to know the exact size you need so that you will not have to scale the bitmap in Flash. You can get away with a little bit of scaling (20 percent larger or smaller) but, in general, avoid scaling bitmaps in Flash.

As for actually setting the resolution setting in a bitmap program, which program you are using will determine the actual name of the command. Here are some common ones:

- In Adobe Photoshop select the Image | Image Size command and change the Pixel Dimensions fields.

- In Macromedia Fireworks use the Modify | Image Size command and modify the Pixel Dimensions.

- In Corel Photopaint access the Image | Resample command. Set the Width and Height in the Image Size section appropriately. Also, make sure the units are set to pixels.

- In Microsoft Photo Editor, use Image | Resize, set the Units to pixels, and then set the Width and Height fields.

- In Windows Paint use Image | Attributes. Set the Units on Pixels. Then set the Width and Height fields.

> ▶ **TRY THIS**
>
> Using a bitmap you have created (or one that you download from the Web), try your hand at manipulating resolution in whatever image-editing package you have available.

Setting Color Depth

As it relates to color depth, the main thing you need to be aware of is making sure the images you import into Flash are RGB based. Often images that are recycled from print publications are handed off in CMYK format rather than RGB. Here are common ways to make sure images are in RGB form:

● In Adobe Photoshop access the Image | Mode submenu. Select the RGB Mode option.

● Macromedia Fireworks automatically converts CMYK-mode files to RGB when they are opened.

● In Corel Photopaint use the Image | Convert To menu and select RGB Color.

● Neither Microsoft Photo Editor nor Windows Paint allows you to change CMYK images to RGB.

File Formats

A final consideration about bitmaps is the file format you choose to use. Flash supports a wide variety of files, but most of the time you will use either PNG or GIF. You do not want to use JPG.

Portable Network Graphics (PNG) Format

If you are importing bitmaps into Flash, PNG is the format you will use most of the time. It is a very robust format that permits either 24-bit or 8-bit data. It uses lossless compression and permits the inclusion of transparency information. PNG's transparency is much more robust than GIFs. It supports 8-bit (256 levels of) transparency, whereas GIF only supports 1-bit transparency (either totally opaque or totally transparent).

GIF Format

While GIF can be used for general importing of 8-bit data, for static, 8-bit images I would use PNG instead. Where GIF is handy is if you want to import animated GIF files. When animated GIFs are imported into Flash, each frame of the GIF file becomes a frame in the Flash file. Granted, you don't want to import a whole slew of animated GIFs (your file size will balloon in a hurry), but every now and then you may need to do this.

Image Series

One final noteworthy element is that if you have a series of images (such as a series of PNG files) Flash can directly recognize them as related to one another. If your files are named with a numeral portion (such as *file01*, *file02*, and so on), Flash will recognize this and ask if you want to import them as a series.

Importing

To be honest, most of the work of getting bitmaps into Flash comes in preparing the images. Once the images are prepared, actually getting them into Flash (and using them) is much less work. Yet, up to this point we have not discussed the concept of Flash libraries, and while there is a chapter devoted to symbols and libraries we need to mention the concept so that things make sense.

When you import certain elements (such as bitmaps or video clips) or create certain elements (symbols), they are automatically stored in the Flash library. You can think of the library as the "data storehouse" in each Flash file. Elements in the library can be used as shared objects in that they can be shared by multiple frames or scenes in a movie. The data is stored once, and can be referred to many times throughout the movie. By using this technique you can significantly reduce your Flash file sizes. When you refer to a library's data (by click-dragging an object from the library to the stage), the stage object is known as an *instance*—that is, a reference to a library object at some point in time in the movie. The library contains the actual data, and what you see on the stage is a reference to that library data.

When you import bitmaps, you can use either the File | Import to Stage or File | Import to Library option. In both cases, the bitmap's data is automatically stored in the library. Because bitmaps are usually larger than vector componentry, this is only logical: it keeps you from overloading the stage with data. However, when you only import to the library, an instance of the bitmap is not placed on the stage. Figure 7-4 shows the library window open (Import to Stage was used).

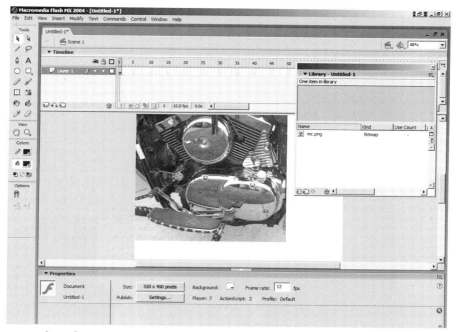

figure | 7-4

Import to Stage was used to import the bitmap, which places the bitmap in the library and creates an instance to it on the stage.

TRY THIS

Using a bitmap image you have created (or one from the Web), try the two importing options to see the difference. If you use Import to Library, open the Flash library (Window I Library) and click-drag the object from the Library panel to the stage. You'll have to select the object in the list, and then click-drag from the preview window in the library to the stage. This creates an instance of the bitmap on the stage.

Library Settings

Because the library is the "storehouse" for the data of certain elements, through the library you can establish default settings for certain things. One of those things is the default compression options for bitmaps.

If you access the library and double click on a bitmap element, a dialog box will open that allows you to set options related to the bitmap, as shown in figure 7-5. To be able to set a compression default, you must deselect the *Use document default quality* checkbox. When you do this, Flash allows two types of compression: Photo (JPEG) and Lossless (GIF/PNG). For the most part, you will likely use the Photo setting. The only time you should use Lossless is when it is absolutely imperative for the image clarity to be maintained. In all other instances, use JPEG.

figure | 7-5 |

The Bitmap
Properties dialog
box is accessed
via the library.

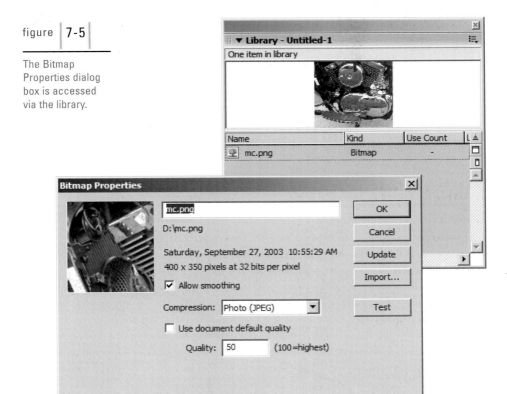

Earlier I said you should never use JPG files to import bitmaps into Flash. The reason is that most of the time you will be using Flash's JPG compression on bitmaps once they are in Flash. If you recompress an already compressed JPG image, particularly doing it twice with JPG, your images will end up being larger than they need to be and they will look poorer than need be.

Once you have the Bitmap Properties dialog box open, you can play around with the various compression settings. As you do, the little preview window will show you the effect of your settings on the bitmap. Realize that if you drag the cursor over the preview window, you can pan around to see different parts of the image with the compression settings applied to it.

> ### TRY THIS
>
> Get a feel for the effect of the various compression settings in Flash by importing a bitmap and then using the Bitmap Properties dialog box to experiment. Make sure you try JPEG at various quality settings. Do you notice the degradation that occurs in the image?

MANIPULATING BITMAPS

Once you have a bitmap instance on the stage, there are a lot of things you can do with it. The cool thing about stage instances (of anything, actually) is that each instance can have its own specific properties (as it relates to size, scale, orientation, and so on). Now, granted I have preached against scaling bitmaps in Flash, but you can get away with a reasonable amount. Just don't go haywire with it. Now, in addition to this, you can do a couple other cool things.

Using Trace Bitmap

One of the things you can do with a bitmap is to convert it to a vector representation by having Flash trace it. It is not all that exact (Flash does no better at raster-to-vector conversion than any other package), but Trace Bitmap can be used to create some stylized versions of bitmap images.

As shown in figure 7-6, you can convert a bitmap to vector representations. To use Trace Bitmap, you select the bitmap on the stage and select Modify | Bitmap | Trace Bitmap. The dialog box shown in figure 7-7 is shown. To obtain optimum results, set the *Curve fit* option to Pixels and the *Corner threshold* setting to Many Corners. Once you use the command, Flash will remove the original bitmap instance from the stage. The resulting vector trace will be composed of fill elements. In general, the less detailed the image the more successful the trace.

figure | 7-6 |

Comparing the bitmap to its vector trace.

Original   Trace

figure | 7-7 |

The Trace Bitmap dialog allows you to customize how the trace will be generated.

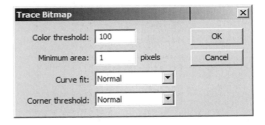

TRY THIS

Try using the Trace Bitmap command by importing a couple different images. When you select images for this task, select one that is moderately complex versus one that is more simplistic, so that you can see the entire range of capability.

Break Apart

Another interesting thing you can do with bitmaps is "edit" them, as well as use them as fills. To do this, however, you must use Break Apart on the bitmap. Once a bitmap is broken, it is no longer a referenced to the library. Instead, it becomes a self-contained stage object. Now, I likely need not mention what happens to file size if you do this to a lot of bitmaps, but the fact that you can edit bitmaps and use them as fills does come in handy from time to time.

Editing

Once a bitmap is broken, you can use many of the painting tools on it. For example, you can use the Eraser tool to split it into pieces. You can also use the Arrow tool to bend or bow the edges, as shown in figure 7-8.

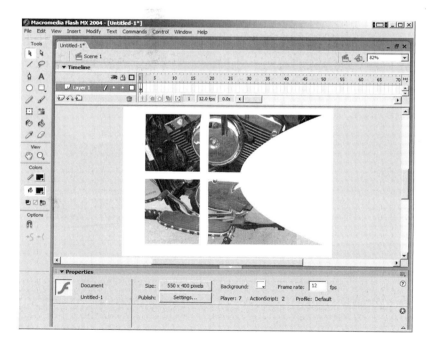

figure 7-8

Once a bitmap is broken, you can manipulate it with many of the toolbar tools.

Using as Fill

A final "effect" you can create with a bitmap is to use it as a fill. Once broken apart, if you use the Dropper tool on the bitmap the bitmap will be picked up as a fill. You can then use the Paint Bucket to fill something with it. Once the bitmap is a fill, you can transform it, too, as shown in figure 7-9.

figure | 7-9

Bitmaps can be used as fills by picking up the element with the Dropper.

Used As Fill   Transformed Fill

SUMMARY

In this chapter you have examined the various things you can do with bitmaps. Again, the main thing to remember is to only use bitmaps when you really need them. More often than not you can get away without using bitmaps. But, if your design calls for one here or there, it is acceptable to use them when you need them.

in review

1. What controls the visual clarity of an image?

2. What controls the color fidelity of an image?

3. Foundationally, why are bitmaps so large?

4. What are the two general types of compression techniques for bitmaps? What is the difference between them?

5. What kind of extra data is typically associated with bitmap images? What is this type of data generally called?

6. As it relates to bitmaps and Flash, what is the most time consuming part?

7. Which file format should you generally use for importing bitmaps into Flash?

8. What are the similarities and differences between Import to Stage and Import to Library?

9. What does Trace Bitmap do? What does it create?

10. What must you do to use a bitmap as a fill element?

↗ EXPLORING ON YOUR OWN

1. Bitmaps are often part of designs that must include photos of products. Create a design that specifically integrates bitmaps (likely you'll need to think of a company site that needs to have bitmaps). Create a working prototype of the main page in Flash.

2. If you create a portfolio web site that uses Flash, bitmaps will inevitably be a part of it. Sketch out what your portfolio page might look like. How will you integrate bitmaps (assuming they will be needed)? Bring that page to life by creating a prototype of it.

sound

8

charting your course

Like bitmaps, sound assets in Flash movies are one of those things that can quickly escalate the size of your files. However, audio is probably one of the more important elements to include, but planning is necessary. While bitmaps can be avoided in many cases, audio on the other hand has become almost a necessity. Flash does a superb job of importing files and a relatively decent job with the control you have over those sounds once they are in the file. But like anything, effectively using sound in your movies is dependent on you. In this chapter, we'll take a look at several issues that should help you better understand audio elements and how to use them in your movies.

 goals

In this chapter you will:

● **Learn about the attributes of sound files**

● **Find out what you need to do to prepare your audio files for use in Flash**

● **Discover how to import sound and set its compression options**

● **Learn to use audio in Flash**

AUDIO ATTRIBUTES

Throughout this chapter you will find many similarities between audio and bitmaps. Both are a "direct quantification of naturalistic material." I hate to use that phrase but it best sums up why audio and bitmaps are the way they are. Both are direct captures or samples of what we humanly hear and see.

It shouldn't be surprising to find that, as with bitmaps, sound files have two distinctive characteristics: audio clarity and audio fidelity. The former has to do with the representativeness of the audio clip (as compared to what you hear naturally), and the latter has to do with the descriptiveness of the clip at any point in time (how faithfully it represents the sound at a point in time). While we don't need a lengthy expository on acoustical physics, a little more info related to these characteristics is in order. Just as you must prepare bitmaps before importing, so too must you prepare audio before importing. To prepare audio, you must typically adjust the audio clarity and (sometimes) the audio fidelity.

Audio Clarity

There are several technical ways to describe audio clarity. If you are comparing it to bitmaps you could simply say it equates to resolution. Yet, with audio, resolution is actually controlled by something called sampling rate. Sampling rate is simply how often (over time) the audio is represented digitally (the higher the sampling rate, the better the audio clarity). Common sampling rates include 44 kHz, 22 kHz, and 11 kHz. More than likely 44 kHz is familiar to you (it is the rate used for audio CDs).

Now, most audio files in computer multimedia—and in Flash files—are actually 22 kHz. Given that the majority of users in the world still have those cheap dinky speakers that come with most systems, 22 kHz is plenty for the general public. There may be cases where greater clarity is needed, warranted, or available, but for the intents and purposes of your Flash development, I'd stick with 22-kHz files.

Audio Fidelity

As it relates to audio fidelity, this is controlled by the bit-depth of the audio clip. As bit depth controls the range of color for each pixel in a bitmap, bit depth controls the range of frequencies that can be defined in an audio clip at any point in time. Most audio files apart from Flash are already 16-bit audio files. And conveniently enough, that is exactly what you need in Flash.

PREPARING AUDIO

While various bitmap editors are quite common, sound tools are less apt to be found on the majority of users' desktops. Sonic Foundry Sound Forge is a common tool on the PC, and Bias Peak is common on the Mac, but to buy either requires a little bit of a budget. And, of course, there are packages that go off the scale as far as cost is concerned. Suffice it to say that you can spend as much as your heart desires on an audio package—from as little as 50 bucks to well over 10,000.

Yet, if you are searching for tools, just about any rudimentary sound editor should permit you to do the basics—namely, modify the sampling rate of a clip. However, if you invest in a tool, often other quite helpful functionalities are available. More than likely, though, you'll need to shell out a little cash to get an audio editor, since such utilities have yet to be included in most operating systems.

Getting Material

One of the major cautionary notes concerning sound is that of copyrights. In the educational arena, we have some liberties, but even those must be taken advantage of cautiously. In short, if you are going to use a piece of music or even certain sound clips, make sure you have the necessary permissions. While "CD ripping" programs are readily available on the Web, it makes it no more legal to use them on material that is not your own.

Recording Your Own

If you have some musical ability, you can create your own content, too. I have a synthesizer and so often I'll sample material into my Mac or PC using it. In the last few years getting material from musical instruments into the computer has gotten amazingly easy (or at least easier). The safest way to avoid copyright hell is create your own content, rather than trying to talk somebody else into letting you use his or her stuff.

Prepping Raw Material

Once you've got some raw sound files to work with, there are several things you can and should do to it prior to plugging it into Flash. Most of what you can do is going to depend on your sound package, but some of these include:

- *Resampling:* The most critical feature of a sound package is the ability to change the sampling rate. If you record your own material, or if you use some stock material, more than likely the clips will be in 44 kHz. While it is entirely possible to import such files into Flash, it is likely way more than you need—particularly for the Web. Resampling lets you reduce the sampling rate down to what I would suggest using, 22 kHz.

- *Normalizing:* This basically adds volume consistency throughout a clip. It "stretches" the sound over time so that there is a consistent level throughout the clip. If you are recording your own material, normalizing is a must.

- *Clipping or cropping:* This removes "dead space" at the beginning and end of a clip. Realize that having "no sound" playing in a clip takes as much file size as places where there are things playing. Trimming dead space is a necessity!

- *Equalization:* Like just about any stereo today, most audio packages will let you change specific sets of frequencies in a clip. This can be used to get rid of hisses, as well as punch up lows, mediums, or highs in the clip.

- *Effects:* Depending on how robust the package is, it may permit you to add effects such as flange, distortion, reverb, and the like. Use these if you wish, but use them sparingly and purposefully. Overusing them is like watching a PowerPoint presentation that uses every transition available.

Formats

When dealing with computer audio, there are typically two types of files you'll run into: WAV and AIFF. Typically you will want to stay with AIFF files—particularly if you are going back and forth between multiple platforms. If you are Mac-only, go with AIFF. If you are PC-only, go with WAV.

IMPORTING SOUND

Importing sound is not that much different from importing bitmaps. You can choose to use the Import to Stage or Import to Library option. The peculiar thing is when you choose to import to the stage. Rather than displaying sound as an element in the library only, sound is shown in the timeline and is attached to the current frame. But before we get into all that, let's discuss file formats and sound properties.

File Formats

While it's not necessary to get into all the nitty-gritty of all the formats supported, a quick gander at the Import dialog box reveals the various sound files Flash can import, as shown in figure 8-1. The three predominant ones you'll likely use are WAV, AIFF, and (to most legalists' disdain) MP3. However, importing MP3s into Flash has the same negative consequences as importing JPEG files into Flash. Recompressing lossy compressed data is never good. So, while it may be tempting to integrate MP3s into Flash, I would avoid it.

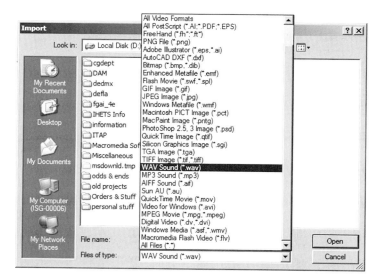

figure | 8-1

The Import dialog box reveals the audio formats that are available.

Sound Properties

Regardless of how a sound file is imported (to stage or to library), it will show up in the library, as shown in figure 8-2. You can set up compression settings for sounds in the library just like setting compression for bitmaps.

figure 8-2

The Sound Properties dialog box, accessed via the library, allows you to set the compression options for the sound.

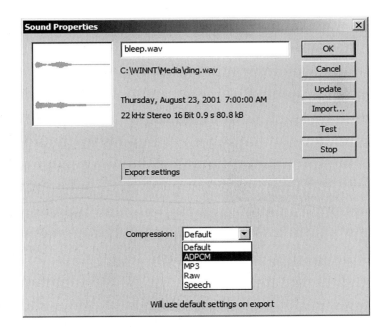

Flash provides four compression options for your use:

- *ADPCM:* This option is best for short sounds, such as sounds associated with buttons (basically, effect-type sounds).

- *MP3:* This option is best for music and longer sounds.

- *Raw:* This option does nothing to the clip. It leaves the clip as raw, uncompressed sound data.

- *Speech:* This option, well, is for voice-over. It is optimized for the range of human speech.

One of the things you should notice in figure 8-2 is the Test button. This is a nice feature in that it lets you experiment with the different compression types and settings before committing to it.

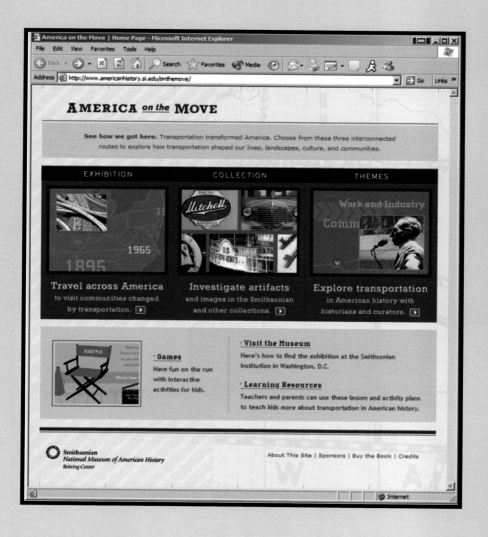

figure 1

The Smithsonian National Museum of American History uses Flash to provide a unique glimpse of American history *(http://www.americanhistory. si.edu/onthemove/)*. In the design of any web site, one of the challenging things is to organize the content and make it easy to get to. This web site does a superb job of providing unique navigation controls to get to the content.

| figure 2 |

The Nasher Sculpture Center uses Flash to provide access to information about the artwork house there *(http://www.nashersculpturecenter.org)*. One of the cool things about Flash is that you can give people a glimpse of things that they might otherwise not be able to see (unless they were there). This web site provides an interesting way to view not only the Nasher Sculpture Center but also the art you can see if you visit it.

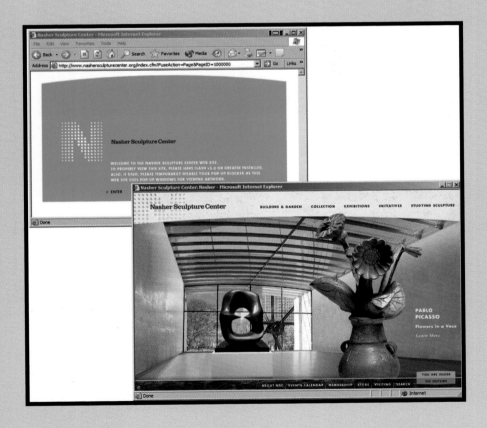

| figure 3 |

Many news organizations use Flash to supplement their traditional media, such as is exhibited on this Washington Post web site *(http://www. washingtonpost.com/wp-srv/world/asia/centralasia/afghanistan/ returntoafghanistan/returntoafghanistan.htm).*

This example also shows how video can be integrated with Flash to provide a unique experience for the end user.

| figure 4 |

Illuminating the Renaissance provides a unique way to review art-work online—providing zooming and panning features for many of the works of art *(http://www.getty.edu/art/exhibitions/flemish/)*.

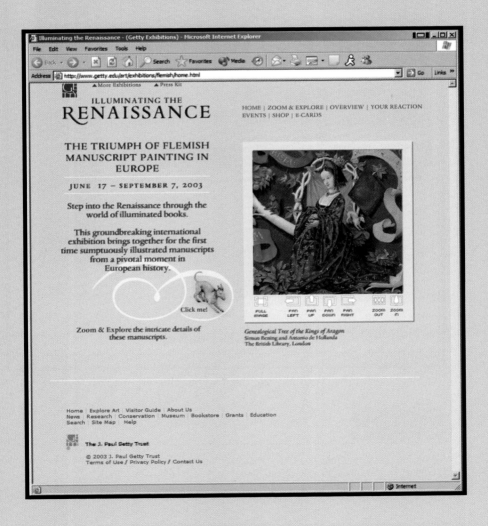

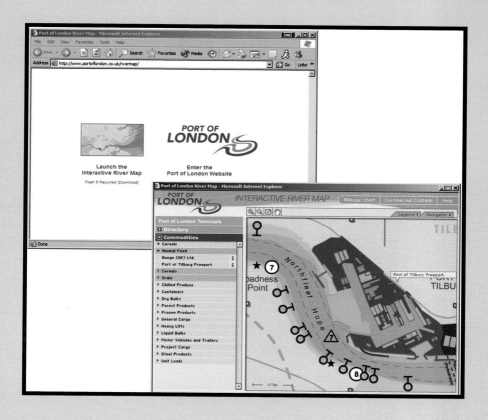

The Port of London web site provides interactive map content online *(http://www.portoflondon.co.uk/rivermap/)*. While the web site shown here requires a hefty amount of programming to pull off, it nonetheless shows an exceptional example of such a thing. With multilevel zoom capability and a lot of ground-level detail, just about any port authority you'd like to find can be found.

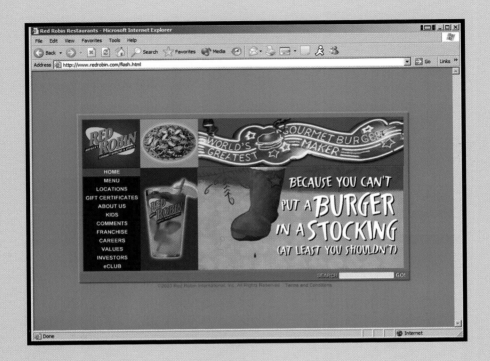

figure 6

Red Robin uses a Flash introduction (and a little humor) to attract its customers *(http://www.redrobin.com/)*. Although this site shows a little holiday spirit, Red Robin routinely presents an interesting advertisement on the front of their site. What strikes me most often about this one is that the animation and message are so uniquely tied together.

| figure 7 |

A very good example of a long-playing movie is demonstrated at Broken Saints *(http://www. rokensaints.com/)*. This example displays a superb combination of Japanese-style artistry and Flash. From the sound and graphics to the styling of the menus, this site is well crafted.

| figure 8 |

Learn about jet engines through GE's web site *(http://www.geae.com/
education/engines101/)*. Since I travel a lot, this site really captured my
attention. It is nicely done with all kinds of useful (and reassuring)
information.

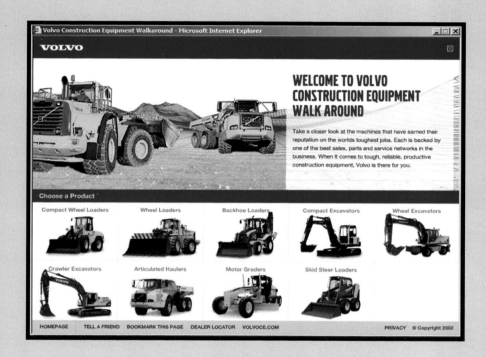

| figure 9 |

The Volvo Construction Equipment Walkaround web site *(http:// global.volvoce.com/walkaround/)* displays an innovative approach to educating the consumer and potential buyer about the various features of Volvo's construction equipment. The site effectively uses photos throughout the site.

| figure 10 |

This stylized portfolio site demonstrates the outstanding work of Projector Studios *(http://www.projectorstudio.com/)*. Since many students focus on portfolio-oriented web site creation, I thought I'd include one of the best I have seen. The minimalist approach works very well here—notice the purposeful use of white space in this design.

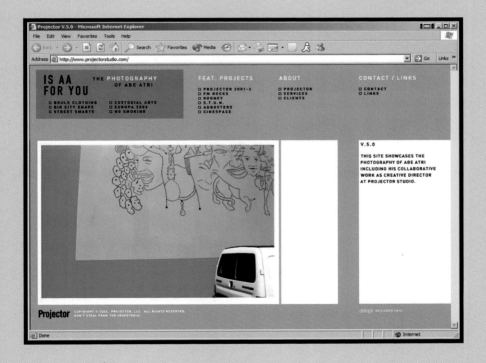

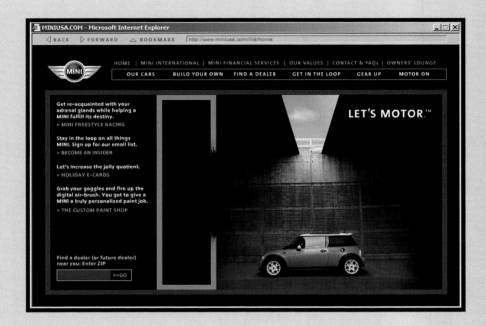

| figure 11 |

The MiniUSA web site is an innovative approach for an innovative product *(http://www.miniusa.com/)*. Not long ago I began investigating these nifty little vehicles and found this site easy to use and quite attractive. The site includes several hidden elements that pop up every now and then, making navigation fun as well as informative.

| figure 12 |

The Barbie web site uses Flash almost exclusively *(http://www.barbie.com/)*. This site designed for kids puts Flash to the test—almost the entire site is Flash based. Based on my daughter's reaction, this is "a really cool site [Dad]."

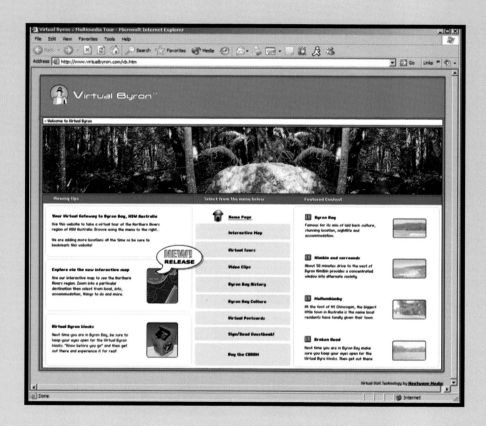

| figure 13 |

The Virtual Byron web site provides a progressive approach to the virtual tour *(http:// www.virtualbyron.com/)*. This web site utilizes intriguing effects and transitions and provides instant access to just about anything you would like to know about the Byron Bay area.

| figure 14 |

The Road Runner portal provides a truly unique integration of Flash into user interface design *(http://www.rr.com/flash/index.cfm)*.

| figure 15 |

The National Park Foundation *(www.nationalparks.org/Home.asp)* uses Flash to provide up to date information on its homepage. This site utilizes an interesting mix of technologies—a good example of judicious use of Flash.

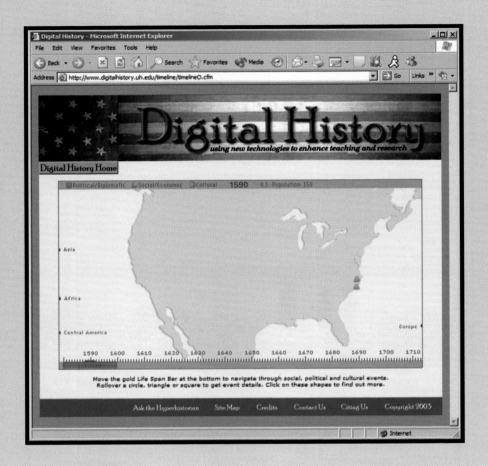

| figure 16 |

The University of Houston's Digital History web site (*www.digitalhistory. uh.edu/timeline/timeline0.cfm*) uses interactive Flash componentry to provide a unique view of US history.

TRY THIS

Experiment with the compression settings in the library. Import a sound or two and then adjust the compression settings. What difference do you notice between the various compression types and settings?

USING AUDIO IN FLASH

Now that you understand how to import and create compression settings, let's do something with some audio in Flash. There are several things you need to know about.

Assigning Sound to a Frame

The first thing about using sound in Flash is to realize that sound is "attached" to frames, not objects. To assign a sound to a frame, you import the sound and then select the frame where you want the sound to start playing. To assign the sound to the frame, you use the Properties panel. Figure 8-3 shows a sound assigned to a frame. Note that the Sound drop-down menu will display all sounds in the current file's library.

figure 8-3

Sounds are assigned to frames using the Properties panel.

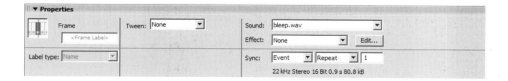

In figure 8-3, you see several other options that appear when you assign a sound to a frame. In the next three sections, we'll discuss what these options do.

Sync Settings

The Sync settings in Flash define how the sound plays. There are two general settings: Event and Stream. Event sounds must be totally downloaded before they begin to play, whereas streaming sounds begin to play before they are totally downloaded. Thus, you want to use Event for the Sync if the sound you are playing is short—such as a sound effect for a button. If the sound you are adding is lengthy—such as a musical background or a narration-type piece— use Stream as the Sync.

One other important thing to note about Event versus Stream is how the sound is coordinated with frame playback. Sounds that are set to Stream are actually coordinated (at least in a rough sense) with the content in frames. So, if you are trying to time music with graphics, you'll want to use Stream Sync. Additionally, if the main timeline stops, a sound set to Stream will stop.

Don't think for a moment that Flash is "exact" in its sequencing of audio and graphics, even if you do select Stream for the Sync. There is always some variability from machine to machine in the synchronization of graphic elements and sounds. This is mainly due to the fact that Flash's content is mostly vector. You can get graphic and audio to time together pretty closely, but it is never exact from machine to machine.

Event sounds, on the other hand, are not coordinated at all with what is displayed on screen. Event sounds play independently of the timeline. Once the play-head encounters a sound set to Event Sync, the sound plays regardless of what is happening on the stage. Even if the main timeline stops, an Event sound will continue to play.

Event and Start Syncs

Another peculiarity of sound in Flash is the existence of the Event, Start, and Stop Sync options. Event and Start are essentially the same: both play independently of the timeline, should be used for short sounds, and both must be totally downloaded before they start to play. Where they differ is that a sound set to Event Sync, if encountered twice before the original instance finishes playing, will start playing again, concurrently. When you start working with actions later in the book, keep this in mind if all of a sudden a sound seems to be going haywire. Needless to say, if you chose Start instead of Event, it won't play over the top of itself.

Looping and Repeat

While the Repeat drop-down menu likely doesn't need lengthy explanation, I do wish to at least acknowledge it. If you choose, you can set a sound to repeat a certain number of times. Or you can choose Loop, which will cause the sound to repeat indefinitely. Do be careful of looping things indefinitely, as things like this really irritate some users. At the least, if you include a looping sound clip—such as background music—make sure you provide a way for the end user to shut it off.

Effects

A final noteworthy element as it relates to sound in Flash is the Effects drop-down and the Edit button. There may be times when you will want a sound clip to fade in, fade out, or some other such effect. The Effects drop-down provides the following default effects that can be quickly assigned:

- *Left Channel:* Plays the entire sound in the left speaker channel

- *Right Channel:* Plays the entire sound in the right speaker channel

- *Fade Left to Right:* Makes the sound pan from the left speaker to the right speaker

- *Fade Right to Left:* Makes the sound pan from the right speaker to the left speaker

- *Fade In:* Sets up the beginning of the sound so that it fades in

- *Fade Out:* Automatically fades out the end of the sound

- *Custom:* Allows you to create your own custom effect by click-dragging the volume control using the Edit button

Editing

If you apply an effect to a clip, or if you want to create your own custom effect, click on the Edit button in the Properties panel. This presents the Edit window, where you can use the sound-editing controls to apply volume changes to the clip, as shown in figure 8-4. These controls allow you to define a volume, per left and right speakers, as well as control how much of the clip is played. Notice the Effects drop-down also at the top of the dialog box.

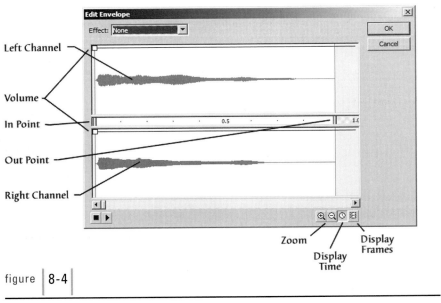

figure 8-4

The Edit window allows you to customize how the sound is played back.

To adjust the volume of either speaker, click-drag the volume controls in the window, shown in figure 8-4. By adding multiple points within the Preview window, fade-in and fade-out effects within the window are created, as shown in figure 8-5. If you were to select Fade In or Fade Out from the Effect drop-down, a similar set of points would be created for you automatically at the beginning or end of a clip. Fade-ins and fade-outs on a single clip must be manually created.

To control how long a clip plays, click-drag the In or Out points as needed. This allows you to play only a specified portion of a clip, even though the entire clip exists in memory. Note that even if you use clipping the entire sound clip will be output in the resulting SWF. In such cases, it would be more effective to edit the clip in a sound editor and import only the part you need.

Located below the Preview window are controls for playing and stopping the sound, in addition to zoom controls and display options, as shown in figure 8-4. The Display Frames button is help-

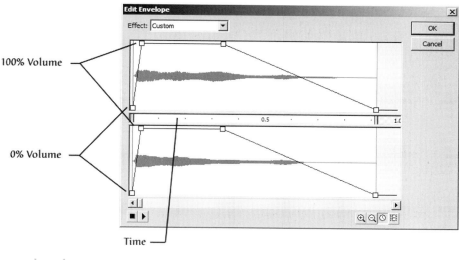

100% Volume

0% Volume

Time

figure | 8-5

You can set up your own effects by adding points to the volume lines.

ful when you are trying to synchronize a sound clip with specific graphical components in specific frames. Additionally, you normally use it with streaming sounds only, not event sounds, because only streaming sounds are "timed" or synchronized with the timeline. When you click on this button, the Preview window shows the sound clip in relation to the current frames. The Display Time button, the default, shows the length of the sound clip in relation to time.

When you select the Display Frames button, the playback speed is assumed to be the currently set frame rate (as defined in the Modify | Movie dialog box). Thus, the sound clip is displayed against the current frames, based on the movie frame rate. Yet, remember that sound is time based and will play consistently. The frame rate will vary, depending on the complexity of elements being displayed and the speed of the computer on which it is being played.

Although you can use the Display Frames button to help you synchronize audio and graphics, it is not 100-percent accurate. The best-case scenario when designing movies is to try to shoot for a target machine. Then, test, test, and test some more on both faster and slower machines. In reality, there is no way of creating an audio and graphics presentation for the Web using Flash that is 100-percent the same on every computer. Machine performance, at least as far as video cards are concerned, varies too greatly. The only thing you can do is shoot for the middle 50 percent of the audience. They are more alike than they are different.

SUMMARY

In this chapter you have examined audio as it relates to Flash. You should now have a general understanding of audio attributes and the things you need to do to prepare audio for use in Flash. We've also examined importing, setting compression options for clips, and using those clips. In the next chapter we'll sort of combine what you know about bitmaps and audio and turn our attention to video in Flash. "Video in Flash," you say? Indeed, Flash has some very powerful capabilities as it relates to video—as you will see.

in review

1. What is resolution as it relates to audio?

2. What resolution should you use for audio in your Flash files?

3. What is audio fidelity? What is the fidelity of most computer-based audio?

4. What two formats should you use for audio? When would you use each?

5. How do you import sound into Flash?

6. Where do you set the compression options for sound files?

7. What types of compression schemes does Flash allow for audio? When should you use each?

8. Sounds are assigned to what in Flash?

9. What are the different Sync options related to sound and what do they do?

10. What kinds of sound effects can you do in Flash?

↗ EXPLORING ON YOUR OWN

1. How might you approach a Flash piece that is designed to market a company? How would you approach the audio for the piece?

video

charting your course

Video is becoming an increasingly important part of the web experience. While you must still keep bandwidth issues forefront in your mind (you must always consider the end user's connection speed in what and how you deliver content), as web connections get faster and cheaper, video use will continue to grow. This is the main reason you see video capability in Flash MX 2004. At some point video will be a necessity on the Web. It's not quite there just yet, but when your end users are blessed with an ADSL or direct Ethernet connection, there's nothing prohibiting you from taking advantage of it today.

There are any number of things you can use this for, not least of which is distance education. As long as the end user has an adequate connection, video is viable. And, Flash provides some pretty robust features and capabilities when dealing with video. Thus, this chapter will highlight some of these aspects—chiefly how you prep and integrate basic video in MX 2004.

 *goals*

In this chapter you will:

● **Find out about the general characteristics specific to video assets**

● **Learn to prep video for Flash**

● **Discover how you can import or link video clips in Flash**

VIDEO ATTRIBUTES

As when working with other media assets, there are several attributes that are unique to video that are worth mentioning. Since video includes both a graphic and audio component, the things you already learned about bitmaps and audio apply to video as well. However, there are a couple other characteristics that are specific to video.

Frame Rate and Size

When dealing with video, you must deal with both frame rate, typically measured in frames per second (fps), as well as frame size (image dimension) of the clip. Frame rates on other media forms (such as broadcast video, movies, and so on) typically float somewhere around 30 fps. When dealing with multimedia-centric video, particularly assets streaming from the Web, you are talking about a frame rate significantly less than 30 fps—more like 12 to 15 fps (or even less). Understand that this mainly has to do with getting the total file size, and more aptly the streaming rate, down to something the end user's bandwidth can handle.

When we talk about stream rate what we are referring to is the amount of sustainable data flow the user's connection can hold at a constant rate. We'll return to this issue in the last chapter, when we talk about Flash's Bandwidth Profiler, where you can simulate a Flash file download to see how it would perform on various connection speeds. Ultimately, if a video clip's stream (or even a Flash file's stream) is interrupted, the element typically pauses momentarily until the data being streamed is enough to continue playback. Thus, you want the stream (or download) rate to be greater than the rate required for playback. So, ultimately, to reduce the streaming rate required for a video clip you can reduce the number of frames per second.

A second thing that is imperative with video clips is to reduce the frame size (image size). Essentially, if you cut the frame size in half, you also cut the total file size in half. Where fps affects the streaming rate, frame size affects the amount of time that the stream rate must be maintained. Usually it is a combination of these two items that are reduced to get the file and stream rate required small enough that it can be adequately presented to an end user given the limitations of bandwidth. Frame sizes for video clips are typically a maximum of 320 pixels by 240 pixels (if end users have a DSL or better connection), all the way down to 160 pixels by 120 pixels (for modem users).

Even at 160 by 120 pixels, a user must really want to see a video clip if they are willing to wait on a modem to download it. Anytime you are considering video in Flash, determine if you might deliver your content another way, such as using static graphics with audio. Often content in a video clip can be communicated in alternative (and less bandwidth consuming) ways.

Compression

As with bitmaps and audio, compression is an important item. Flash provides its own ability to compress and integrate video within SWF files. When you import a video clip, Flash can use its own compressor to crunch the video down to a manageable size. Thus, it is best to import uncompressed video into Flash—letting it use its own compression algorithm on clean, uncompressed data.

There are two types of general compression algorithms used on video clips: spatial and temporal compression. Spatial compression compresses each individual frame and is also called *intraframe* compression (it treats each frame independently). Temporal compresses across frames or from frame to frame and is called *interframe* compression. Typically, spatial compression is best for clips that do not change a lot from frame to frame (such as a "talking head" clip). Temporal compression is best for clips that have a lot of changes in each frame, such as a clip that pans across a landscape scene.

Flash MX 2004's internal video compression uses the Sorenson Spark compressor. It is a very robust, yet compact, compressor that is an interframe compressor. Thus, it excels with clips that have a lot of changes from frame to frame. We'll talk more about the Sorenson compressor a little later in this chapter.

Streaming Rate

Already I have mentioned the streaming rate and what it is. Another term for the stream rate—a term common to web-based video—is *bit rate*. It basically means the number of bits per second you need to maintain smooth video playback. You will see this term (or settings related to bit rate) as you begin working with video in Flash.

File Formats

A final noteworthy element is the issue of file formats. There are numerous video formats, but a limited number that Flash will directly support. The most common ones you will likely be using are QuickTime (QT), MPG, and Windows AVI.

Now, as I mention video formats, realize that MPG is an actual compression format, while QT and AVI are more aptly described as "container" formats. By container I mean that a QT or AVI file may use any number of codecs (compressors/decompressors) on the data inside them. Additionally, a QT or AVI file may also include data that is in raw, uncompressed form. While you can import compressed video files into Flash, it is best to use raw, uncompressed footage whenever possible. It goes back to that "compressing an already compressed" item issue. Anytime you repetitively compress something with lossy codecs (all video codecs are lossy based), you enter noise into the file, decrease the visual quality, and end up with additional data in the element. In the next section we'll take a couple minutes to talk about prepping video for use in Flash.

PREPARING VIDEO

Preparing video is not an easy task; it takes much more time and effort than most people realize. If you already have material recorded, the task is somewhat easier. But if you must set up the shot, shoot it, get it into the computer and prep it for the Web, there is much involved. When people ask me how much time it takes (for proposals and such) I suggest figuring out how long you think it will take and then double it.

Acquiring Source Material

The limits of this book won't allow us to go in-depth into all aspects of getting good material. Heck, one could spend an entire two to four years in a college or institution learning to do any number of jobs related to the creation of video content. Who am I to think I can do it in a few paragraphs of one chapter in a book?

But I do wish to acknowledge that successful video integration on the Web (or in other multimedia products) is all about good source and careful planning. First, as I will acknowledge again, make sure you even need video for what you're doing. More often than not, video is a want and not a need.

Second, if you are going to include video, use as clean a source as is possible. Recording with a DV camera provides cleaner source than snagging VHS copy. Video-editing machines are often preferable over quick-and-dirty capture cards. If you have a digitized video clip already available, an uncompressed clip is better than a compressed clip (sure, it will be larger to start with, but once Flash crunches it down, the end results will be far better). Whatever you can do to get the cleanest and best source possible, do so.

Now, ultimately I acknowledge that more often than not you have to work with what you've got. But try to get the best you can as it relates to video. Even the best video on the Web will push most end users' connections. Nothing is worse than a user on a slow connection waiting to download a video clip, only to find that it wasn't worth the wait.

Sorenson Squeeze

In conjunction with the release of Flash MX (where video emerged as a part of Flash), an add-on tool called Sorenson Squeeze was released. By default, Flash includes a standard version of Sorenson's Spark compressor. Squeeze gives you greater flexibility by allowing you do much more than what can be done in Flash. This tool, as shown in figure 9-1, is designed for those who intend on doing a lot of video integration with Flash. It gives you several preset options for streaming rates and allows you a wide range of creation capabilities. If you plan on doing a lot of video, Squeeze may be something you'll wish to purchase. Sorenson's web site provides additional details about what Squeeze can do (*http://www. sorenson.com/*).

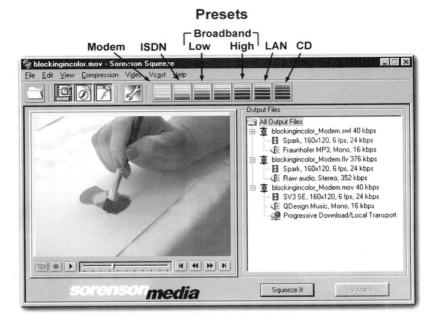

Presets

Modem   ISDN   Broadband — Low   High   LAN   CD

figure | 9-1 |

Sorenson Squeeze is an addition tool you might want to purchase if you are doing a lot of video integration with Flash.

NOTE: If you wish to install and experiment with Sorenson Squeeze, a trial version is available on Sorenson's web site

IMPORTING VIDEO

If you decide to use video as part of a Flash project and you have your clean, source material ready to import into Flash, you have a lot of the work done. Yet, even once you get to the point of getting it into Flash, there are still several decisions to be made. In general there are two ways to get video into Flash: embedding the clip so that it is saved as part of the Flash file or by linking the Flash file to an externally stored video clip.

Embedding Versus Linking

Before you ever start fiddling with video in Flash you do need to decide how you want the clip integrated into Flash. Embedding a video clip into Flash makes it so that the clip is stored inside the FLA (and the eventual SWF file). From that point, no additional plug-ins are needed (that is, beyond the Flash plug-in). The fact is that this is the simplest way to integrate video into Flash. When the clip is imported, you choose to embed, set some options related to how the clip is encoded, and you are on your way. From that point on the video file becomes a native Flash element and all you deal with are FLA and SWF files.

An alternative method for integrating video is to link a QuickTime movie to the Flash SWF file. Note that it only works with Quick-Time and it requires that you export the Flash movie as a QuickTime movie, instead of as a Flash web-ready file. This latter point is the "negative point" associated with using video linking. When you export Flash content as a QuickTime format, some of the interactivity and scripting you can include in the Flash file doesn't work so well (or requires a work-around to function properly). If you are creating Flash files that are going to be delivered apart from the Web, for instance as part of a CD or DVD-ROM, linking may be something you'll use. But, I would recommend embedding video clips most of the time. And, since embedding is what you will use most often, that is what we will focus on for the remainder of this chapter.

Video Wizard

The Video wizard in Flash MX 2004 is a wonderful addition to the product and a great improvement over what Flash MX could do. When you import a video clip, the wizard automatically pops up to assist you with settings relative to video. The first thing you'll need to do is select whether you want to link or embed the video clip. Again, more often than not you will want to select Embed, as shown in figure 9-2.

figure | 9-2 |

The Video wizard first asks you to select whether you want to link or embed the video clip.

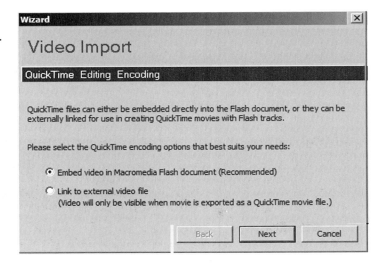

Editing

Once you have selected to embed a clip, you are given the option to insert the entire duration of the video clip into Flash, or you may choose to "edit it" and only include a specific section or sections of it (see figure 9-3). Just as a note, if you had linked the clip (instead of embedding it) you would not have the option of editing the clip (it simply inserts the clip in its entirety in the Flash movie).

figure | 9-3 |

When you choose to embed a clip, you can edit the duration of the clip.

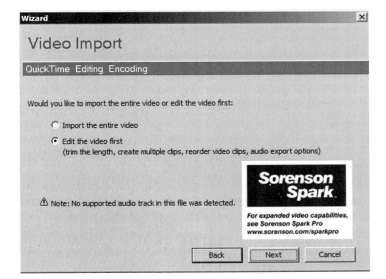

If you choose to edit the clip, the wizard shows the options displayed in figure 9-4. Using the In and Out markers, shown in figure 9-4, you can selectively choose what portion of the clip you want inserted into Flash. Set the markers and click the Create Clip button. Clicking this button adds the selected portion of the clip to the pane on the left of the dialog box.

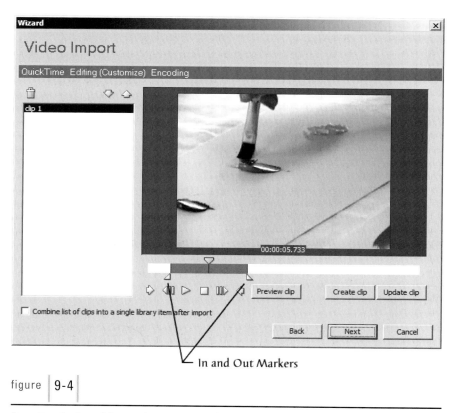

figure | **9-4**

By setting the In and Out markers you can select a specific portion of the clip to play.

In addition to being able to select a single portion of a clip, you can add multiple pieces from the clip to create an entirely new clip (where all the pieces are reassembled into a single element in Flash) or several partial clips that end up being separate video elements in Flash (see figure 9-5). If you want to combine all the pieces into one, you check the *Combine list of clips* checkbox. Also, once a clip is listed in the pane on the left, double-clicking it will reselect the In and Out markers associated with it.

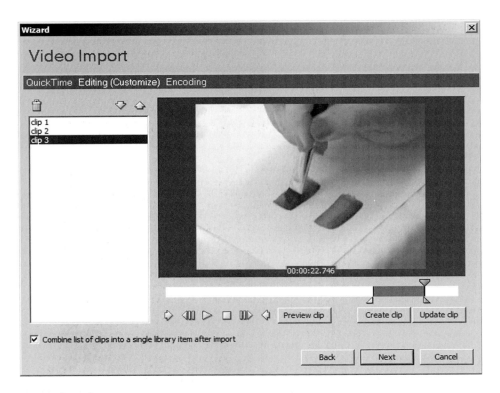

figure | 9-5 |

You can select multiple pieces of a clip that are either stored separately or as a single element in Flash.

Compression

Once you have set the editing options, you then must establish the compression settings associated with the clip and advanced settings, as shown in figure 9-6. Once you select a setting (or create your own) for both of these, Flash applies the compression and advanced settings to the clip in real time as it imports.

Let's first examine the Compression Profiles. Flash offers several default compression profiles for you to use. The profiles include:

● 56 kbps modem

● Corporate LAN 150 kbps

● Three different DSL settings (256, 512, and 718)

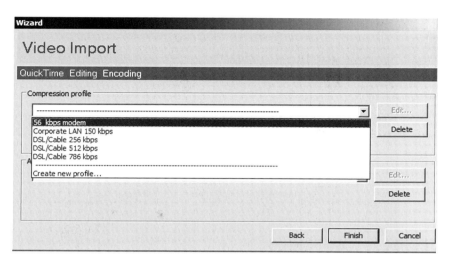

figure | 9-6 |

Flash provides several compression profiles you can use.

In addition to the default profiles, you can establish your own custom profile by choosing *Create new profile* from the Compression Profile drop-down menu. Figure 9-7 shows the dialog that lets you establish a new compression profile. When you set up a compression profile, you can base the compression on either bandwidth (which I recommend) or by quality.

figure | 9-7 |

The dialog box for setting up your own compression profile.

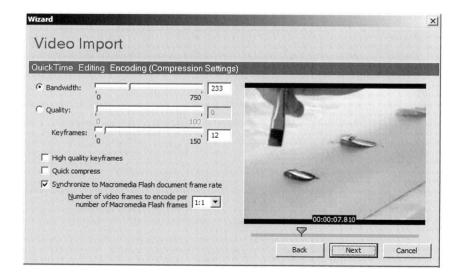

Part of creating a compression profile is defining the number of keyframes in the video clip. In general, the more keyframes the bigger but better looking the file. As you will recall, I mentioned that Flash's compression scheme uses intraframe compression, where compression is applied over a range of frames (the range is defined by a keyframe and its following frames, up to the next keyframe). Keyframes are written in their entirety (basically not compressed at all), while between frames are comparatively written.

Thus, the Keyframes slider controls the number of keyframes (and essentially how many frames are between each keyframe). Depending on how alike a keyframe and its following frames are determines the effectiveness of compression and the size of the resulting file.

The *Number of video frames to encode per number of Macromedia Flash frames* drop-down list is pretty important. It determines the number of video frames to match against Flash frames. Generally, you want there to be synchronization between the number of video frames and Flash frames (working with a 1-to-1 ratio is easiest). In general, it is best to prep videos outside Flash such that they are already set to a frame rate of 15 fps, as previously mentioned. Then, matching the video to Flash is easy: select the 1 to 1 option.

Advanced Editing

One final cool thing Flash lets you do is apply advanced settings to a clip while you import it, as shown in figure 9-8. The Advanced settings are:

- *Color adjustments:* This allows you to do hue balancing, as well as adjustments to saturation and gamma. Hue allows you to apply a color overlay to a clip, thereby adding that color to the clip. Saturation allows you to shift color, and gamma allows you to add neutral gray to the clip.

- *Brightness and Contrast adjustments:* These allow you to fiddle with the overall brightness or contrast in a clip.

- *Scaling:* This allows you to adjust frame size of the clip while you are importing.

- *Clipping:* This is a beauty! The ability to crop to a particular section of a clip is extremely handy.

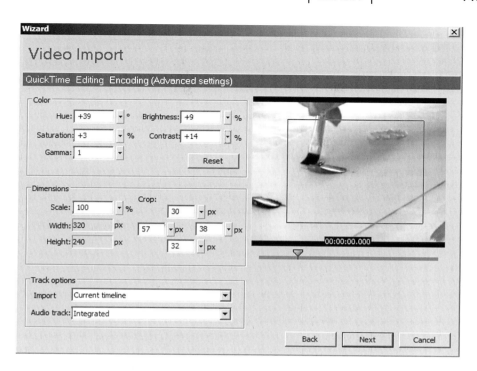

Finishing the Import

Once you have made all the settings in the Video wizard and you click Finish, Flash will encode the clip with the settings you have chosen and place the clip on the stage (or in the library, depending on how you imported). If you import to the stage, Flash will prompt you, wanting to know if you want it to extend the frame you are inserting into to match what is needed by the video clip. You will want to say yes. Once the clip appears on the stage, you can play the Flash movie, which will in turn play the video clip.

figure | 9-8

The Advanced Settings allow you to adjust color, brightness, contrast, and frame parameters.

SUMMARY

In this chapter you have reviewed quite a bit of information related to video. Realize, however, there is much more study you can do concerning the creation of video and the use of it on the computer. The fact is, there is just not enough room in this book to say all I'd like to say. In this chapter you just get the quick and dirty. But I would encourage you to do further reading along these lines. As I said, as bandwidth gets faster and cheaper video will become even more important than it already is.

in review

1. What is the typical range for frame rates for web-based content?

2. What does frame size for video clips refer to?

3. What are the two types of compression schemes for video and what is the difference between the two?

4. What is the streaming rate for web video? What is bit rate?

5. What are the three common video formats you'll likely deal with as it relates to web-based video?

6. Before you decide to use video on the Web, what question should you first ask?

7. What are the differences between linking and embedding a video clip in Flash?

8. When you edit a video clip with the Video wizard, what does it allow you to do?

9. What is the Keyframes setting in the Compression Profile for?

10. What kind of advanced settings can you create in relation to video (what attributes can you manipulate)?

↗ EXPLORING ON YOUR OWN

1. Download some appropriate video source material from the Web and try to integrate it into one of your own designs in Flash.

2. Download some appropriate video source material from the Web and try working with the linking capability in Flash.

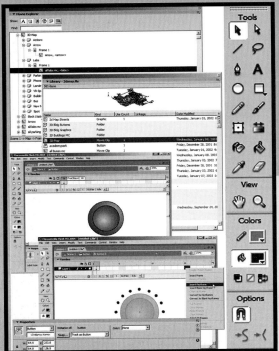

symbols and libraries

charting your course

When we discussed assets in prior chapters, we briefly touched on the issue of symbols—specifically, the fact that when you import a bitmap, sound, or video clip, Flash automatically inserts the element into the library. And, to set the default compression options for those elements you do so through the library.

However, there is much more that can be said about symbols as well as the Flash library. In this chapter we'll chat about the various types of vector symbols you can create as well as the myriad uses of libraries, including transferring symbols from one Flash file to another and sharing symbols across files using shared libraries. We'll start with some conceptual things you should know about symbols and move on from there. The latter part of the chapter will address issues related to libraries.

 goals

In this chapter you will:

- **Examine several conceptual items related to symbols so that you understand how they work**

- **Learn to create the three primary types of Flash symbols that are vector based**

- **Find out about using libraries to transfer symbols across files**

- **Discover how to create shared libraries**

SYMBOL CONCEPTS

Symbols are not really a new concept. Many different graphics packages give you the ability to create a reusable, graphical component—the earliest being CAD packages. However, while the concept is similar, Flash symbols behave uniquely and have their own characteristics, as you will soon see.

Symbols and Instances

Symbols are simply reusable components you create or import in Flash. There are three types of symbols you can create and four types that are automatically created when you import external media assets. In the next section we'll discuss the three types of symbols you can create in Flash. You have already seen three of the automatically created symbols: bitmaps, sound, and video. The fourth type, fonts, allows you to store font descriptions in a Flash library.

The main thing to understand about symbols (regardless of symbol type) is that the symbol is the actual data that describes the element, while an instance is simply a reference to the symbol. This means that once you have a symbol created, you can make multiple references to (or instances of) it on the stage. Recall that you create an instance of a symbol by click-dragging the symbol from the library to the stage. Once multiple instances of a symbol are created, each instance operates somewhat independently of the other instances. Each instance can have a different location, size, orientation, and color effect on the stage, even though all the instances refer to the same library symbol.

The key to understanding how symbols and instances work is to realize that while instances can have different stage properties, if you change the symbol in the library (such as accessing the symbol and scaling it), all instances will change to reflect the change in the symbol itself. So, the key is to understand those things you can change concerning instances (and how they don't affect everything else) and how changes inside a symbol do affect everything else. By the time you complete this chapter you'll have a good handle on this.

Instance Properties

When you create instances of a symbol, each instance can have its own properties on the stage. Figure 10-1 shows several instances of the same symbol, each with varying properties. Understand that even though all of the instances are referenced back to the original symbol in the library, each can have its own size, location, skew, orientation, and color effect setting.

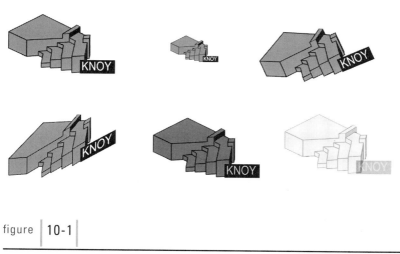

figure | 10-1 |

Each symbol instance can have its own properties, even though all the instances refer to the same symbol.

Nesting Symbols

In addition to acknowledging symbols and instances, you should also realize that you can nest symbols inside of one another. It is really quite common to insert one symbol inside of another symbol. As you are getting up to speed this may be confusing at first. Often I recommend that newcomers to Flash use the Movie Explorer to examine the hierarchical structure of symbols in a file. Figure 10-2 shows a series of nested symbols as viewed through the Movie Explorer.

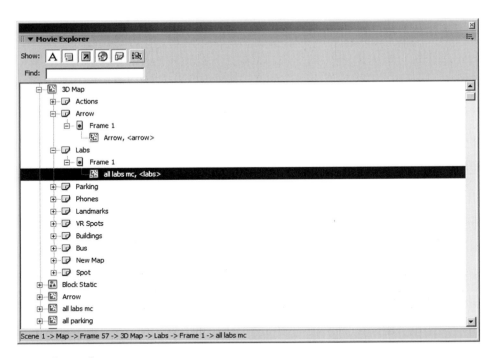

figure | 10-2

The Movie Explorer can be used to view the hierarchy of nested symbols.

Symbol Types

There are three types of symbols you can create in Flash. These are graphic symbols, button symbols, and movie clip symbols. Each of these different types of symbols has specific functionalities and so-called rules. There are also specific situations in which you should use each. Graphic and movie clip symbols are similar in that both have their own timeline. You can think of these types of symbols as "sub-timelines" within the main movie timeline. Button symbols, on the other hand, have a special timeline that allows you to set up states for a button. Let's look at each of these more closely.

Graphic Symbols

Graphic symbols are symbols that have their own timeline, very similar to the main movie timeline. When you create a graphic symbol into the main movie timeline, you are actually nesting the graphic symbol's timeline into the main movie's timeline.

What makes graphic symbols unique is the fact that they are synchronized with the main movie timeline when they play. When one frame of the main movie plays, one frame of the graphic symbol plays. Similarly, when the main movie timeline stops, so does a graphic symbol. Another unique thing about graphic symbols is that you cannot insert sounds into them, nor can you nest a button symbol in them. So, in this way they are somewhat more limiting than movie clip symbols.

So, the question you'd like to ask is, "when should you use a graphic symbol?" Typically, graphic symbols are used for static elements, or for elements you want tied or synchronized with the main movie timeline. For example, if I were going to create a character-based walk cycle, I would likely use graphic symbols for all the parts of the character I want to animate. When I create the animation, I would animate the graphic symbols. Realize that this is just one example. Generally, 90 percent of the time you'll use graphic symbols for static components that will themselves be animated.

Button Symbols

The second type of symbol is the button symbol. Button symbols are special in that, instead of a time-based timeline, they have four frames. Three of the frames represent "button states," while the fourth defines the hot area for the button. So, when you create a button you define content in an up frame, an over frame, and a down frame. As well, you place content in a "hit" frame, which defines the "hotspot" for the button. You'll see an example later in this chapter that constructs a button from scratch.

The thing to note about button symbols is that they play independently of the main timeline. So, if the main timeline stops, a button will continue to function. Also, realize that a button symbol only allows you to create the visual activity of the button. To have the button do something, you must attach code to it.

Movie Clip Symbols

The final type of symbol is the movie clip. It is somewhat like a graphic symbol except that it plays independently of the main movie timeline (if the main timeline stops, movie clip symbols continue to play). Movie clips can also contain any type of object, including sounds and all other types of symbols.

Movie clip symbols are the most extensible type of symbol. However, most of the time you will use movie clips to perform specific types of animation. Let's return to our walk cycle example. When something is walking, there are two things happening: the movement of the parts of the individual and the simultaneous movement of the individual across the stage.

To create an animated walk cycle (although this is a very simplified description), you would create the arms, legs, torso, and head of the individual as separate graphic symbols. Then you would insert those graphic symbols into a movie clip. Inside the movie clip you would position the parts over time so that it looks like the individual is walking "in place." In the next chapter we'll get into setting up animation.

Once you have the parts inside the movie clip such that they look like the individual is walking in place, you would insert the movie clip into the main timeline. Once inserted, you would animate the movie clip moving from one side of the stage to the next. This makes the individual look like he or she is walking across the stage. Conceptually, these are the types of scenarios you use movie clips for: animating something that is itself animating. Might sound confusing, but as we get into animation in the following chapters this will make more sense.

Library and Identification

Now, with all these various types of symbols, you're likely thinking, "How do you tell them all apart?" When you access the library, as shown in figure 10-3, you will note that the different types of symbols are graphically represented using different icons. When an instance is on the stage, you can determine what type of symbol it refers to by selecting it and looking at the properties panel.

CREATING SYMBOLS

Now that we have looked at some of the conceptual things, let's get down to business and examine how you create symbols. The next three sections will build upon one another. In looking at creating different symbol types, you will learn how to create an animated button.

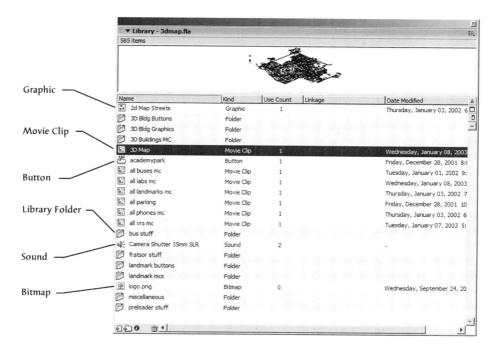

Graphic

Movie Clip

Button

Library Folder

Sound

Bitmap

figure | 10-3

The library uses different icons to represent the different types of symbols.

Graphic Symbols

When creating symbols (regardless of symbol type), you can either convert existing stage material to a symbol or build a new symbol from scratch. To do the former, select some stuff on the stage and choose Modify | Convert to Symbol. To do the latter, choose New Symbol from the Insert menu.

To create the beginnings of our button, we'll use New Symbol. When you select Insert | New Symbol, Flash presents the dialog box shown in figure 10-4. In this dialog, you give the symbol a name and you set its behavior (what type of symbol it is). The bottom of the dialog box shown in figure 10-4 contains a bunch of other stuff we'll discuss later. Once you name the new symbol and set its behavior, clicking OK creates the symbol and opens the timeline for it so that you can start putting stuff in it.

figure | 10-4 |

The New Symbol dialog box is where you give the symbol a name and set its behavior.

The button I will eventually create is a simple round button. So, I create my static graphic content inside the graphic symbol as shown in figure 10-5. For now, all I need is the "normal" button state—that is, what it looks like when the user is not messing with it. Note that the content is created around the small crosshair that appears in the center of the screen. The crosshairs represent the registration point (origin) for the symbol.

When you are all done creating content in a symbol, you can click the Scene 1 link in the "edit path" to get back to the main movie's timeline (see figure 10-5). When you return to the main movie timeline you will not see the graphic symbol (at this point the symbol only exists in the library). This is similar to when you use Import to Library. Once you use New Symbol to create a symbol, you must manually drag the symbol from the library to the stage to create an instance of it.

Edit Path

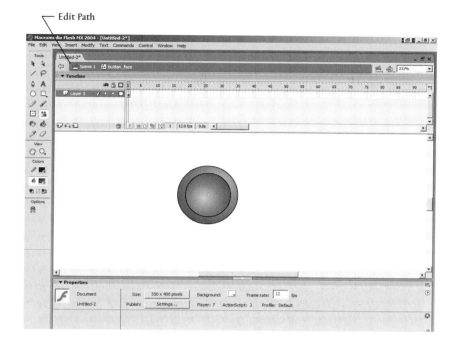

figure | 10-5 |

Graphic content is created inside the graphic symbol's timeline.

TRY THIS

Plan out your own button symbol. What will the button look like? Once you have it in mind, create a graphic symbol you can integrate into a button symbol following the next section. Create it and store it in a Flash file for later use.

Button Symbols

Now that I have the graphic symbol, let's put it into a button symbol (so that we can make an actual button). To do this, we'll use the Convert to Symbol command rather than the New Symbol command.

With the graphic symbol on the stage, I'll select it and choose Modify I Convert to Symbol. I set the behavior to Button, give it a name, and click OK. This process places the graphic symbol inside a new button symbol. However, you won't see a difference on the stage—that is, unless you click on the item and look at its properties in the Properties panel.

Now, although the graphic symbol has been nested inside a button symbol, we have a little more work to do to make a functioning button. If you double click on the button symbol on the stage, the button symbol's timeline is opened. Now you are working inside the button. As shown in figure 10-6, the button's timeline is different from other symbols, as well as the main timeline. It provides four unique frames in which you can place content.

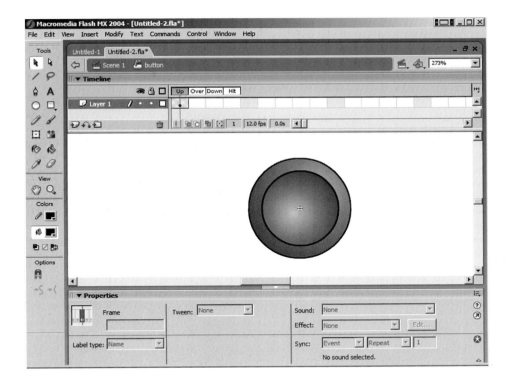

figure | 10-6

A button symbol's timeline provides four specific frames.

To set up a button, you must place content in the four frames. The first three are associated with different user states of the button. The last frame ("hit") defines the hotspot for the button. To duplicate the content from one frame to another, you right click and select Insert Keyframe, as shown in figure 10-7.

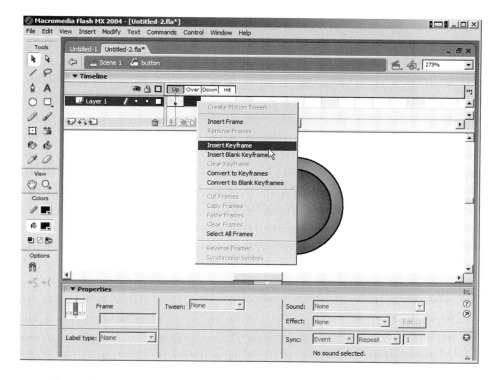

figure | 10-7

Duplicate content from one frame to the next using the Insert Keyframe option.

Once you have created keyframes in all four frames, click on the Down frame. In this frame you will want to modify the graphic symbol so that when the user clicks on it the button appears to press in. With the playhead over the Down frame, use the Free Transform tool to rotate the button 180 degrees, as shown in figure 10-8.

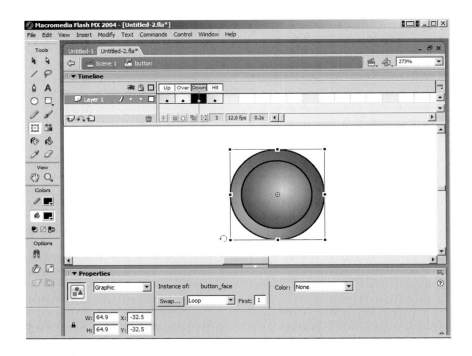

figure | **10-8**

Rotate the graphic
symbol in the Down
frame.

Before we move on, let's also add a sound to the button—so that
when the user clicks on the button a sound is played. You'll need to
find an appropriate sound and import it so that you can use it in
the button symbol. Once you have imported a sound, click on the
Down frame to make it the current frame. Then use the Sound
drop-down menu in the Properties panel to assign the sound to the
frame. Set the Sync drop-down to Start.

Now let's return to the main timeline and see the button work.
Click on the Scene 1 link in the edit path. Then select Enable
Simple Buttons in the Control menu. Now move the cursor over
the button and click on it. The Enable Simple Buttons menu option
allows you to work with rudimentary buttons and see them work.
Once you have seen a button work, however, make sure you turn it
off. Otherwise, you won't be able to select the button with the
Arrow tool.

In this section, you have learned to make a graphic symbol and
then use that graphic symbol in a button. Let's modify the Button
symbol so that it also includes a movie clip symbol as an animated
state for the button. The movie clip symbol will be played when the
user rolls over the button.

TRY THIS ·

Using the graphic symbol you designed earlier, now insert that graphic symbol into a button and create all of the necessary button states for it to work. Once you have successfully created your button, try moving the hit content around and see what effect it has on the button.

Movie Clip Symbols

For the animated state of the button, I'll create a simple set of circles around the button that will appear and animate when the user rolls over the button. To get the placement of the circles correct, in the main timeline I created the circles around the button as simple fill elements, as shown in figure 10-9.

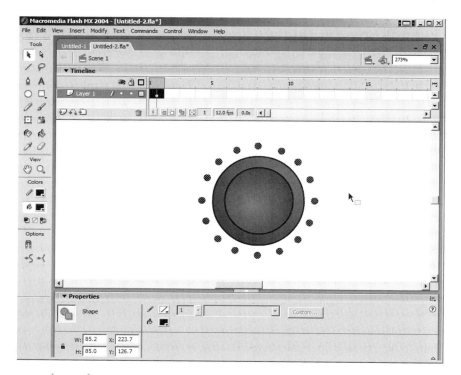

figure | 10-9

Placing the fill elements that will be in the movie clip.

Once the fill elements are created, select them all (just the fills, not the button symbol) and use Modify | Convert to Symbol. I set the behavior on movie clip and give it a name. Note that when you use Convert to Symbol the elements on the stage are converted to a movie clip. We don't want the symbol here (it goes inside the button), we only created it on the stage to get the placement right. As such, once you have created the movie clip symbol, delete it from the stage.

Although you deleted the movie clip instance from stage, it still exists in the library. At this point you need to insert the movie clip into the Over frame of the button. Double click on the button symbol to open its timeline. In the button symbol, place the playhead on the Over frame and open the library. Drag the newly created movie clip from the library to the stage such that the center of the movie clip is aligned with the center of the graphic instance on the stage, as shown in figure 10-10.

figure | 10-10

Insert the movie clip symbol in the Over frame of the button and align it.

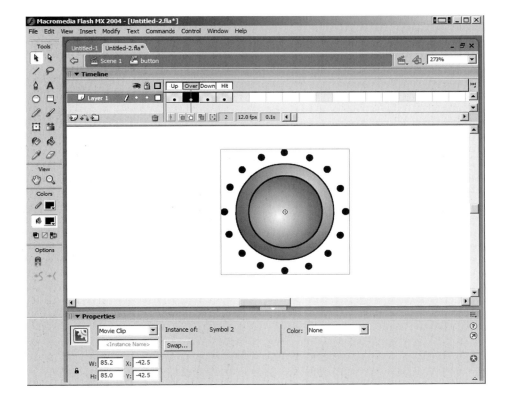

Now that the movie clip is inserted into the button, we need to add some animation inside the movie clip (right now the movie clip is actually static). Double click the movie clip to open its timeline. To do the animation (all we're going to do is rotate the circles), we must convert the fills to a graphic symbol. While you are inside the movie clip, select all the fill elements and use Modify | Convert to Symbol on the fills. Choose Graphic as the behavior and give the element a name. Click OK.

Now that the fills are a graphic symbol, you need to extend the graphic instance to frame 15 so that we can do a little animating. In the timeline, right click in frame 15 and select Insert Keyframe, as shown in figure 10-11. This creates a keyframe in frame 15 and extends the duration of the instance in frame 1 to frame 14. Note that in the next chapter we'll examine animation in more depth. For now, simply follow along.

figure | **10-11**

Insert the movie clip symbol in the Over frame of the button and align it.

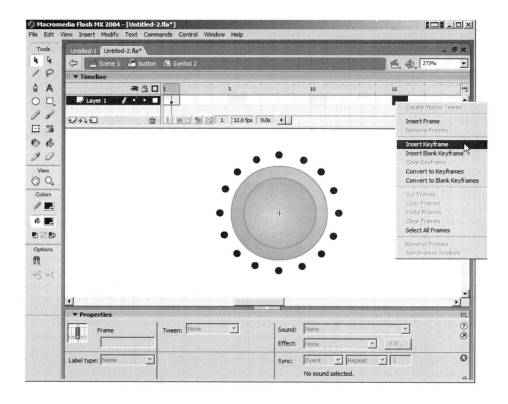

Once the graphic's duration is extended, select any frame between 1 and 14 in the timeline. In the Properties panel, set the Tweening drop-down to Motion. Then set the Rotate drop-down to CW (clockwise). This sets up the graphic so that it rotates once over 15 frames.

Now you basically have everything set up for your animated state. Click on the Scene 1 link in the edit path. When you have a movie clip in a button, you cannot use the Enable Simple Buttons option to test the button like you did before. Instead, you use the Control | Test Movie option. Use this option to see the button work. In summary of what you just worked on, take a moment to acknowledge the structure of the movie clip:

● Button symbol

● Graphic symbol

● Movie clip symbol

● Graphic symbol

To create the animated button, you nested both a graphic symbol and a movie clip symbol into the button. The move clip symbol itself contained a graphic symbol. As you work with Flash, being a good developer is dependent on knowledge of symbols—and nesting those symbols inside one another. As you start building movies, think about how you can effectively use symbols.

EDITING SYMBOLS

In the last section you examined how to create the various symbol types and got a pretty good feel for how they are interrelated and can be nested inside one another. Before we move on to libraries, let's acknowledge some other important things to realize about symbols.

Accessing Symbol Data

Already you have seen that you can access a symbol's data by double clicking an instance of it on the stage. The nice thing about accessing a symbol this way is that content not in the symbol is dimmed out while still giving you a way to see the symbol "in context" of other elements in the main timeline.

Realize that you can access a symbol's data in a couple other ways. If you right click on a symbol instance, you can use the context menu to select Edit or Edit in a New Window. The Edit in Place option is the same as double clicking the instance. Or, you can double click a symbol name in the library, which will open the symbol's timeline.

Swapping Symbols

The ability to swap symbols allows you to use one symbol instance as a placeholder for others. For example, if you want to create a series of buttons, say for an interface, you can create one button and create several instances of it in some arrangement on the stage. Then, as you create the remaining buttons you can use the Swap Symbol button in the Properties panel (see figure 10-12) to exchange one symbol for another.

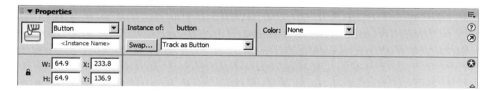

figure | 10-12

The Swap button allows you to change the symbol associated with any symbol instance.

Changing Symbol Behavior

There may be times when you want to convert one type of symbol to another behavior type, such as changing a symbol from a graphic to a movie clip, or vice versa. This is relatively easy to do, but you must change the symbol behavior in two places. The first place is to change it in the library (access the library, right click the symbol name, and change the Type submenu setting). The second place you must change the behavior is on every instance of that symbol on the stage—which can be a pain if there are a lot of instances of the symbol you want to change. Nevertheless, to change the behavior of a symbol instance, select the instance and change the Symbol Behavior drop-down menu (in the upper left) of the Properties panel.

Breaking Symbols

A final issue to acknowledge is the ability to break symbols using the Break Apart command. When you use Break Apart on a symbol, the symbol is "disassembled" to its component parts. If you have a basic symbol that contains only groups, lines, fills, and so forth, Break Apart disjoins the instance from the symbol and leaves groups, lines, fills, and so forth on the stage. If you use Break Apart on a symbol that itself contains other symbols, it breaks the main symbol (you end up with component symbols as separate elements). So, as it relates to symbols, you can think of Break Apart as a command that breaks the hierarchy of elements from the top down, and what you end up with depends on what is inside the symbol. And, regardless of what is in a symbol, if you consecutively use Break Apart on a symbol, at some point you'll end up with a bunch of stage objects.

LIBRARIES

Already you likely have a good sense of some of the basics concerning libraries in Flash. In the final portion of this chapter, I wish to extend your view a little—showing you some additional (and quite powerful) things libraries provide.

Current Library

Already you have seen that you access the current file's library using the Window | Library command. One of the things we have not yet acknowledged is the ability to create library folders, in which you can group symbols that logically belong together.

For example, if you have a symbol that is composed of several other symbols (such as our button example in the prior section) it might make sense to create a folder to contain all the parts of a particular symbol. Along these lines, whatever organizational strategy you decide to employ in the library is up to you. The important part is that you at least use some sort of strategy to organize stuff in the library. Otherwise, you'll get to the end of developing a movie and have a whole slew of symbols in the library—making future work with the movie file a memory (rather than a management) task. I would suggest that as you build your movies, take the time to create an organizational structure inside your library. It will save you time later.

> ## ▶ TRY THIS
>
> Open the file in which you created a button symbol. Access the library and try creating a folder or two and adding symbols to the folder. Also, take a look at the Library panel's menu to see what other commands you have available to you.

Standard Libraries

In addition to the library that exists as you add symbols to your movie, Flash comes with several "standard" libraries that are installed with the application. If you access Window | Other Panels | Common Libraries, you can open and access some pre-created symbols that ship with Flash. If you pull symbols from these libraries, they are automatically added to the current file's library.

> ## ▶ TRY THIS
>
> Examine some of the various standard libraries that come with Flash. You'll find a variety of things, from relatively simple buttons to complex interaction components. Take a little time familiarizing yourself with the symbols that are there.

External Libraries

Being able to share symbols from one file to the next is a pretty cool feature. When you open the standard libraries that come with Flash and pull symbols from them to your own files, the symbols become part of the file you are working with. In actuality, any Flash file that contains symbols can be opened and "borrowed" from. If you use the File | Import | Open External Library command, you can borrow symbols from any file. When you open an external library, you cannot edit the library; that is, you cannot create folders, delete symbols, or add symbols to it (to do that, you must open the file directly with the normal File | Open command).

One thing you will notice as you start working with libraries is that you can open several libraries at once—making it sometimes difficult to determine which panel is the current file's library. The easy way to tell the difference is this: the current file's library has a white background, while external libraries (including the standard or common libraries) have a gray background.

Shared Libraries

Rarely (if ever) should you create one big honking Flash file, slap it on a page, and call it a web site. Rather, most web sites that use Flash use several pieces of Flash content that are used for various parts of a site. As such, those different pieces often have certain elements that are the same. When this is the case, Flash provides the ability to create a special library, called a shared library, which allows you to share symbols across multiple Flash files. This is an extremely powerful capability and lets you further reduce the comprehensive data transfer requirements of your web site.

Setting up a shared library in Flash is pretty easy. It requires two basic steps. First, you must create a Flash file that will be used as the shared library. In it, you identify the symbols (in most cases, all of the symbols in a shared library are shared) to be shared. The second step is to use those shared symbols in subsequent files. Let's examine how these two things are done.

Setting Up a Library for Sharing

To set up a shared library, open a new Flash file and stock it with the symbols you intend on sharing. Shared libraries typically have no content on the stage or in the timeline (the only things in them are symbols).

Once you have symbols in the library, you must tell Flash each of the symbols you will want to share (again, in most cases that means all of the symbols). And, even if there are symbols that make up other symbols you must manually set up each one to be shared.

To set a symbol up so that it is shared, right click on the symbol's name and select Linkage. This will open the Linkage Properties dialog box, as shown in figure 10-13. To set up a symbol so that it is shared, you must enable the *Export for runtime sharing* option and put a name in the URL field. The name you put in the URL field is the name you intend on using for the SWF version of the shared library. Yes, Flash can only use SWF files in shared libraries; you cannot put an FLA file name there.

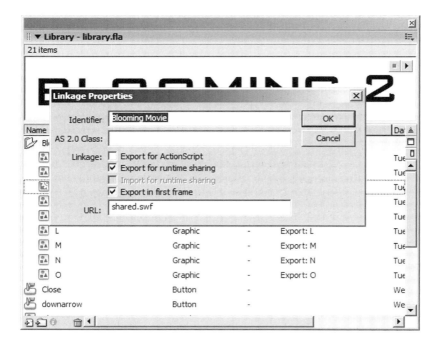

figure | 10-13

To set up symbols so that they can be shared you use the Linkage Properties dialog box.

Using Shared Symbols

Now, to use a shared library's symbols in other movies, you first use Import | Open External Library to open the external (shared) library. Once it is open, you can see the symbols that are shared, as shown in figure 10-14. Notice the Linkage column, which shows the name it will be imported as. To get the shared symbols from the shared library to the current file's library, simply drag the symbols from one library to the other.

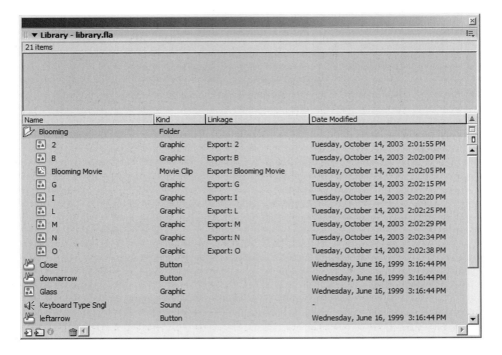

Name	Kind	Linkage	Date Modified
Blooming	Folder		
2	Graphic	Export: 2	Tuesday, October 14, 2003 2:01:55 PM
B	Graphic	Export: B	Tuesday, October 14, 2003 2:02:00 PM
Blooming Movie	Movie Clip	Export: Blooming Movie	Tuesday, October 14, 2003 2:02:05 PM
G	Graphic	Export: G	Tuesday, October 14, 2003 2:02:15 PM
I	Graphic	Export: I	Tuesday, October 14, 2003 2:02:20 PM
L	Graphic	Export: L	Tuesday, October 14, 2003 2:02:25 PM
M	Graphic	Export: M	Tuesday, October 14, 2003 2:02:29 PM
N	Graphic	Export: N	Tuesday, October 14, 2003 2:02:34 PM
O	Graphic	Export: O	Tuesday, October 14, 2003 2:02:38 PM
Close	Button		Wednesday, June 16, 1999 3:16:44 PM
downarrow	Button		Wednesday, June 16, 1999 3:16:44 PM
Glass	Graphic		Wednesday, June 16, 1999 3:16:44 PM
Keyboard Type Sngl	Sound	-	
leftarrow	Button		Wednesday, June 16, 1999 3:16:44 PM

figure | 10-14

When you open a library that is set up to share, the shared elements are identified by the content in the Linkage column.

SUMMARY

In this chapter you have examined a host of issues surrounding symbols and libraries. You have learned about the three main symbol types, when to use them, and how to create them. As it relates to libraries, you now know how to share libraries and symbols, and how to create shared symbols.

1. Knowing about symbols, how will it impact your designs? What strategies can you use to efficiently and effectively use symbols in your designs? What limitations might the three basic symbol types impose on your creations?

2. What is the difference between a symbol and a symbol instance?

3. What are the three different types of symbols in Flash? What is the difference between each type?

4. When would you use a graphic symbol? When would you use a movie clip symbol?

5. What is the difference between New Symbol and Convert to Symbol?

6. What does the hit frame in a button symbol do?

7. When would you swap a symbol?

8. If you need to convert a graphic symbol to a movie clip symbol, how do you do it?

9. When you import a symbol from an external library, what happens in the current file?

10. How do you set up a shared library?

↗ EXPLORING ON YOUR OWN

1. Try your hand at creating an interface that utilizes the range of buttons available in the common libraries.

2. Try creating a portfolio interface using what you have learned in this chapter.

ADVENTURES IN DESIGN
A LITTLE VIDEO APPLICATION

Flash opens up quite a range of possibilities when you start considering all it can do. With its video capabilities, one of the things you should realize is that Flash is not just for the Web but can also be used for CD or DVD materials. This section describes a small video application that was designed to highlight my trip up Diamond Head (see figure B-1). Since creating this, I have had several opportunities to create these types of things and actually make money doing it! Once you have created one of these, it makes it pretty easy to replicate—by simply creating a new interface for the application and interchanging the video within it.

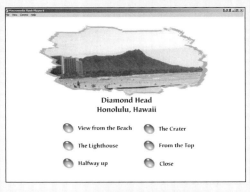

Figure B-1. The interface for the little video application.

Project Example

This project actually started because my wife wanted a way of easily viewing videos—thus, enter Flash. However, I began by sampling the video clips from our Sony HandyCam into the computer. Once there, I did a little editing on the clips and got them into Flash using the Video wizard. I ended up creating a little video interface, shown in figure B-2, which would allow me to control the video clip. The video interface was actually created as a shared library component. Also, each video clip was a separate file that was loaded into the main movie (using the *loadmovie()* action). Note that most of the actions needed for this project are described in

Figure B-2. The video interface for the clips.

Chapter 14. As an additional source of "how-to," see the Flash Help menu, as it does a pretty good job with specifics.

Once the video interface was completed, I then designed the main interface for the application (shown in figure B-1). I wanted something that looked a little elegant but not stodgy. Then I created the buttons for the interface. Clicking on them simply loads the associated video clip onto the screen, as shown in figure B-3.

Your Turn

Now it's your turn to try something like this. There are basically two different ways you can go with this. If you have access to video equipment, try creating your own Flash application that lets users view some of your clips. If video equipment is not available, try just creating an interface to be able to view some of your own artwork—like a small portfolio interface that lets you view specific images you have created.

1. Start by deciding whether you are going to use video or imagery for your project. Obviously, there is much less work involved in doing an image-based viewer as opposed to a video-based viewer.

2. Next, decide how you'll display the work. In my example, I created a little video interface into which I could place any of my clips. If you are doing an image-based viewer, you will have to consider how you will make all the images fit (seldom does all of one's work conform to the same aspect ratio or size).

3. Once you figure out what work you will show, create an interface that can be used to access your content. Keep in mind that when you design interfaces, simplicity is key. Don't make users jump through 20 hoops to get to what they need to see. "Simple" is a key term in interface design.

4. Implement your project as a set of files that can be burned to CD or DVD and distributed.

Figure B-3. When you click on the button, the video is loaded and displayed.

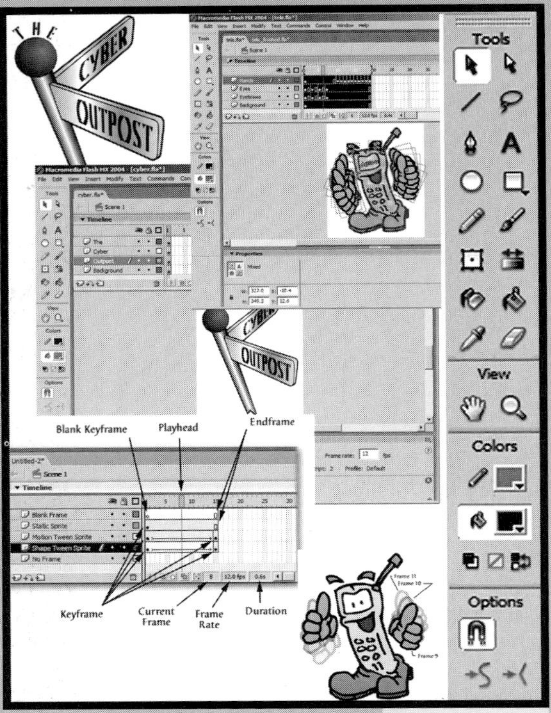
THE
CYBER
OUTPOST
Tools
View
Colors
Options
Blank Keyframe
Playhead
Endframe
Keyframe
Current Frame
Frame Rate
Duration

11

keyframe animation

charting your course

I'll open this chapter by saying, "I've said all the things in the past 10 chapters to prepare you for these latter five chapters." The first 10 chapters dealt with all the various things you really have to know before you can ever start creating animation or integrating interactive elements. Now we get to do some of the fun stuff—namely, use Flash's animation tools.

This chapter will begin with the basics of using keyframe animation techniques to create the most rudimentary type of animation, cel animation. In cel animation, you create each individual frame that appears in the animation. The positive aspect of this is you have a lot of control and the negative is that it is time consuming and often monotonous. A lot of times the only way to create a particular animation in Flash may be through the use of frame-by-frame animation. Following this chapter we'll cover two additional types of animation: motion and shape tweening. Motion and shape tweening are the heart of Flash's animation capability. However, we have to start with the basics in this chapter first.

 goals

In this chapter you will:

- Learn to add, delete, and modify frames in the timeline

- Discover the five main frame indentifiers and what they represent

- Find out how to create frame-by-frame animation in Flash

FRAME BASICS

To start learning how frames work, we'll use a simple example in which we want things to appear on the stage over time. I'm going to work with the example shown in figure 11-1, in which I want the words on the sign to individually appear over about 4 or 5 seconds. The first thing to do is consider that the movie will be playing at the default of 12 frames per second. Thus, each word will take about 1 second to appear and there will be a pause of 1 second at the beginning and the end of the small movie.

figure | 11-1|

A simple animation in which the words appear on the stage over time.

To make things more interesting, the first word (*The*) will appear a letter at a time. So, each letter in the word *The* will appear on increments of 1/3 of a second (or at every four frames). Anytime you start to do an animation you should begin by thinking about the timing of the sequence. You need to have a pretty good feel for not just what will happen but when it will happen.

Creating, Naming, and Populating Layers

To begin this animation, I am starting with a basic "flat" graphic that resides on a single layer. To begin the animation process, I need to split the graphic up onto different layers so that I can more easily animate it. I will place the word *The* on one layer, *Cyber* on another layer, and *Outpost* on another layer. The remainder of the elements will be on a totally separate layer. Because I am not animating anything else, it is perfectly acceptable to just leave all the other stuff on a "background" layer.

To get everything onto its own layer, I use a pretty specific process. I select the word *The* on the stage and use Edit | Cut. Then I add a new layer and use the Edit | Paste In Place command. The Paste in Place command pastes the element I cut in the exact location I cut it from. If I had used a normal Paste command, it would paste the element in the center of the screen instead.

Once I am finished with the *The* text, I repeat the process for the other two words, such that I end up with four layers. Typically, once you have your stuff arranged on the various layers you will want to rename the layers to something other than the default of *layer1*, *layer2*, and so forth. If you double click on a layer name you can change its name. Figure 11-2 shows my layer structure after separating the pieces onto different layers.

figure | 11-2 |

The layers created for the various pieces that will appear on the stage.

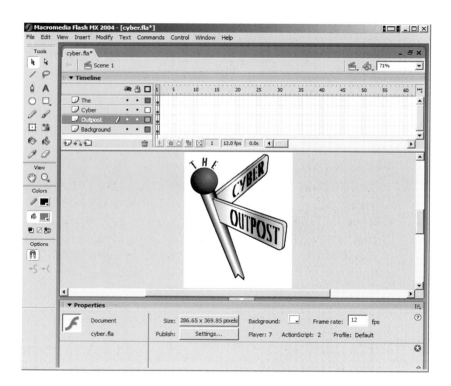

Rules of Frames

Now that the content is separated onto different layers, I can begin defining the keyframes and actually creating this basic animation. In figure 11-2, you will see that as content is placed on each layer, by default a keyframe is created in frame 1 of each layer. Keyframes are identified as filled, black circles in the timeline. In general, a keyframe defines a specific location, orientation, size, or color (that is, alpha, brightness, or tint) of some object on the stage. Keyframes are the basis for all animation in Flash, regardless of whether you are creating frame-by-frame, motion, or shape animations.

Before I continue on with my example, it would be helpful at this point to acknowledge the different types of frame representations Flash uses and what they mean. Then we will return to the example at hand.

Frame Identifiers

There are five different types of frames that can appear in the main timeline. Figure 11-3 shows them. In addition, the timeline provides several other items you should be aware of, such as the current frame indicator, the frame rate indicator, and the element duration.

As shown in figure 11-3, the first layer, (named *Blank Frames*), shows the representation for a set of frames that contain no objects. When creating animations in Flash, you build the timeline from the left side using blank frames. For example, if you want an object to appear at frame 15, you insert blank frames up to frame 15 and then place a keyframe in frame 15.

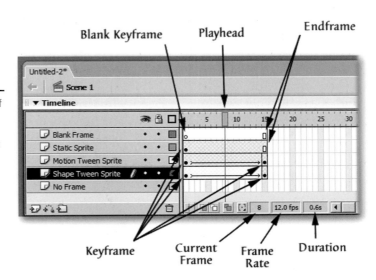

figure | 11-3 |

The various types of frame representations in the timeline denote the different types of frames.

The second layer shown in figure 11-3, named *Static Sprite*, shows a sprite (an object in the timeline) that simply exists on the stage, beginning at frame 1 and ending at frame 15. Note that it begins with a keyframe, which is an initial definition of the objects' respective location, size, orientation, and color as defined on the stage. A black circle identifies a keyframe. The sprite extends to frame 15, in which there is the endframe indicator (a small, hollow rectangle).

Sprites in the timeline are completely adjustable as far as their starting point (keyframe) and duration (endframe) are concerned. You can click-drag a keyframe to move when the objects appear on the stage (represented by the keyframe). Similarly, if you hold the Ctrl key (Command on the Mac) and click-drag the endframe indicator, it changes the duration of the sprite, which is the amount of time the object appears on the stage.

If you click-drag the endframe indicator and do not hold Ctrl or Command, the sprite is extended, but a keyframe is placed in the last frame. Clicking on the center of a sprite selects a single frame within a sprite, and double clicking on a frame within a sprite selects the entire sprite. When an entire sprite is selected, you can click-drag it to another location in the timeline.

The third and fourth layers shown in figure 11-3 (layers named *Motion Tween Sprite* and *Shape Tween Sprite*, respectively) are the two types of tweened animation Flash can create. Notice that both types of tween sprites begin and end with a keyframe. As with static sprites, you can click-drag these keyframes to adjust starting time and duration. Because this book is printed in grayscale, you do not see the one significant difference between these two representations, which is that motion tween sprites are displayed as blue in the timeline, whereas shape tweens are displayed as green. You'll see these two types of frame representations in the next two chapters.

Also note the last layer, *No Frames*. This layer currently has no frames defined within it. Usually when you create a new layer a blank keyframe is automatically added to frame 1. The important thing to note is that when a layer has no frames at all, if you select it and try to draw, paste, or import, Flash will tell you it cannot perform the operation because no frame exists. Thus, you can do nothing with a layer if it has no frames.

DON'T GO THERE

When editing objects on the stage, the editing affects the nearest left keyframe of the current layer. If the playhead is between a keyframe indicator and an endframe indicator, the objects in the keyframe to the left are modified. Thus, when you want to edit a keyframe, such as change the position of an object on the stage for that keyframe, you can select any frame between the keyframe identifier and the endframe indicator to make the change. Pay close attention to where the playhead is located and what layer you have selected when transforming objects on the stage.

Building from the Left: Blank Frames

figure | 11-4 |

Holding Shift while selecting two frames vertically selects all frames across the layers.

Now that we have some of the frame basics out of the way, I will continue with the Cyber Outpost animation I was building. Let's begin by extending the duration of all the timeline keyframes (sprites) to frame 56. There are many ways to do this—the easiest being to click in frame 56 of the uppermost layer. Then, while holding the Shift key, click in frame 56 of the lowermost layer. This selects frame 56 across all the layers, as shown in figure 11-4.

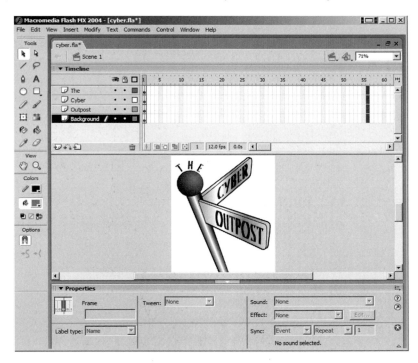

With the selection in the timeline, right-click and choose Insert Frame in the context menu. This will extend the duration of all keyframes (sprites) to frame 56. Note that there are myriad ways to extend the duration of the objects (this was just the quickest in this context).

With all of the sprites extended, we can start fiddling with keyframes to create the animation. In this example, I will work backward in the timeline—starting with the last element to appear on the stage. I could also work forward if I wanted to. I'll begin by right clicking in frame 44 of the *Outpost* layer and choosing Insert Keyframe. This splits the sprite into two pieces (by adding a keyframe), as shown in figure 11-5.

figure | 11-5

Inserting a keyframe splits the sprite into two pieces.

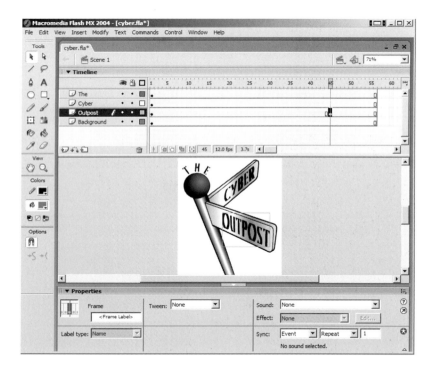

Since the *Outpost* text (which is what is on the *Outpost* layer) will only appear on the stage at frame 44, I need to delete the content in the sprite in the first sprite. To do this, I will select any frame between frame 1 and frame 43 of the *Outpost* layer and hit the Backspace key. When I delete the content on the stage, the timeline will then show a blank keyframe, as shown in figure 11-6. This is the basic process we'll use throughout the remainder of this example.

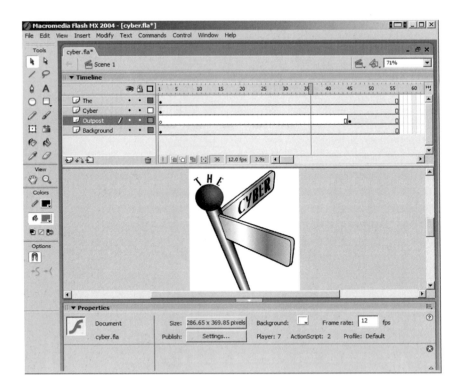

figure | 11-6

Deleting content on the stage changes the sprite to a blank representation.

Let's turn our attention to the *Cyber* layer. I'll do the same basic thing with it. With it, I create a keyframe at frame 32, and delete the content in the first sprite. Now the *Cyber* text will appear at frame 32 and play through the rest of the movie.

Now I'll deal with the *The* layer. Even though I am going to have it so that each letter appears progressively, I will start out the same basic way I did with the prior two layers. The *T* for the text *The* will appear on the stage at frame 12. So, I will start by inserting a keyframe at frame 12 and deleting the content of the first sprite. Then I need to create two more keyframes, one at frame 16 and one at frame 20. When I do this, I will end up with copies of the *The* text in three places, (frames 12, 16, and 20), as shown in figure 11-7

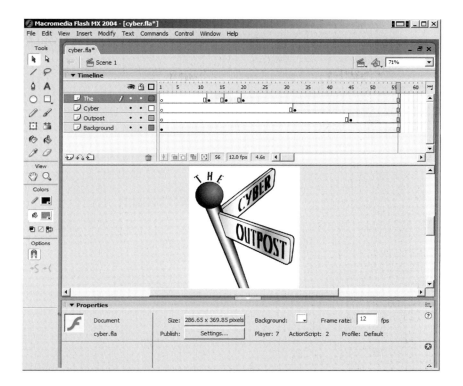

figure | 11-7

Set up three keyframes for the *The* text.

Once the keyframes are set up, I need to modify the content on the stage so that each sprite has the appropriate letters. Frames 12 to 15 need only the *T*, frames 16 through 19 need the *T* and *H*, and frames 20 through 56 need the entire word. The key when working with animation is to make sure the playhead is in the right place when you start editing the stage content (it is very easy to mix things up and edit in the wrong place). To remove the *h* and *e*, I need to make sure the playhead is somewhere between frames 12 and 15. To remove the *e*, I need to make sure the playhead is somewhere between frames 16 and 20. (Again, it is critical to pay attention to where the playhead is when you start working with animation.) This is similar to making sure which layer is current when you work with content on the stage. Figure 11-8 shows the final timeline setup for this simple animation.

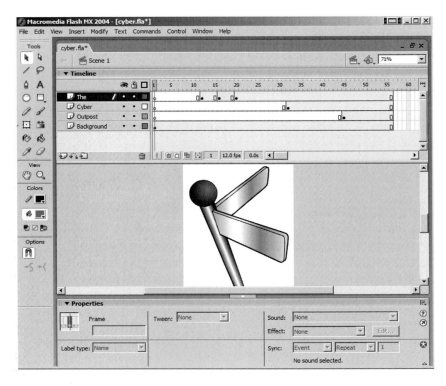

figure 11-8

The final timeline setup for the Cyber Outpost animation.

Modifying Timing

Once you have set up an animation and you play it, you may find that the animation plays slower than you thought it actually would. In the Cyber Outpost animation, even though I planned it out as it relates to timing, it plays slower than I would like. To speed up the animation I could increase the frame rate. However, often this is not the recommended thing to do. Rather, it would be better to reduce the number of frames in the timeline to make things happen quicker.

You can do this relatively easily. If you select a frame across multiple layers (using Shift while selecting a specific frame across multiple layers or by click-dragging across multiple layers), you can then use Shift + F5 (Edit | Timeline | Remove Frames) to delete a frame across all layers. If I cut all the durations in half, as shown in figure 11-9, it gives me a faster animation. This is (in most instances) preferable to increasing the frame rate for playback.

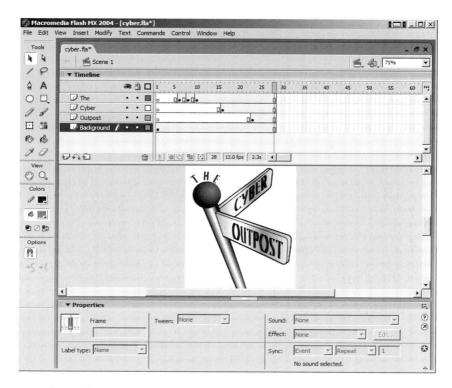

figure | 11-9

Cutting the sprite durations in half speeds up the animation.

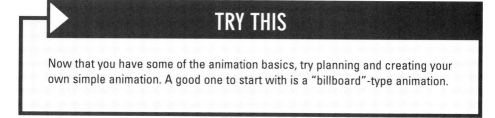

TRY THIS

Now that you have some of the animation basics, try planning and creating your own simple animation. A good one to start with is a "billboard"-type animation.

CREATING FRAME-BY-FRAME ANIMATION

Now that you have a good feel for how frames work, let's do something a little more complex and learn about some of the additional animation tools that Flash provides. The example I will be working with is shown in figure 11-10. I will animate the hands, eyebrows, and eyes of the character. Each of these elements will be animated to make the character look like it is doing the "chicken dance." It's a little cheesy, but you'll learn about some important commands and tools in the process.

figure | 11-10 |

The telephone character that will be animated.

Due to the limits of this book, I won't go into the planning behind the character. However, I have already laid out the timing for the character. Anytime you are doing an animation, you should start with storyboards to get a relative sense of the timing and key movements in the animation.

Preparation Work

As when we worked with the Cyber Outpost animation, I will first start by grouping the various parts that will be animated onto layers. In this animation, I will also use graphic symbols to try to cut down the file size.

I will start by making each part that will be animated a symbol. I will make the left hand, the right hand, each eyebrow, and each eye a symbol. Once each of these is a symbol, I will place each set of items onto its own layer. There is a layer for the hands, the eyebrows, the eyes, and the background (the things that won't be animated). Figure 11-11 shows the layer structure I will begin with.

figure | **11-11**

The layer structure that is set up prior to animating the phone.

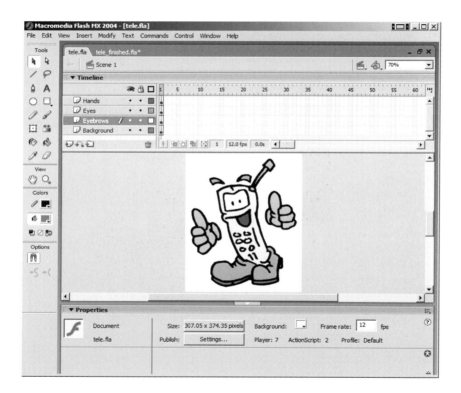

Creating Movement

To begin creating this animation, I will extend all the frames out to frame 19. The first thing to move in the animation will be the eyebrows and the eyes. They will move simultaneously. As the character looks left, the left eyebrow will come down, and as the character looks right, the right eyebrow will come down. Thus, I place a keyframe at frames 3, 5, and 7 in both the eyebrow and eyes layers.

Next, I need to set the position for the eyes and eyebrows in two of the new keyframes. The keyframes in frame 7 will make sure I end up with the eyebrows back in their original starting position. I place the playhead in frame 3 (or 4) and modify the left eyebrow so that it is shifted down. I also modify the eyes so that they look left, as shown in figure 11-12.

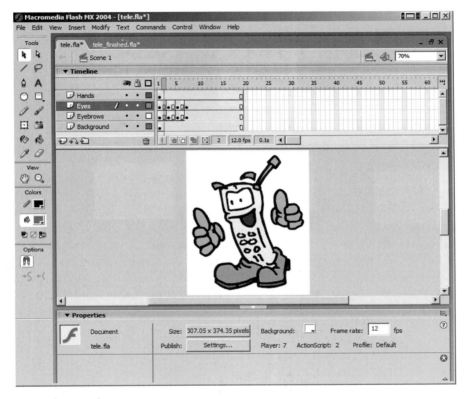

figure | 11-12

Position the eyes and the left eyebrow.

Now I will perform the same operation with the playhead in frame 5 or 6. I shift the right eyebrow down and move the eyes so that they look right, as shown in figure 11-13.

figure | 11-13 |

Making the changes to the right eyebrow and eyes.

With the movement set up for the eyes and eyebrows, I now turn my attention to the hands. The hands will eventually rotate up and down, but there are some special tools in Flash that make doing this a little easier.

To begin I will place a keyframe at frame 10 of the hands layer. With frame 10 of the hands layer selected, I will use the Free Transform tool to rotate the hands slightly (the rotation of the hands will occur over two frames). So, the hands will reach their apex (highest point) at the second frame. Figure 11-14 shows where the hands are in frame 10.

Original Position

New Position

figure | 11-14 |

Rotating the hands slightly in frame 10.

To create the second position for the hands (their apex position), I create a keyframe at frame 11 and rotate the hands to their highest point. Figure 11-15, shows the three positions for the hands.

figure | 11-15 |

The three positions
for the telephones
hands.

Onion Skinning

Before we move on, let's take a break for a minute. I would like to
acknowledge an important animation tool, onion skinning, that
you should know about.

The Onion Skin button, shown in figure 11-16, shows a representation of "before and after" frames adjacent to the current frame.
Surrounding frames are shown transparently with the current
frame. In reality, the Onion Skin command was how I created fig-
ures 11-14 and 11-15.

When you click on the Onion Skin button, two small markers
(called onion markers) appear around the playhead, as shown in
figure 11-16. You can move the onion markers to reveal more or
fewer frames concurrently on the stage. When building frame-by-
frame animations, you can turn Onion Skin on to see the frames
around the current frame—allowing you to make the on-stage
changes from frame to frame smoother. However, you can only edit
the current frame, which is displayed opaque. Semitransparent

figure | 11-16 |

The onion skinning
feature allows you to
compare adjacent
frames.

objects are not editable. In Onion Skin mode, you can move the playhead to the point (frame) you want to edit while still being able to see the frames immediately adjacent to it.

Copying, Pasting, and Reversing Frames

Let's continue with the example I was building. We have the hands moving into an apex position, and we now need to animate them back to their original position. I could do this by creating keyframes and repositioning the content on the stage, but there is an easier way. Here's where I'll show you a nifty trick in Flash.

To start this, I need to delete frames 12 through 20 in the hands layer. I click-drag across the end of the sprite (starting at frame 12 across frame 20) to select it. Then I right click and select Remove Frames from the context menu, as shown in figure 11-17.

What I need to do is create the hands moving back to their original position. Rather than recreating this, I will copy the three frames that have the hands moving up, paste them at the end of the hands layer, and then tell Flash to reverse the order of them—essentially creating the movement of the hands into their original position using what I have already created.

figure | 11-17

Selecting and deleting the frames in the hands layer.

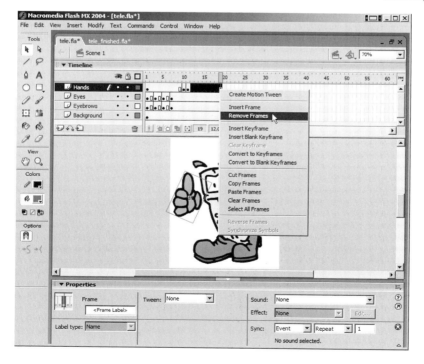

With the old frames deleted, I click-drag across frames 9 through 11 to select them. I right click on them, select Copy Frames, and then right click in frame 12 and choose Paste Frames. Once the frames are pasted at the end of the hands layer (they become frames 12 through 14), I click-drag across them to select them and then right click and select Reverse Frames. Now I have an animation of the hands moving up, and then back to their original position. Cool, huh?

To finish out this animation, I need to rotate the hands the other direction and have them move back to their original position. Basically, the process here is the same. I create two frames and position the hands so that they rotate in the opposite direction. Then I copy those three frames, and paste and reverse them, to make the hands rotate back to their original position.

Edit Multiple Frames

A common question people ask is how to scale an entire animation once it has been created. As simple as it may sound, scaling the telephone animation requires you to select all elements on all layers at one time, across multiple frames.

Flash provides a feature similar in function to Onion Skin, called Edit Multiple Frames, which allows you to view the content of a number of frames at the same time. Unlike Onion Skin, in the Edit Multiple Frames mode all objects are shown as opaque and are editable at the same time. If Edit Multiple Frames and Onion Skin are both enabled, Edit Multiple Frames overrides Onion Skin.

When using Edit Multiple Frames, all objects are opaque on the stage (as opposed to the transparency used with Onion Skin). Thus, it is difficult to tell what is on each layer when Edit Multiple Frames is used. In addition, it is easy to mistakenly move the wrong objects, so you do have to be careful when using this feature. However, Edit Multiple Frames is the simplest means of scaling all objects in a movie at the same time.

If I wanted to scale the prior example down on the stage (but maintain the animate I created) I could select the Edit Multiple frames button, shown in figure 11-18. When I do this, markers (similar to onion skin markers) appear. To select everything in the telephone animation, I drag the markers so that they totally encapsulate the frames in my movie, as shown in figure 11-18.

Once I have the markers placed, I click on the stage and use Edit | Select All. This selects all content on all layers, as shown in figure 11-19.

With all the content selected across all layers, I can then use the Free Transform tool to scale all of the elements. Using this technique allows you to treat all content across all layers as a single unit (temporarily, that is), without converting the content to a symbol.

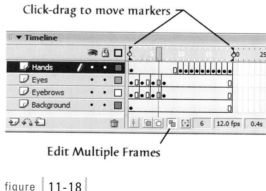

figure | 11-18 |

Edit Multiple Frames allows you to edit everything at once.

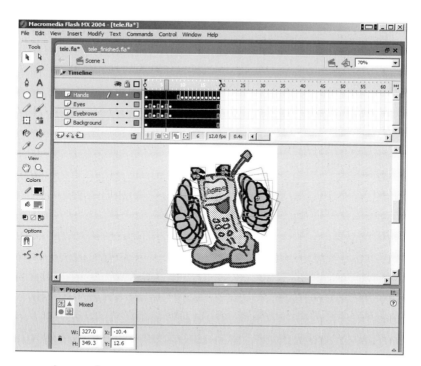

figure | 11-19 |

Once Edit Multiple Frames is enabled, using Select All selects all content cross all layers.

SUMMARY

In this chapter we have covered many of the basics related to animation. The critical things you should have picked up are how frames work (both adding and deleting as well as identifiers) and how to construct basic frame-by-frame animations. Again, I realize that frame-by-frame animation creation is quite tedious (and monotonous). But sometimes frame-by-frame may be the only way to solve a particular problem. In the next chapter we focus on creating motion tween animations. Motion tweens help reduce some of the time-consuming and monotonous aspects of cel animation.

in review

1. How should you go about beginning an animation project? What planning should you do before you ever sit down in front of the computer?

2. How do you rename a layer? Add a layer? Delete a layer?

3. How can you seamlessly move an object on the stage from one layer to another while maintaining the object's location, position, and size?

4. What is a keyframe? What does it define?

5. What are the five main types of frame identifiers?

6. What is a sprite?

7. What does Onion Skinning do? Why might you use it?

8. What does Edit Multiple Frames do? Why might you use it?

9. Give an applied example of why you might use the Reverse Frames option.

↗ EXPLORING ON YOUR OWN

1. Now that you understand the basics of animation, plan and create a simple animation designed to describe a process or a task. Use all the available tools in Flash. For example, you may choose to integrate photographs into your animation as well as sound. Experiment with various techniques.

2. Develop a short story and create an animation using cel techniques.

3. Try doing a simple animation of a logo of your choosing.

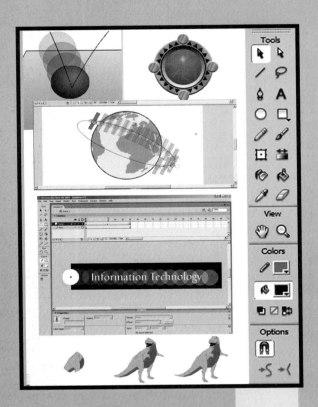

motion tweening

charting your course

In the last chapter you began learning about animation through the creation of frame-by-frame animation. And, while creating cel animation can be laborious, at times it may be the only way to create what you are wanting.

In this chapter we're going to get into motion tweening. With motion tweening, you basically create keyframes and then allow Flash to create the in-between frames automatically. Likely about 75 percent of the time you'll be able to create what you want using motion tweening. The other 25 percent of the time you'll either use shape tweening (discussed in the next chapter) or cel animation. So let's get started!

 goals

In this chapter you will:

- Learn the basic rules of motion tweening
- Find out how to tween position, size, orientation, and color effect
- Discover what timeline effects are and how they are used
- Use motion guides to create animation based on paths
- Find out about masks and how they are used

MOTION TWEEN BASICS

Motion tweens allow you to animate a change in position, size, orientation, or color effect of an entity on the screen. Thus, you can animate an object moving across the screen, scaling up or down, or rotating in either direction. As it relates to animating a color effect, you can animate an object such that its alpha (opacity) changes, its overall "tint" changes (this adds an overlay color to the totality of an object), or its brightness changes (such that the object transforms to white or black). All of these things are possibilities when you are using motion tweens, and they can be performed in any combination simultaneously.

Now, before we jump into a motion tween example, let's acknowledge a few rules that you should be aware of concerning motion tweens. First, motion tweens are designed such that they only work on overlay objects. That means you can perform a motion tween on a text entity, a symbol, or a group. You cannot use a motion tween on stage-level objects (lines, fills, and so on). And, from a file size perspective, you should *always* use symbols as the basis for your motion tweens.

Due to file size issues, I recommend never using a motion tween on a text entity or group. Instead, convert those items to symbols and then animate them.

The second motion tween rule to be aware of is that you can only use a motion tween on one object per layer. Trying to motion tween several objects at the same time on the same layer will break the motion tween. If you want to simultaneously animate three or four items, each of the items needs to be on its own layer. For example, if I wanted to animate the letters of a word flying in from all directions, each letter would need to be a separate layer (and each one should be a separate symbol).

The final rule associated with motion tweens is that there are a couple of special features that exist for motion tweens. These include guide layers and layer masks. Guide layers allow you to specify a specific path for motion, whereas layer masks allow you to mask out other elements. In the subsequent sections of this chapter we will look at these two facilities.

Animating Size and Position

To learn about animating size and position, let's do a simple example of a ball bouncing across the screen. Figure 12-1 shows the setup for this, in which I have created a plane for the ball to bounce on as well as the ball itself. The first step here is to convert the ball to a symbol so that I can start the animation process. I will have the ball bounce over 30 frames, so I extend the frames for the ball and background layers out to frame 30.

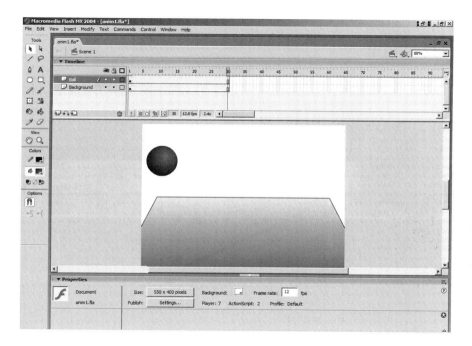

figure | 12-1

The setup for the basic animation includes a plane and the ball.

With the frames extended, I will add a keyframe to frame 30 of the *ball* layer. When you do motion tweening, you generally set up two keyframes in the timeline that have some difference. In this case, the two keyframes will define two different positions. So, in frame 1 the ball will be off the left side of the stage and in frame 30 it will be off the right side of the stage, as shown in figure 12-2.

figure | 12-2 |

In frame 1 the ball is off the left side and in frame 30 the ball is off the right side.

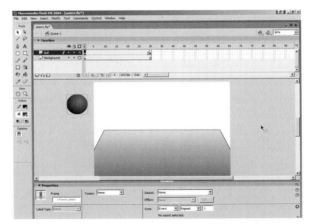

Frame 1

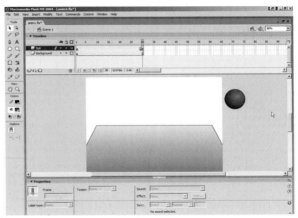

Frame 30

Once the two opposing positions are established, I can set up the motion tween. To set up the motion tween I can select any frame in the *ball* layer between 1 and 29 and then select Motion from the Tweening drop-down in the Properties panel. This sets up the motion tween—which is indicated by the change in the timeline, where the frame identifier is changed to a blue background with an arrow. Whenever you create a motion tween, the timeline will show a successful tween set up this way. If it shows a dotted line with no arrow, it tells you that it was not successful. If this happens, make sure you followed the two rules I mentioned earlier.

Once the motion tween is set up, moving the playhead in the time-line will show the ball animating from its position in frame 1 to its position in frame 30. Note that Flash interpolates or creates the in-between frames based on the differences between the two opposing keyframes.

Now, let's make the ball bounce. We already have it moving across the screen, so I place the playhead in frame 15 (the point at which it will bounce). Once the playhead is there, I move the ball on the stage down so that it will look like it is bouncing on the plane, as shown in figure 12-3. Because the motion tween is already set up, when I create a new keyframe in frame 15 (by moving the ball on the stage) the motion tween is automatically adjusted: the ball now animates down and right to the bounce point and then up and right to the offscreen position on the right.

figure | 12-3 |

Adding the bounce to the ball at frame 15.

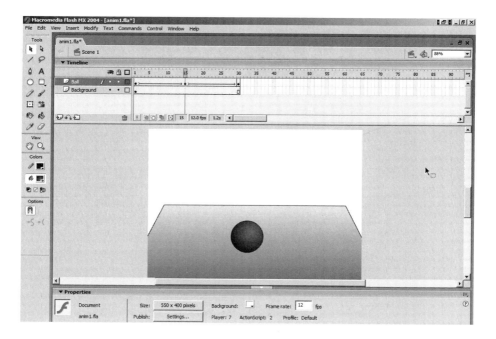

Now that the ball is bouncing we need to add one more element to it to make it look better; that is, the ball is rubber and needs to squish a little as it bounces. To do this, we need to add two more keyframes around frame 15 and then disproportionately scale the ball. So, I add a keyframe at frame 13 and frame 17. Then I access frame 15 and scale the ball vertically (just a little) so that it will look like it squishes as it bounces, as shown in figure 12-4.

Before we move on, I want to acknowledge why we added keyframes at frame 13 and 17. We added those keyframes to constrain the squish over time. Had I not added those keyframes, the squish

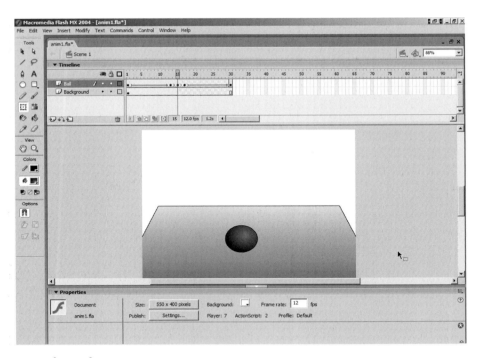

figure | 12-4

Making the ball squish when it bounces.

would have started at frame 1 and ended a frame 30. Since the squish was to occur near frame 15 only, the two keyframes constrain the squish to two frames before and two frames after the bounce.

In this example, you have learned to animate two types of transformations: position and disproportionate size. Let's add one more thing to make this animation look a little more real—a shadow— while also learning about proportional size scaling in animation.

To create the shadow for the ball, I need a fill element with a fuzzy edge. Also, the shadow as it is "projected" onto the plane needs to be the same color as the plane (in this case it will be gray). I create an elliptical fill element that will serve as the shadow and I convert it to a symbol. To get the size, shape, and position of the shadow element just right I create the fill "in position" with the playhead at frame 15, as shown in figure 12-5. Also, I place that element on its own layer so that I can animate it (keep in mind that I cannot place the shadow element on the *ball* layer). Each animated element must be on its own layer.

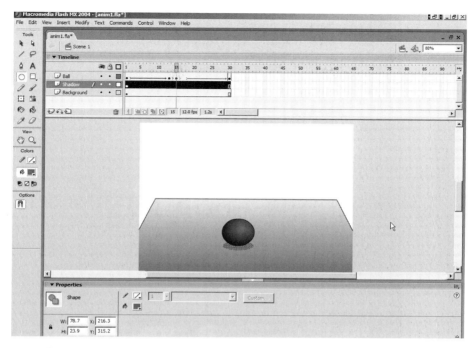

figure | 12-5

Adding the element that will be used as the shadow.

Now, to retain the "frame 15 position" of the shadow element, I insert a keyframe at frame 15 in the *shadow* layer. Then I move the playhead back to frame 1 (which puts the ball to the far left). I now move the shadow element over so that it is vertically inline with the ball, as shown in figure 12-6.

Once the shadow is in place, I need to scale it down a little. In the real world, as a spherical object moves toward a plane its shadow gets bigger. So, the shadow needs to be small when the ball is far from the plane. Figure 12-7 shows the size reduction on the shadow.

Now, we need to create the same effect on the shadow at frame 30. To make it easy, I will copy frame 1 and paste it at frame 30. Then I move the shadow to the right side of the screen, as shown in figure 12-8.

The last thing to do is to assign motion tweening to the *shadow* layer. While you can use the process described before and use the Properties panel, there is a shortcut. If you right-click in a frame

figure | 12-6|

Moving the shadow into position in frame 1.

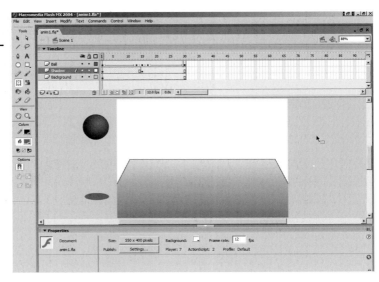

figure | 12-7|

Scaling the shadow down at frame 1.

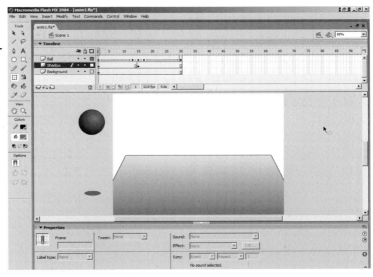

between frames 1 through 14 you can quickly select Create Motion Tween from the context menu. Do the same thing somewhere in frames 16 through 29, and voilà!—you have your motion tweens quickly set up.

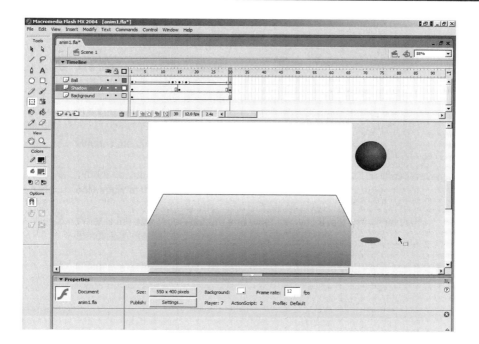

Animating Orientation

Aside from animating position and size, you can also animate orientation. In this example, we'll create a wheel rolling across the screen. To do this we will need a movie clip that contains the rotating wheel. Then we'll animate the movie clip moving across the screen.

figure | 12-8

Adding the keyframe for the shadow in frame 30.

To begin the setup for this animation, I start with a ground plane and the wheel shown in figure 12-9. Note that I have already converted the wheel to a graphic symbol inside a movie clip. I have placed the movie clip on a separate layer from the plane. The first thing to do is to animate the wheel inside the movie clip. So, I access the movie clip's timeline by double clicking on it.

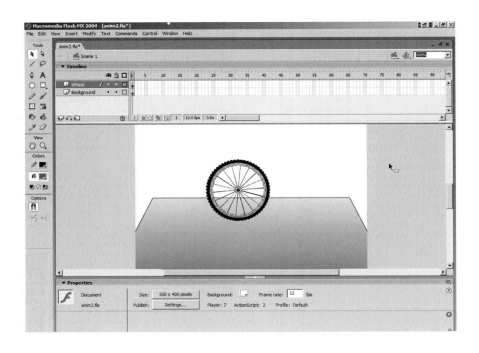

I want the wheel to do a full rotation in 2 seconds. So, with the movie clip timeline open, I will insert a keyframe at frame 24 (this movie will use the default of 12 frames per second). As shown in figure 12-10, I select any frame between frames 1 and 23 in the timeline and set up the motion tweening in the Properties panel. I set the Tweening drop-down to Motion and then set the Rotate drop-down to CW (clockwise). I want it to rotate one time, so I enter a value of 1 in the times field. The rotation of the wheel is now successfully set up.

Now if I return to the main movie timeline and use Test Movie, the wheel rotates but it does not move across the screen. I need to animate the wheel moving across the stage in the main timeline to do this. In the main timeline, I will have the wheel move across the screen over 5 seconds. I extend the duration of the sprites (both the wheel and the background) in the timeline out to frame 60. As I did in the last exercise, I create an ending keyframe in the *wheel* layer and then position the wheel off the left side of the stage in frame 1 and off the right side of the stage in frame 60. I then quickly set up the basic motion tween for the *wheel* layer so that it animates.

I want to acknowledge two things about this little animation. First, if I try to use Control I Play to see the animation, the wheel will

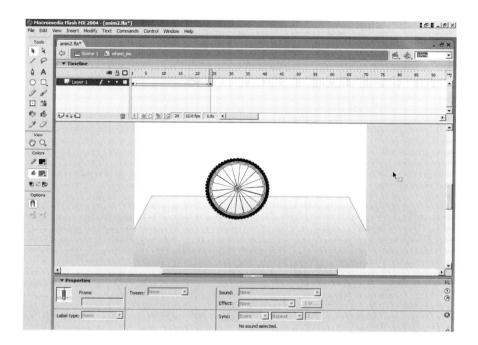

move across the screen but the movie clip will not play. To see this whole thing work, I must use Control | Test Movie.

The second thing to acknowledge is that when I use Test Movie and see my results, the wheel "hiccups" as it rolls. When I created the wheel animation inside the movie clip, the first and last frames where in the same position, which caused the wheel to have two frames, with the wheel in the original starting position, and thus the wheel appears to pause when it plays. Anytime you want smooth continuous motion in a movie clip (or even in a looping segment of the main timeline) you have to do something special to make it so that it flows smoothly.

To fix the pause in the wheel movie clip, I will access that timeline. What we need to do is remove the last keyframe so that the pause is gone—but if we do this, the motion tween will be broken because there are no longer two opposing keyframes for the tween to interpolate. So, here's the trick: insert a keyframe in the timeline in frame 23 (the next to last frame). You can then delete the last keyframe, while maintaining the animation that was set up. I then pull frame 23 over to frame 24 (holding Ctrl or Command while click-dragging frame 23 to frame 24). Now if I use Test Movie the wheel no longer has a hiccup in it.

figure | **12-10**

Setting up the motion tween so that the wheel rotates.

Before we leave this example, let's make it a little more interesting by adding a shadow to the wheel while it is rolling across the screen, which is actually a lot easier than you might think it is. I will begin by creating a new layer underneath the *wheel* layer; let's call it *shadow*. Then I select all the frames in the *wheel* layer, right-click on the selection, and select Copy Frames. Then select all the blank frames in the *shadow* layer, right-click, and select Paste Frames. In essence, we just made a duplicate layer of the wheel animation, which we will transform into a shadow.

To make things clearer for myself, I hide the *wheel* layer by clicking on the dot in the *wheel* layer underneath the "eye" icon in the time-line. I am going to begin by adding a color effect to the instance of the wheel in the *shadow* layer in frame 1. Select that instance of the wheel and then use the Properties panel to change the Color drop-down to Tint. Choose a gray color for the tint to be applied to the instance and set the opacity of it to 100 percent, as shown in figure 12-11.

figure | 12-11

Applying a tint to the movie clip so that it looks like a shadow.

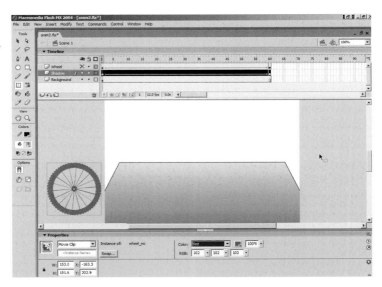

Now that the shadow is the right "color," I need to scale it down and position it correctly. In frame 1 of the *shadow* layer, I select the wheel and use the Free Transform tool to disproportionately scale it. I turn on the wheel layer so that I can position it correctly in relation to the object on the *wheel* layer, as shown in figure 12-12. Note that I have aligned the bottom of the shadow with the wheel, but I have offset the shadow to the left a little so that it looks like the light source is above and to the right of the wheel.

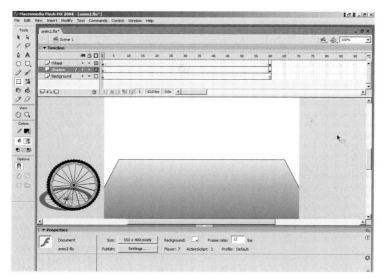

figure | 12-12

Scaling and align-
ing the shadow to
the wheel so that it
looks right.

Once the shadow is in the right place in frame 1, I need to set up
its position and size in frame 60. I could repeat what I have done to
frame 1 in frame 60, but instead I will copy frame 1 of the *shadow*
layer and paste it into frame 60 of the *shadow* layer. Then, in frame
60 I move the shadow into its correct position, as shown in figure
12-13. Using Test Movie, the wheel now has a shadow that follows
it correctly as it rolls along.

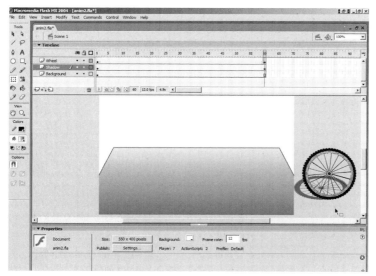

figure | 12-13

The ending position
for the shadow on
the right side of the
screen.

TRY THIS

Given the prior example, design a simple animation that uses motion tweening to make an object roll across the screen. You could use just about any cylindrical object for this, such as a coin, a wheel, and so on.

Animating Color Effects

In the last section you began to see the power of color effects. Color effects you can apply to animation include:

- *Alpha:* Changes the opacity of an item from completely opaque to transparent

- *Brightness:* Applies either a white or black to the totality of the object

- *Tint:* Applies a color you select, in the amount you select, to the totality of an object

- *Advanced:* Allows you to simultaneously apply any or all of the prior three effects

Before we move on to timeline effects, let's look at one more example that uses the Alpha color effect to do a fade-in/fade-out transition. Unlike some multimedia authoring programs, Flash does not provide a great number of transitions you can apply to your content. Thus, you must build most of them manually using motion tween animations. Later in this chapter we'll look at masks, which can be used for transitions too. Here, let's just look at getting something to fade in and fade out.

Figure 12-14 shows a simple object that I want to have fade in over 1 second (12 frames), stay on screen for 4 seconds (36 frames), and fade out over 1 second (12 frames). I have already converted this object to a symbol. Now, given my animation parameters I will create a keyframe at frames 1, 13, 48, and 60.

Once the keyframes are set up, I need to set the opacity of the object to 0 percent in frame 1 and frame 60. Thus, I access frame 1 in the timeline, select the object on the stage, and use the Properties panel to set the Color to Alpha at 0 percent, as shown in figure 12-15. I do the same thing at frame 60. Now, with a quick

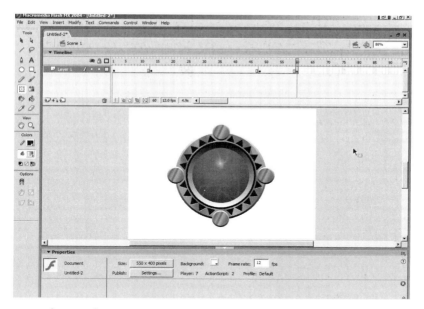

figure | 12-14

Setting up the keyframes for the object to fade in and fade out.

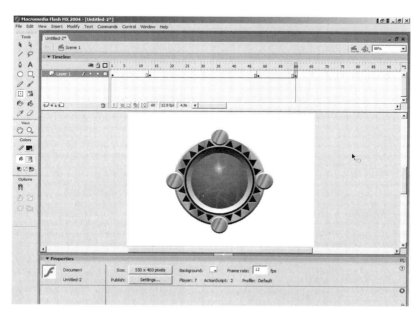

figure | 12-15

Assigning the Color setting Alpha to the object in frame 1.

> ▶ **TRY THIS**
>
> Now that you know how to make things fade in and out, try it on an object of your own choosing. Keep in mind that to fade an entire object or set of objects it must be a symbol.

right-click between frames 1 and 12 and again between frames 48 and 59 I apply a motion tween using Create Motion Tween from the context menu. Once the tweens are assigned, the fade in and fade out are created.

TIMELINE EFFECTS

Timeline effects are designed to help you accomplish simple animation tasks more quickly and easily. Applying them is pretty straightforward: select an element on the stage and then select Insert | Timeline Effect. Once you apply a timeline effect, the objects to which the effect is applied are "encased" in a self-contained graphic symbol.

There are essentially three types of timeline effects. All of them can be found in the Insert | Timeline Effects menu. Within the *Assistants* submenu are what I would call "utility" effects, such as those for copying items to the grid or for distributed duplication (often called power duplication). The Effects menu includes effects for such things as blur, drop shadow, and explode. And the final grouping is the Transform/Transition grouping, which is somewhat self-explanatory.

While the limits of this book don't allow lengthy expository on each, I would like to briefly mention them so that you know what is there. Most of them are pretty straightforward as it relates to use. Thus, the effects include:

- *Assistant | Copy to grid:* Allows you to quickly create a rectangular array of an object. This timeline effect aids in visual object creation. In essence, the effect duplicates the selected objects based on your entry of number of columns and rows and the associated spacing between them.

- *Assistants | Distributed Duplication:* This timeline effect is a great addition to Flash. It lets you create duplicated items that subsequently vary in spacing, size, and color.

- *Effect | Blur:* Animates the edges of the selected objects such that they blur with an eventual fade-out of the object. You can control the duration, direction, and resolution (visual quality) of the blur.

- *Effect | Drop shadow:* This effect allows you to quickly create a drop shadow of the selected objects.

- *Effect | Expand:* This timeline effect allows you to create an animation of two or more symbols expanding or contracting (as it relates to their position on the stage). You can control starting and stopping positions, separate scale factors related to height and width, and establish the duration of the animation.

The Expand effect is the only one that will not work with stage-level objects. Also, you must select more than one symbol for the Expand effect to work.

- *Effect | Explode:* As its name implies, this effect can be used to make items randomly separate from one another.

If you use overlay objects with the Explode effect, the objects will randomly separate and shrink, but the objects will not be broken into subsequent pieces. However, if you use a stage object, Flash will automatically break the object up into small pieces as a part of the effect process.

- *Transform/Transition | Transform:* The Transform effect allows you to easily create basic transformation animations (that is, a change in position, size, orientation, or color). You can control the animation duration, beginning and ending alpha settings, and easing (speeding up or slowing down).

- *Transform/Transition | Transition:* This effect allows you to create basic fade and wipe transitions automatically. You can control the duration, direction, and easing.

> ▶ **TRY THIS**
>
> Before we move on, take some time to experiment with the timeline effects. Try creating some basic animation with the Transform effect or try using the Assistants effects to get a better understanding of what they do.

MOTION GUIDES

Certain animations you create will require that an object travel along a specific path. When the path is linear, you can manually force the object to move from one point to another, as you have already seen. But what about making an object move along a curvilinear path? Granted, you could manually set it up by positioning keyframes all along the duration, but that is more work than is necessary. Flash provides a feature called a motion guide—where you define an object to be used for the path of motion for another object. You can also allow a single motion guide to be used for multiple objects. Let's take a look at this feature and see how it works.

Curvilinear Paths

To show an example of a curvilinear path, let's return to the ball example we used earlier. This time I'll make the ball bounce a couple of times, and rather than using the manual technique I used earlier I will use a motion path. Also, I am going to make the ball bounce toward the screen so that it is a little more interesting.

I'll start with the same setup as before: the ball (a graphic symbol) on one layer and a ground plane on another. The first thing I will do is create the motion path. If I select on the *ball* layer and click on the Motion Guide button in the timeline, a blank motion guide layer is added to the timeline, as shown in figure 12-16. Note that the *ball* layer is shifted over in the timeline, meaning that the motion guide will affect it.

The first thing I will do in this animation is to draw the motion path for the ball on the guide layer I created. You can create it using any of the drawing tools, but I prefer using the Pen tool because it offers more control (when combined with the Subselection tool). Figure 12-17 shows the path I created. Note that you don't have to

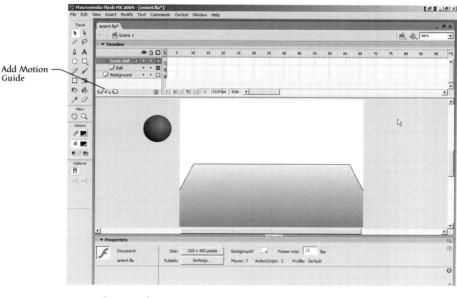

figure | 12-16

Adding a motion guide for the *ball* layer.

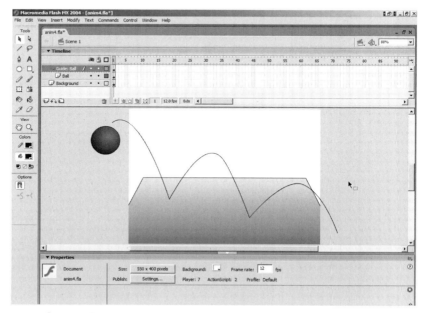

figure | 12-17

The motion path is drawn on the motion guide layer.

perfectly draw the path—you can come back and adjust it after the animation is set up, which I will likely have to do on mine once I see the animated results.

The next thing I will do is extend the duration of the frames out to frame 60, so that the animation takes about 5 seconds. I can always come back and adjust that later if it is too fast or slow.

With the duration extended, I will set up the ball so it follows the motion guide. I begin by attaching the ball to the left end of the path, as shown in figure 12-18. When working with motion guides you will want to make sure that the View | Snapping | Snap to Objects option is selected. If this is selected, when you move the ball near the line it will snap to it. Before I leave this step, I am also going to size the ball down some, because as the ball approaches the screen it needs to get bigger so that it looks like it is coming toward me.

The next step is to create a keyframe in frame 60 of the *ball* layer and attach the ball to the right end of the motion path. Then I set

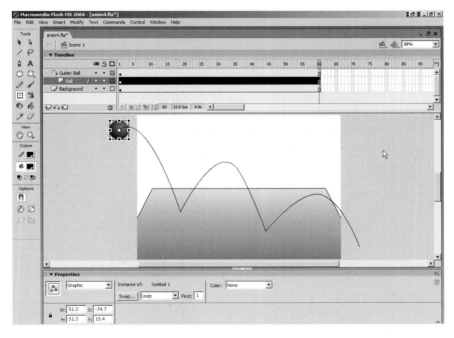

figure | 12-18

Attaching the ball to the left end of the path.

up the motion tween by right-clicking a frame somewhere between frame 1 and frame 59 and selecting Create Motion Tween. If I move the playhead I see that the ball is now following the path. However, the animation still needs some tweaking to make it look more realistic.

To make the animation more realistic, I want to do a couple things. First, like before, I want the ball to squish when it hits the ground plane. In addition, to make it more physically correct, I want it to slow down (ease) into the apex of each bounce. Because the easing occurs over a larger set of frames (as compared to the squish), I will start with it.

To set up the easing, I need to separate the ball tween into pieces. To do this I will place a keyframe at each place in the *ball* layer that the ball hits the ground plane. If you create your own example like this, the frame numbers won't be the same—but in my example it is at frames 17 and 40. This splits the one big tween into three separate segments but retains the original movement of the ball I set up.

Now to set up the tweening. I select a frame in the first tween and modify the easing setting so that the ball will ease in (that is, slowly enter and then speed up toward the end). Since the first tween is near its apex already as the animation starts, I will only use −10 for its easing value. I will set the easing value of the other two tweens (since they are each a full bounce to bounce cycle) at −60, as shown in figure 12-19. In all three instances, the ease-in applied to the ball will make it slowly enter the apex and then speed up toward the bounce. What I am trying to accentuate is the fact that as the ball goes up it is fighting gravity. When the ball comes down, gravity accelerates it slightly.

With the easing applied, I can now set up the squish for the ball. Just as I did in the earlier example, I will add two keyframes around each bounce point (to constrain the squish) and then disproportionately scale the ball. The only difference is that I will squish the ball ever so slightly and the keyframes will be one frame apart, as shown in figure 12-20.

One final touch that will make this look more realistic is adding a shadow, like I did in the original ball example in this chapter. I could choose to use either the technique I used earlier or use another motion guide. It will actually be easier to use a motion

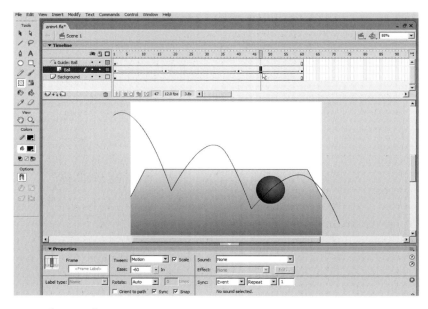

figure | 12-19

Setting up the easing value for the tweens.

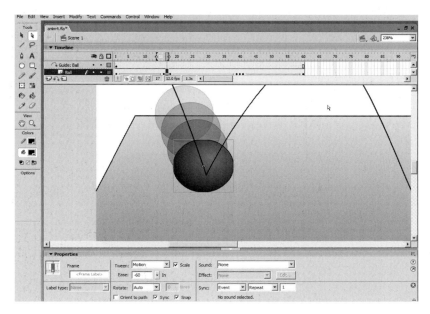

figure | 12-20

Adding the squish to the ball.

guide here because the shadow needs to move at an angle that it correctly meets the ball at the bounce point.

To begin, I will add a *shadow* layer and then apply a motion guide to that layer. Next I create a linear path for the shadow and attach the shadow to the beginning and ending of the path. Figure 12-21 shows the basic setup, with the shadow attached to the beginning at frame 1.

As you can see in figure 12-21, with the shadow set up on a linear path the shadow doesn't quite line up with the ball when the ball is supposed to be touching the ground plane. Because I am using easing on the ball's animation, I need to do some fine tuning to the shadow so that they do line up. To do this, I create a keyframe in the *shadow* layer at frames 17 and 40 (the bounce point for the ball) and then I nudge the shadow to the correct place. Note that it is often helpful to lock the guide layer when you are trying to work with the object that follows the path. Once I nudge the shadow, I really only have one more thing to do: make the shadow grow and shrink as the ball moves up and down.

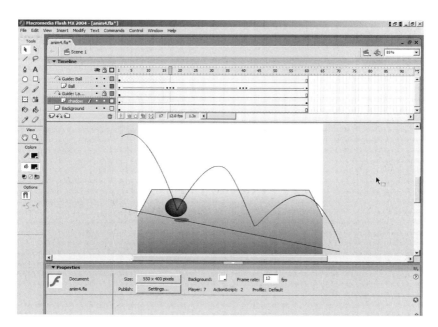

figure | 12-21

Adding the linear path for the shadow to follow.

To make the shadow grow and shrink I will start by making it simply grow as it moves along the path. Thus, I modify the shadow in frame 1 so that it is small and grows to maximum size in frame 60. However, because I have a keyframe at frames 17 and 40, I must also appropriately size it there too.

Once I have made this overall "growth" occur, within each bounce apex the shadow needs to be modified too (even though the shadow grows in size as it moves toward the screen, it grows and shrinks within that as the ball moves up and down). To accomplish this I add a keyframe in the *shadow* layer at the two visible apexes of the ball (in my example, frames 28 and 50). In these two keyframes I scale the ball down slightly to get this effect.

While this example may on the surface seem very simple, as you can see there is actually a lot going on—and motion paths make creating it a lot easier. Once I have the animation set up, the final step is to hide the two motion paths. Figure 12-22 shows a composite of all of the frame so that you can get a feel for what it looks like given the static nature of textbooks.

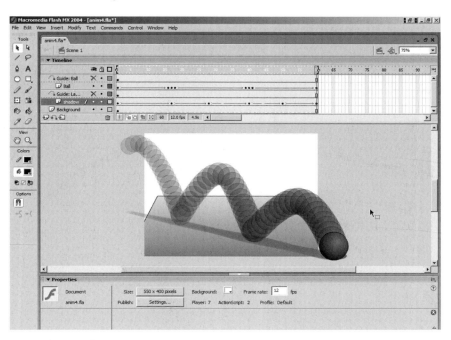

figure | 12-22

The final bouncing ball animation in composite form.

Closed Paths

Working with closed paths is pretty similar to linear and curvilinear, but let's look at a quick example to drive it home. The simple animation I will create is an animation of a satellite rotating around a graphic of the earth. The parts for this animation are shown in figure 12-23. As is standard, the earth and the satellite are both graphic symbols on different layers.

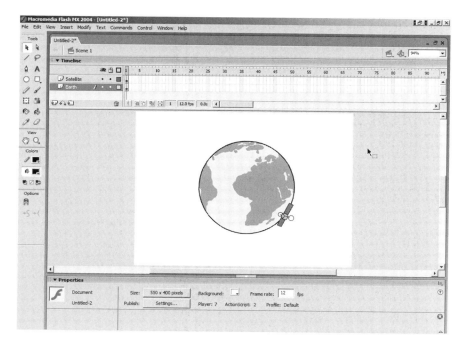

figure | 12-23

The pieces that will be used to demonstrate a closed motion path.

DON'T GO THERE

Anytime you are working with motion guides make sure you have the View | Snapping | Snap to Objects option selected. Otherwise, the motion guide animation won't work correctly.

The first step is to select the *satellite* layer and add a motion guide that will be applied to the *satellite* layer. Then I draw an ellipse and rotate it into position, as shown in figure 12-24. This ellipse will be used as the motion guide. This animation will occur over 30 frames, so I will also extend the duration of the sprites to frame 30.

Now, to get an object to rotate around the path I access the keyframe in frame 1 and snap the satellite instance to the path. Then I create a keyframe at frame 15 and move the satellite halfway around the ellipse. Then, in the final keyframe (add one at frame 30), I position the satellite back in its original position (I just copied the keyframe in frame 1 and pasted in frame 30).

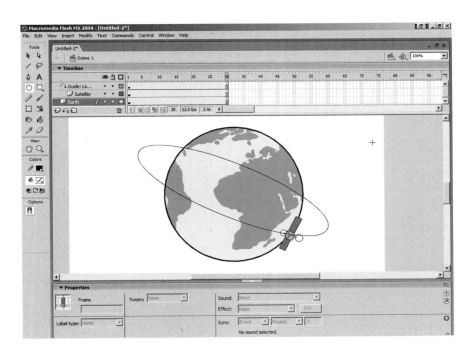

figure | 12-24 |

Adding the motion guide layer and adding the elliptical closed path.

Now one of the things that invariably happens when using closed paths is that Flash gets confused as to the direction of the animation. Figure 12-25 shows all of the frames composited. Note that Flash animates the satellite halfway around the ellipse, but has it return in a cycling motion, rather than proceeding all the way around the ellipse. Another error (which is also exhibited in this example) is that the object may proceed in the wrong direction (this goes left first, rather than right).

To fix this animation, all we need to do is add one more keyframe to define a position for the satellite as it rotates around the earth. If I select frame 8 in the *satellite* layer (halfway point between 1 and 15), the animation will occur correctly, as shown in figure 12-26.

Now we have two more things to fix on this before we are done. The first is the hiccup I had when I did the wheel animation earlier in this chapter. If I loop this animation, there will be a pause in it because the first and last frames are the same. To fix this, I add a

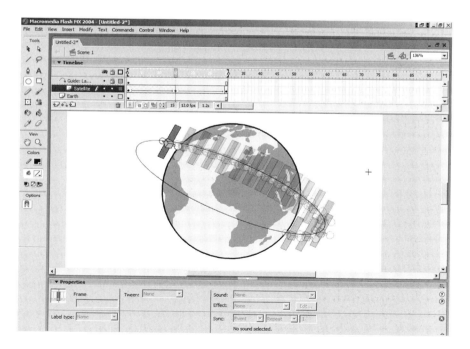

figure | 12-25

What typically happens with minimal keyframes in closed path animation setup.

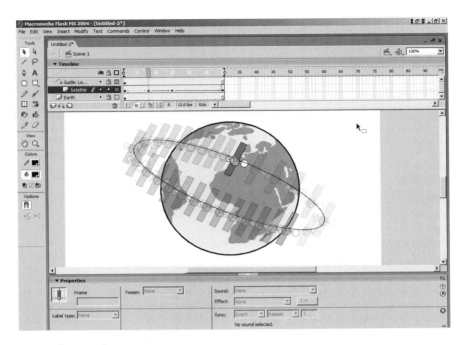

figure | 12-26 |

Correcting the animation by adding a single keyframe.

keyframe at frame 29 in the *satellite* layer, delete the last keyframe (frame 30), and then shift frame 29 to frame 30.

The other problem with this animation is the fact that the satellite doesn't yet go "behind the earth." To solve this, I will create a partial copy of the earth symbol on a layer above the motion guide. I begin by creating a new layer above the motion guide and copying the earth symbol (in the same location) to that layer.

Now I need a custom copy of the earth symbol—so I use Break (to separate the instance from the symbol). As shown in figure 12-27, I edit it by removing the bottom half of it. I have hidden all other layers so that you can see just the edited copy of the earth.

With the modified earth graphic in place, if I turn the other layers back on the satellite will appear to go behind the earth. Figure 12-28 shows a composited version of the animation so that you can get a feel for what it would look like.

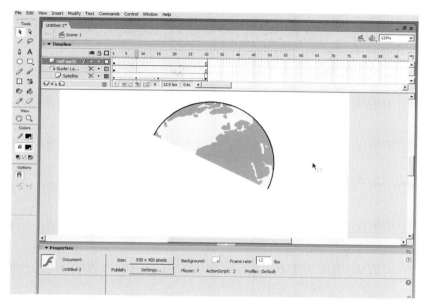

figure | 12-27 |

Creating the 3D illusion.

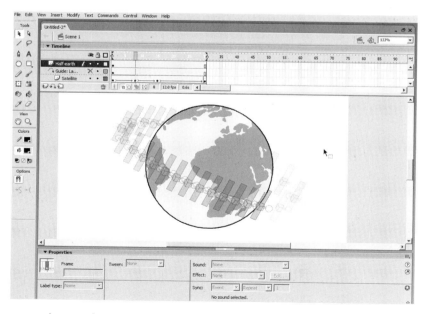

figure | 12-28 |

The final composite animation.

TRY THIS

Now that you have seen an example of a closed path animation, try creating your own. In reality just about anything that moves around a closed path could be created.

MASKS

While mask layers are not limited to animated content—they can be used in a static way to create specific graphical effects—they are definitely more interesting when you use them in an animation. When you use a layer-type mask layer, there are at least two layers involved: the mask layer itself and the masked layer. Basically, content in the masked layer only shows up in the areas of the mask layer that have content in them. Said another way: the blank areas of the mask layer hide the content on the masked layer.

Let's take a look at a quick and dirty example to show this concept. Figure 12-29a shows a circle created on a layer. Figure 12-29b shows a square that overlaps a circle; the square resides on a second layer. If we change the layer containing the square to a mask, with the layer containing the circle as the masked layer, we get the result shown in figure 12-29c.

figure | 12-29

When a mask is applied to a circle on one layer (a) and a square on another layer (b), the result is a portion of the circle contained within the square (c).

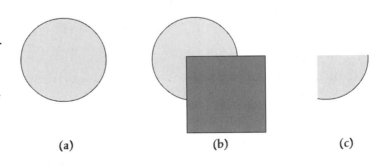

(a)   (b)   (c)

The key thing to keep in mind when working with masks is that you can animate them. Thus, you can animate content moving through a mask, or you can animate the mask itself. Also, realize that only fill elements on a mask layer have any effect at all. For example, the lines on a mask layer do nothing to the content being masked. Additionally, fills that have transparency that are used on mask layers don't create a transparent mask. All fill elements on a mask layer are treated as opaque.

Text Effects

Let's do a quick text effect to help understand how masks work. In figure 12-30 you see some text and a circle. I will create an animation that has the circle pass over the text, as if the circle were a spotlight. At this point, the circle is a symbol on one layer and the text is on another layer. This animation will occur over 30 frames.

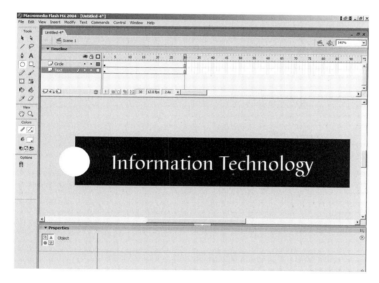

figure | 12-30

The basic setup for the mask animation.

Next, I create a basic motion tween animation of the mask moving across the text from one side to the other and back again. If I wanted I could adjust the easing to make it more interesting. Figure 12-31 shows half of the animation.

To finish up this little example, I want the animated circle to mask out the content on the text layer so that the text only shows where the circle is during the animation. Thus, the circle layer will be the mask and the text layer will be the masked layer. If I right-click on

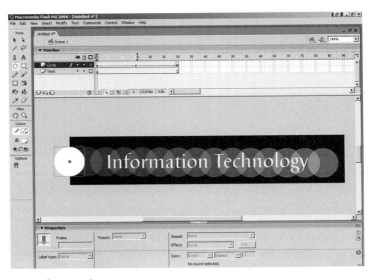

figure | 12-31

A composite of half the animation.

the circle layer's name, I can select Mask from the context menu. When you do it this way, Flash will automatically assume that the next layer down in the timeline will be the masked layer. This is how quick and easy it is to set up a masking scenario!

TRY THIS

Create your own animation using the technique described in this section. Select some word or phrase that has meaning or relevance to you and then create a spotlight effect that reveals it on the stage. Don't be afraid to go beyond what I have described here. Try doing something outside the box and creative!

Transitions

Before we wrap up this chapter I need to address how important masks are to building transitions. Masks are the foundation for most of the transitions beyond the basic fade-in and fade-out type of transition. Let's go through one final example before leaving this chapter.

Figure 12-32 shows a basic static graphic on the stage into which I want to transition in an interesting way. Here I am going to use a circular mask to reveal the object. There are other techniques you could likely think of employing once we complete this—so there is not necessarily one best way. This is just one example.

In this example I will use a circular mask and have the mask open up over 1 second, display the content for 3 seconds, and close over 1 second (60 frames at 12 fps). Thus, as always I create a layer for the circle that will be the mask and a layer for the content to be revealed, and extend the frames to frame 60. Then in the circle's layer I insert a keyframe at frames 12 and 48. At frame 12 the circle will be at its largest point (revealing all the content) and at frames 1 and 60 the circle will be small. Figure 12-33 shows the setup.

Once the animation for the circle layer is set up, the last thing to do is to assign the circle layer as a mask layer. Figure 12-34 shows a couple of screen shots from the final transition animation.

figure | 12-32

A basic object that we will use for the transition animation.

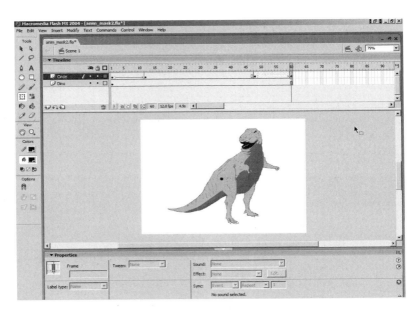

figure | 12-33 |

The frame setup for the transition animation.

figure | 12-34 |

Screen captures from the final animation.

SUMMARY

In this chapter you have taken a look at the basics of motion tweening. The main things to keep in mind are the rules associated with motion tweens. You can only use one motion tween per layer and you should always strive to use symbols as the basis for the things you are animating. You have also gotten a preview of timeline effects, motion guides, and layer masks. Hopefully your brain is buzzing with all of the possibilities these capabilities offer you. There really is no end of what you can do with Flash's motion tweening tools. However, now we get ready to turn our attention to shape tweens. While they are less common in actual practice, they are no less powerful.

1. What are the rules you must keep in mind as it relates to motion tweens?

2. How do motion tweens differ from frame-by-frame or cel animation techniques? What are the advantages of each? What are the limitations of each?

3. What are the four things you can animate with a motion tween?

4. What does the easing function do?

5. What are the four different color effects that can be applied to symbols and what does each do?

6. What are timeline effects? When might you use a timeline effect as opposed to building an animation manually?

7. What is a motion guide and when would you use it?

8. When you want to use a closed motion guide, what is the one thing you must keep in mind?

9. What is a layer mask and when might you use one? What are the limitations of layer masks?

10. Given what you know about motion tweens, how might it impact the way you approach animation design? What things should you consider in your designs?

↗ EXPLORING ON YOUR OWN

1. Now that you have the basics of motion tweens under your belt, choose a logo (one of your own or one you know of) and do an interesting animation with it using motion tweening.

2. Create an interesting text-based animation using motion tweens. Be creative in your selection of font, color, word choice, and the way you animate it.

ADVENTURES IN DESIGN

BANNER ADVERTISEMENT

Banner ads are one of those things we all love to hate as we surf the Web. However, the reality is that there is big money in banner ads, for the company whose product the ad represents and for those of us who create them! This example will challenge you to consider how to create a banner advertisement in Flash. The key to banner ads on the Web is to present something that will attract the user, but that is small. When you design banner ads, one of the critical things is to have a very, very small file (most companies that hire ad designers place limits on the file size, which is usually about 10 kilobytes maximum). And, while Flash is known for small files, designing around 10 kilobytes is still an admirable challenge.

Project Example

The banner ad I created was for my department at Purdue. It is a pretty simple thing—we simply wanted to advertise our URL to folks. Thus, the animation consists of three screens. The first uses a text effect to reveal the words "Computer Graphics," as shown in figure C-1. The second reveals the words "Purdue University" in a similar fashion. And the final screen uses a different animation technique (a text fly-in) to display our URL, as shown in figure C-2.

The banner ad uses scenes to separate the different content sections. At the end of each scene there is Action-

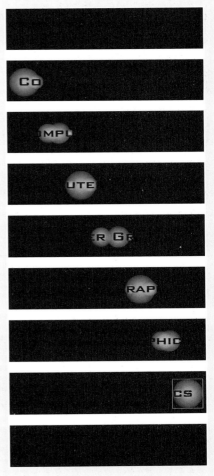

Fiure C- 1. The text effect used in the first two screens of the banner ad.

Script attached to a frame that says:

```
gotoAndPlay("scenename", 1);
```

This causes the banner add to go from one scene to the next. The "scenename" is actually whatever the name of the scene is (you can control this via the Scene panel). Thus, the banner add rotates from scene 1 to

scene 2 to scene 3 and then back to scene 1. Note that I could have placed all of the content in one scene and then had it loop back to frame 1, rather than using three scenes. However, I broke it into different scenes to try to keep the timelines shorter so that I wouldn't have to scroll way out to the right when working. Another issue to note is that my banner ad was about 7 kilobytes in size (and included some sound).

Your Turn

Now it's your turn to try your hand at creating a banner advertisement. You can either create your own fictitious company or product to create a banner for or choose a real company or product. Plan out what message you want the audience to get—essentially, the main reason or purpose for the ad. In my example, we wanted people to understand that "Computer Graphics at Purdue University" could be found at our URL. Once you know the main purpose, design an animation to communicate this—and keep in mind the 10-kilobyte limit on file size.

1. Determine the main message you are trying to communicate to the audience.

2. Plan and design some simple animation to attract or entice the user to pay attention to your ad. Don't make it too complex (or boring). Find the appropriate mix to get them to pay attention to your ad.

3. Decide how you will structure the Flash file for the ad. Scenes or no scenes? Sound or no sound?

Figure C-2. The text fly-in used on the third banner ad screen.

shape tweening

13

charting your course

While frame-by-frame and motion tweening will likely comprise most of the animation techniques you will use, there does exist one more animation type: shape tweening. Shape tweening allows you to morph one stage object to another—and the key is that shape tweening only works on stage objects. Thus, it will not work on groups, unbroken text, or symbols. Similarly, you cannot use it on bitmap images either, which is usually the first thought that comes to peoples' minds when faced with the possibility of shape tweening. Nevertheless, even with the limitations that exist with shape tweening there is still some validity in covering how you set them up and how they can be used. So, let's take a look at the last of the primary animation techniques before moving on to adding interactivity to your movies.

 goals

In this chapter you will:

- Learn what shape tweens are and how they can be used
- Understand the rules governing the use of shape tweens
- Discover how shape hints can be used to control animations created with shape tweening

WHAT ARE SHAPE TWEENS?

As I have already hinted, shape tweens allow you to create morphing animations where one stage-level shape is morphed to another stage-level shape. There are limitations to what can be done with shape tweens, but there are things you can do with them that would be nearly impossible if you tried to do the same things via frame-by-frame animation or motion tweening.

The Basics

Setting up a basic shape tween is relatively easy. Getting it just the way you want may take a little more work, however. Let's go through a quick example to show you how you can use a shape tween. After we talk a little about limitations, we'll then focus on methods for having a little more control and accuracy over how the tween morphs, through the use of something called shape hints.

Shape tweens work relatively well on simple to modest graphic creations. However, complex graphical elements that are shape tweened can really push Flash to the limit—causing the animation to really slow down. I have found that shape tweens work best when simple.

In this little example, I will have the letters of my nickname morph from one letter to the next. I will start by creating the text and choosing a font and size I like for the text. Recall that shape tweens are designed to work on stage-level objects, so once I get the text I want I will use Modify | Break Apart on the text. Using Break Apart on a text element will first split each letter apart as true text objects (so that each letter is a distinct element). If I use Modify | Break Apart a second time, the individual true text elements are then converted to stage-level representations—with each letter being a separate fill element, as shown in figure 13-1.

With each letter as a fill element, I can now get started on the animation. I will have each letter morph to the next, proceeding from left to right (and then back again). All I need to do is create one cycle (that is, left to right) and then I can copy frames and reverse it to make it go back the other way.

There are five letters in my nickname (Jamie), so I will have the animation occur over 20 frames (5 frames for each morph), which will happen pretty quickly. Again, I can go back and add frames later if it is too fast. I will start by extending the duration of the sprite that represents the text out to frame 20. Then I place a keyframe at frames 5, 10, 15, and 20, as shown in figure 13-2.

figure | 13-1

Breaking the text apart so that it can be used in a shape tween.

figure | 13-2

Establish the keyframes for the layer.

Once the keyframes are set up, I need to modify the content in each keyframe such that there is only one letter present in each frame. Thus, frame 1 has the *J*, frame 2 the *a*, frame 3 the *m*, and so on. Figure 13-3 shows frame 10, which contains the *m*.

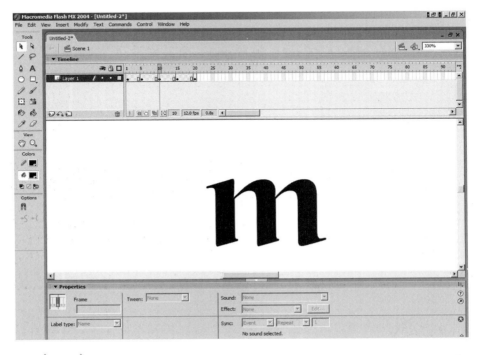

figure | 13-3

figure | 13-3

Delete the appropriate letters in each frame.
Frame 10 should contain the *m*.

With the keyframes established, the last thing to do is to assign the shape tweening to each set of frames. Unlike motion tweening, there is no "Create Shape Tween" option in the context menu. To assign the shape tweening, you must select a frame in the timeline and then use the Properties panel to assign the shape tweening to that set of frames. Like motion tweening, you can select any left keyframe (or any of the copies of it to the right) to assign the shape tween. Figure 13-4 shows the Properties panel with Shape selected in the tween drop-down menu. If a shape tween is successfully established, the frame representation in the timeline should change to an arrow with a green background.

In figure 13-4 you will note that there are a couple of options for shape tweening. Like motion tweening, you can establish easing for the shape tween—such that it either comes in slow and goes out fast or vice versa. More importantly, note the Blend drop-down.

This drop-down provides two options: Distributive and Angular. When you are morphing two objects that are "organic" in nature (that is, they do not have sharp corners and edges), use the Distributive option. When you have more mechanical (or non-organic) objects that have sharp corners, use the Angular option. Because the text I am working with is kind of a mixture (even though I would argumentatively say it is more angular than distributive), you might not notice much of a difference between the two.

figure | 13-4

With the keyframes set up, select Shape in the tweening drop-down menu to set up a shape tween.

TRY THIS

Now that you understand how to set up basic shape tweens, try your hand at some text of your own choosing. You could use your name or really any text you want. Be creative with your choice of size and font in this exercise.

Limitations

As I have already mentioned, shape tweens do have some limitations—the most significant being the amount of computer processing required to render them. Because shape tweens are designed to work on stage objects, if you apply a shape tween to a really complex graphical element the computer can slow down to a severe crawl.

Notwithstanding, you must also realize that people who view your animation may have a machine that is less capable than what you've got. This is why I said earlier that shape tweens are best on simple to modest graphical elements. As Flash morphs the objects in real time, it requires some serious processing behind the scenes—not only as it relates to the main processor in your machine but to the video card processing and throughput. As you think about using shape tweens, just keep this in the back of your mind and design around it.

SHAPE HINTS

If you mess around with shape tweens at all, more than likely your results may need a little tweaking. Seldom can you slap two opposing keyframes down, apply a shape tween on it, and be happy with it. I don't know about you but I always like to tweak things to my liking—and that is just what shape hints are all about.

Shape hints in Flash allow you to put some controls on top of a shape tween. In essence, they are control points that allow you to define a point in the start of the tween and then the point in the end of the tween, which forces Flash to morph the two points exactly in the tween. Let's do a quick example so you can see what I mean.

To show this example, I will work with a basic example of a circle morphing to a star. I want the circle to kind of spin into the shape of the star. Right now, the circle just kind of shrinks to the star. This provides a perfect opportunity to use Shape Hints to get what I want.

figure | 13-5

When Add Shape Hint is selected, the small circle with the letter is inserted into the movie.

With the shape tween already set up, I can start adding control points to the animation. To add a shape hint, I select in frame 1 in the timeline and select Modify | Shape | *Add Shape hint*. This adds a small circle with a letter *a* in it to the stage, as shown in figure 13-5. To use the shape hint I position the point in frame 1. One thing to note is that the user will not see the shape hints when the movie is played back.

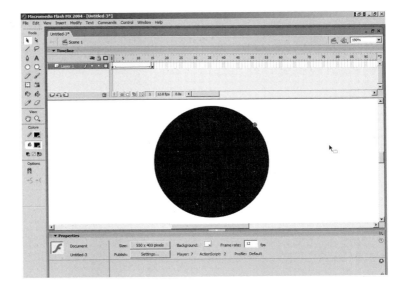

With the shape hint defined in frame 1, I need to access the last frame of the tween and set the point. Once I do this, the point will change to green in the last frame and yellow in the first frame. Now I can add several more shape hints, setting them to the location I want in the first and last frames, as shown in figure 13-6.

Frame 1   Frame 15

figure | 13-6

Addition of all the shape hints to do the morph as desired.

One of the things to note about shape hints is the fact that you are limited in the number you can use; that is, essentially you have 26 shape hints that can be used in any shape tween (because they are alphabetically ordered). However, you will find that seldom (if ever) will you go beyond a maximum of 15 hints (if you do, you may want to reevaluate what you are creating, because it may be too complex).

> ## TRY THIS
>
> Now that you understand what shape hints are and how they work, try using them in a shape tween to control your animation.

SUMMARY

In this chapter you have taken a quick look at shape tweens. Again, you will more than likely use frame-by-frame or motion tweening much more than you will shape tweens. But you should realize that there are times that shape tweens can be used where the other techniques don't apply. The thing to keep in mind is that shape tweens work best on simple things. When you start trying to morph really complex objects, it really starts to fall apart. Also, just as motion tweens are limited to overlay objects, shape tweens are limited to stage objects.

in review

1. What is a shape tween? What does it allow you to do?

2. What is the difference between the Angular and Distributive settings for shape tweens?

3. When might you use a shape tween? Can you think of a creative example where a shape tween might be used?

4. What are the limitations of shape tweens?

5. What is easing?

6. What are shape hints?

7. How many shape hints can you use in your animation?

↗ EXPLORING ON YOUR OWN

1. Try to think of a specific example where a shape tween would be useful. Plan out the animation and put Flash to work to make it happen.

2. Scour the Web and see if you can find at least two examples where shape tweens have likely been used.

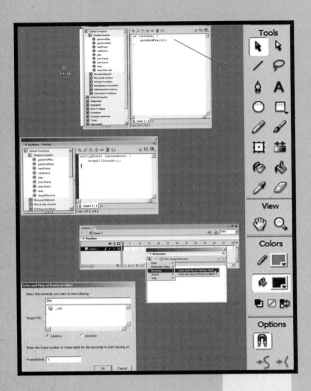

| actionscript, behaviors, and interactivity |

charting your course

Since version 5 of Flash, the scripting capabilities in Flash have been improving consistently from version to version. Along with this, so too has the complexity of ActionScript increased—the name of Flash's scripting language.

It is highly unlikely that any book could provide you everything you need to know about ActionScript in a single volume. If you are like most people, you will have to gather many different books on ActionScripting in Flash if you really want to be an "expert Flash coder." There are numerous web sites, as well, that can be used to supplement your learning.

Quite frankly, there is simply too much you can do to be able to cram all there is to know about ActionScript into one book, or into one chapter for that matter. Thus, my approach in this chapter will be to provide an overview for you—a survey of sorts that will at least make you aware of what is possible. To get really serious with ActionScript, you'll need to do further study for sure, but what I intend in this chapter is to cover the most important points that will get you started.

 goals

In this chapter you will:

- Learn the generalities of setting up ActionScript code and where you place it in movies
- Find out about the Actions panel and how to use it to add code
- Learn about the movie control actions
- Find out about the browser and network actions
- Discover the movie clip control actions and what they do

AN OVERVIEW OF ACTIONSCRIPT

Being able to create ActionScript code in Flash requires that you know two things: you must know (1) when you want something to occur and (2) what you want the code to do at that point. I don't want to dupe you into thinking that's all there is; indeed there is much in the details of these two things. But if you boil it all down, fundamentally these are the two main issues you have to deal with anytime you want to put some code in Flash that does something. Let's first deal with the issue of "when" concerning these two things.

Events

Everything in Flash is based on events within the environment. For example, when the user clicks a button, that is an event. When the playhead moves from frame to frame, each frame that is encountered is also an event. Thus, whenever you want to use ActionScript, probably the easiest thing to consider is when you want something to occur. If you want something to occur as a result of the user interacting with a button, it means you will attach code to a button (so that the code will respond to the events associated with that button). If you want something to occur at a particular time in a movie, you attach code to a frame (so that the occurrence of the frame causes something to happen).

So, in essence, if you can determine when you want something to occur, you will know where you need to add coding in your movie. This sounds simple, but often this is where newcomers get confused—because there are a lot of places you can actually put code in Flash. But if you boil it down to when you want something to occur, the question of where to put code is a lot simpler to answer.

Coding What You Want to Do

The second part of the coding process—the "what you want to do"—is a little more complex. Quite frankly it is more complex because it is in this part of the coding question that you get into all the nitty-gritty programming stuff—such as methods, properties, conditional and looping statements, and dealing with variables. Granted, if you have some background in some other programming environments all of this stuff will probably make more sense than for someone who has never touched a lick of code. But, regardless of which describes you, don't be discouraged! With time and practice, you can learn. This chapter will get you started, but once done with it, more books will undoubtedly be necessary.

NOTE: In this chapter I am not going to get into all the nitty-gritty details of ActionScript, because Macromedia quite succinctly gives you a lot of information in the Help section of the software. I will refer to this from time to time. Take the time to visit it now to see all the things they include. There is a terminology section you might want to review, as well as background on the language, comparisons of ActionScript to JavaScript, and many other things that will give you much more information than I have provided here. Use these materials to supplement what I provide in this chapter.

Let's continue by looking at some simple things concerning how (and where) you place your scripts into Flash.

THE ACTIONS PANEL

Flash has three objects that can react to events: the frame, the button, and the movie clip. These are the three places you can place scripts in Flash. All three of these objects can respond to two primary types of events: events related to the user (mouse or keyboard) and events associated with frames in the timeline.

Frame and Instance Code

ActionScript is assigned within Flash in two ways, depending on whether you want the code to execute when the movie reaches a certain frame (a frame action) or when the user does something to a button (an instance action), as I have already said. Additionally, movie clips, which are also instance actions, can respond to frame or user events. Thus, you can have frame actions or instance actions.

You assign ActionScript to a frame by clicking on a frame and then entering code for the frame using the Actions panel. When code is assigned to a frame, it will execute when the frame is encountered by the playhead.

NOTE: When you attach code to a frame, a lowercase letter *a* will appear in the nearest left-hand keyframe. If adjacent frames are to have different code attached to them, each frame must be a keyframe.

To assign code to a button or movie clip, click on the symbol on the stage and enter the code in the Actions panel, shown in figure 14-1. Actions attached to instances of symbols on the stage are a property of the instance, not the symbol itself. Thus, various copies of a symbol throughout a movie may have different actions assigned to them (just like various instances can have their own scale, size, and location properties).

figure | 14-1 |

The Actions panel is used to assign ActionScript code to frames and symbol instances.

Actions Toolbox List

Script Pane

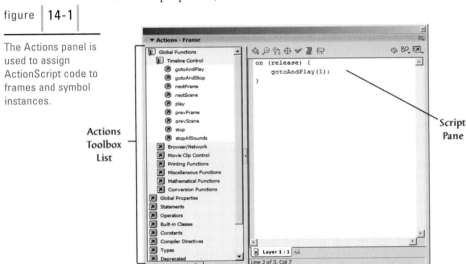

Figure 14-1 shows the Actions panel, with code being assigned to a button. The Actions toolbox list on the left provides access to all available Actions in Flash. The Actions are organized in groupings according to what they do. The grouping names used in the toolbox list are as follows.

● *Global Functions:* Provides access to ActionScript methods that relate to the main movie, movie clips, and buttons. They are arranged in subgroups that include movie control, browser/network, movie clip control, and printing.

● *Global Properties:* Provides access to top-level properties.

- *Statements:* Provides access to command statements such as *if*, *switch*, and *case*.

- *Operators:* Provides access to the global, arithmetic, assignment, bitwise, comparison, and logical operators.

- *Built-in Classes:* Provides access to events, methods, and properties associated with built-in classes.

- *Constants:* Provides access to commonly used values that do not change.

- *Compiler Directives:* Provides access to special commands within ActionScript.

- *Types:* Provides access to specific data-type keywords.

- *Deprecated:* Provides access to ActionScript items that will likely be unavailable in the next version of Flash.

- *Data:* Provides access to the methods and properties associated with data input/output capabilities.

- *Components:* Provides access to special items related to Flash components.

- *Index:* Provides an alphabetical listing of all available ActionScript elements.

Adding an Action

You add ActionScript by selecting either a frame or a symbol instance and then accessing the Actions panel. In the Actions panel, you either double click on an item in the Actions toolbox list on the left (see figure 14-1) or click on an action in the Actions toolbox list and click on the small plus (Add Action) button. To see how a basic action is attached to a button instance, perform the following steps.

1. Open Flash and start a new file.

2. Create a button symbol on the stage.

3. Click on the button and access the Actions panel.

4. In the Actions panel, click on the Global Functions grouping in the Actions toolbox list.

5. Click on the Movie Clip Control grouping.

6. Double click on the *on* item. This adds an *on()* handler to the Code window on the right.

7. Once the *on* handler is added to the Code window, in the Code window you must specify an event in the Code Hint drop-down list. Select Press from the list.

8. Create a blank line beneath the first line of code (*on (release) {*) in the Code window by pressing the Enter key.

9. In the Actions list, click on the Timeline Control grouping (inside the Global Functions grouping).

10. Double click *gotoAndPlay* from the list. This adds the function to the code listing. You will note that Flash needs you to enter one more piece of data in the code listing: the number or label of the frame you wish to go to. Enter a *1* in the parentheses in the code list.

11. Save this file so that you can return to it later.

As you saw a couple of times in this exercise, once you double click on a code item in the Actions toolbox list code is automatically added to the Script pane. Let's examine the following code, which you have added to the Script pane.

```
on (release) {
  gotoAndPlay(1);
}
```

Coding or scripting that responds to an event is called an event handler (or handler, for short) because it has code defined within it that "handles" the event. The handler begins with the event name, such as *on (release)*, as shown in the previous code. The things that are supposed to happen when the event occurs are grouped and appear between the curly brackets. You will also find that the statements between the curly brackets are terminated with semicolons (which are not required unless you have several consecutive statements on a single line).

When you assign an item to a button (such as Play, Stop, or Go To), it is automatically inserted into the event handler *on (someevent)*, where *someevent* is a word such as *release, press,* and so on. This is the event that initiates the handler. All actions assigned to a button must be inserted inside an *on ()* handler. Actions assigned to a movie clip must be inserted into an *onClipEvent (someevent)* handler, where *someevent* again is some word such as *load, enterFrame*, and so on.

One peculiarity to note is that when you insert an action into a frame you will find that no event handler appears. This is because in a frame there is a single assumed event (the occurrence of the frame); that is, there are not multiple frame events, as in other applications. So, the code you enter just kind of "hangs out there," with no event handler wrapping around it. If you are used to coding in other environments, this might seem weird, but that is just how it works in Flash.

Once you have added a single action to a button, you can continue adding more code to the handler; that is, you can have multiple things going on in sequence inside a single handler. To see how this works, perform the following steps.

1. Open the file you were previously working with.

2. Click on the button you had created and open the Actions panel.

3. Click at the end of the *gotoAndPlay(1);* code in the Script pane and press the Enter key to add a blank line beneath it.

4. Find the *StopAllSounds( )* action in the Timeline Control grouping in the Actions toolbox list and double click on it. It is located in the Global Functions | Timeline Control grouping. Note that when you double clicked on the Stop All Sounds action that it was added to the Actions list, as shown in figure 14-2. Once you start adding actions, you can add as many as you want to a single handler.

figure | 14-2

Multiple actions can be assigned within a single handler.

The order in which the actions occur is often important. What if you wanted all sounds to stop before going to another frame? You can easily change the order of actions in the list by continuing with the following steps.

1. Click on the *stopAllSounds()* action.

2. Using Cut and Paste, cut the *stopAllSounds()* and paste it before the *gotoAndPlay()*.

As you can see, the ordering of actions in the list is fluid and can be changed pretty easily. However, what if you want the button to stop the sounds on the down press and to go to another frame when you release? Currently, both actions are assigned to occur upon release of the button. Let's modify the previous example so that it would do this. Continue with the following steps.

3. By manually entering code into the Script pane of the Actions panel, above the current handler enter a new *on()* handler. Set its event to *press*.

4. Cut and paste the *stopAllSounds()* function to the new handler, as shown in figure 14-3. Now the Stop All Sounds will occur upon a press of the mouse, and the *gotoAndPlay(1)* upon release of the mouse.

figure | 14-3

Multiple handlers can be assigned to a single object.

Before moving on, let's acknowledge the button, frame, and movie clip events to which you can respond. As it relates to mouse events (that is, as it relates to the *on()* handler), actions can be set to take place when any one of the following scenarios occurs.

- *Press:* Causes the actions to execute when the mouse button is pressed.

- *Release:* Performs the actions when the mouse button is released inside the object.

- *Release Outside:* Implements the actions when the mouse button is released outside the object. However, the user would have had to begin by clicking on the button.

- *Key Press:* Performs the actions when a particular key is pressed. To use the field, click the mouse in the field and press the key to which you want to respond. Note that not all keys or key combinations can be used. This option is generally limited to alphanumeric keys.

- *Roll Over:* Carries out the actions when the user rolls into or within the boundaries of the object.

- *Roll Out:* Executes the actions when the user rolls off the boundary of the object.

- *Drag Over:* Performs the actions only when the user drags across the object. This is generally used for an object such as a slider or scroll bar.

- *Drag Out:* Runs the actions only when the user drags outside the boundaries of the object.

Frame Events

If you decide you want an action to execute based on a specific point in time within a movie, attach your actions to a frame. As mentioned previously, you click in a frame and use the Actions panel to assign actions to frames, which is very similar to clicking a button and adding it directly to the button. The only major difference between assigning actions to frames and objects is that the *on()* event handler cannot be used in frames. To have a movie stop at a specific frame, perform the following steps.

1. Click on a frame and access the Actions panel.

2. In the Actions toolbox list, click on the Global Functions group and then on the Timeline Control group.

3. Double click on the *stop()* action to add it to the Script pane.

The results of the *stop();* action cause the movie to stop at the frame in which the action exists. Note in figure 14-4 that the "enterFrame" handler is assumed, but is not shown; no *on()* handler is present and no curly brackets are used.

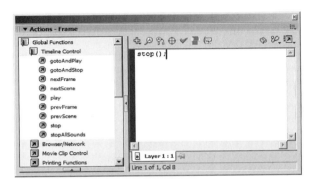

figure | 14-4 |

When actions are assigned to frames, there is no *on()* handler, nor are there curly brackets.

Movie Clip Events

Movie clip events allow you to attach ActionScript code to movie clip instances. To attach an action to a movie clip instance, perform the following steps.

1. Start a new Flash movie and create a movie clip symbol.

2. Click on the movie clip instance on the stage and access the Actions panel.

3. In the Actions panel, select Global Functions | Movie Clip Control from the Toolbox list.

4. Insert the *onClipEvent* handler (select the *mouseDown* event in the Code Hint drop-down that appears).

5. Insert a *stopAllSounds* function inside the *onClipEvent* handler.

If you followed along, the Actions panel should look as it does in figure 14-5. Note that the event handler name for a movie clip is *onClipEvent()*.

figure | 14-5

Actions can also be assigned to movie clip instances.

When you attach actions to movie clips, you can have the actions respond to the following events.

● *load:* Causes the actions to execute when the movie clip is loaded and appears on the stage.

● *enterFrame:* Causes the actions to execute after the keyframe is played; that is, the keyframe in which the movie clip resides.

● *unload:* Actions associated with this event are initiated in the first keyframe following the frame in which the movie clip was removed from the timeline.

● *mouseDown:* Initiates the actions when the left mouse button is pressed.

● *mouseUp:* Initiates the actions when the left mouse button is released.

● *mouseMove:* Initiates the actions whenever the mouse is moved.

● *keyDown:* Actions in movie clips linked to this event execute when a key is pressed.

● *keyUp:* Actions attached to movie clips linked to this event execute when a key is released.

● *data:* Initiates actions whenever data is received into a movie clip via *loadVariables()* or *loadMovie()*.

BEHAVIORS

In the previous section, you examined the rudiments of adding ActionScripting to your files. However, in Flash MX 2004, Macromedia has added some automation to basic scripting through something called behaviors. This is very similar to behaviors in Dreamweaver and Director. They are designed to make the environment easier to use for those who do not know how to (or don't want to) write code.

Indeed, the positive thing about behaviors is that they minimize coding. The negative thing about behaviors is that by only learning how to use behaviors you miss out on learning to write your own code. Additionally, when all you know is how to use behaviors you can only "code" the things in Flash for which a behavior exists.

Using the Behaviors Panel

In previous exercises you saw how you could add code to buttons, frames, and movie clips. In a similar manner, you can use the Behaviors panel to add code to these entities. If you select a frame and then access the Behaviors panel (shown in figure 14-6), its menu can be used to automatically add the required code to a frame.

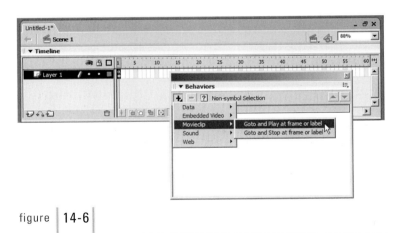

figure | 14-6

The Behaviors panel allows you to easily add certain code snippets.

Once you select a behavior, you are presented with a dialog box asking you for more information. In the dialog box you define the object you want to apply the code to, as well as any other information required by the particular behavior. The behavior added in figure 14-6 was a Go To Frame behavior. Thus, the dialog box in figure 14-7 also asks for a frame label or number. These "extra pieces of information" are actually the arguments for the ActionScript functions that underlie the behavior (behaviors are built upon ActionScript functionality). Recall that when you manually entered the code for a *gotoAndPlay* action in an earlier exercise you had to enter the "place to go" (you entered *1*). This is called an argument.

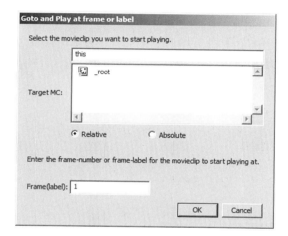

figure | 14-7 |

Once you select a behavior, Flash will ask you for the target object for the code and other specific pieces of information.

ACTIONSCRIPT SYNTAX ISSUES

When dealing with any language, whether it is a spoken language or a programming language, there are rules you must follow for communication. When dealing with Flash, there are four things you need to pay attention to in regard to syntax.

- Structural details such as brackets and semicolons
- Case sensitivity issues
- Comments and what they are for
- Dot syntax

Brackets and Semicolons

One of the first things you probably noticed earlier is that curly brackets ({}) are used in ActionScript coding. There is really nothing mysterious about these characters, and indeed JavaScript, Java, and many other languages use them. They are used to denote logical blocks of code that function as a single unit.

As you write ActionScript, the location of curly brackets in code is not that important, as long as they enclose (delimit) lines of code that should function together. For example, the three items in code example 14-1 would all be valid and interpreted by Flash the same way. The physical location of curly brackets is not imperative, as long as a pair encloses logical code groupings.

Code Example 14-1: Use of Curly Brackets

```
//Item 1
with (_parent.myclip) {
   gotoAndPlay (1);
   stopAllSounds();
}
//Item 2
with (_parent.myclip)
{
   gotoAndPlay (1);
stopAllSounds();
}
//Item 3
with (_parent.myclip) { gotoAndPlay (1); stopAllSounds();}
```

Another syntax issue you must deal with in Flash is the use of the semicolon (;). Semicolons are not important if you are dealing with the first two methods of writing scripts shown in code example 14-1 (items 1 and 2). Although code example 14-1 shows semicolons following *gotoAndPlay (1);*, you could omit these. However, if you are using the style of notation following item 3 in code example 14-1, semicolons are important because they identify where one method ends and another begins.

Case Sensitivity

A common programming question has to do with case sensitivity. It is always a good idea to be consistent in your capitalization of items, regardless of the rules of a particular language. Most, if not all, ActionScript code words are case sensitive. Properties are the only items that are not case sensitive. Over time you will learn what things need to be capitalized and what don't. If something is not working quite right, use the ActionScript Reference in the Flash software to figure things out.

Comments

A common practice in programming is to include internal documentation in code. Comments allow you to leave notes for yourself or others in your code so that you can remember what something does, or anything else concerning the code you might later forget. Comments entered into code are ignored by the Flash player and do not appear when the user views your movie.

In Flash, single-line comments are identified by double slashes (//) that precede them. Code example 14-1 used comments to identify the sections of code that were highlighted. If you need to include multi-line comments, you use a special set of characters. A slash followed by an asterisk (/*) begins the comment, whereas an asterisk followed by a slash (*/) ends the comment. Code example 14-2 shows an example of a multi-line comment format containing these conventions.

Code Example 14-2: Multi-line Comment Format

```
/* This is an example of a multi-line comment.
All of the items written here are ignored by the
player. */
```

Dealing with Dot Syntax and Targets

One of the most crucial concepts in Flash is knowing how to specifically target and talk and objects. By targeting objects such as buttons or movie clips, you can control them. For example, you could tell a movie clip to play, stop, or a number of other things. A target is simply a straightforward way of specifying the location of an object in the movie hierarchy and what you want to do to or with that object. You define a target in dot syntax.

Many of the general actions in Flash do not require the use of targets. For example, the *getURL()*, *play()*, and *loadMovie()* functions (as well as others) do not require a target, as they are automatically directed to the main movie timeline. Thus, when you want to execute one of them you simply place the action within an event handler, as in the following.

```
on (press) {
  getURL("http://www.purdue.edu/");
}
```

If this code were attached to a button, when the button was clicked a new web page would be loaded into the browser. You could also use the *getURL()* function in a frame.

Targeting Movie Clips and Buttons

One of the interesting things about Flash is the level of control you actually have in the environment. You can control movie clips and buttons, as well as other movies. Let's deal with the former of these, movie clips and buttons.

When you add instances of movie clips or buttons to the stage, you can easily control them with ActionScript coding via targets. The primary thing you must do to be able to "talk to" a movie clip or button is to name it in the Properties panel. If you select a movie clip or button on the stage, you will find that the Properties panel provides a field called Instance Name. If you enter a name for a movie clip or button, you can direct commands to it.

For example, one of the properties of a movie clip instance is *_alpha*, which is the opaqueness of the instance. If you wanted to change the opaqueness of a movie clip instance (named *MC1*) using ActionScript coding, you would use a statement such as the following.

```
MC1._alpha=50
```

PROGRAMMING FUNDAMENTALS

Although this section is devoted to a discussion of programming fundamentals, you have already had some exposure to the general terminology. Again, you can refer to the Macromedia Help file if you forget what some of the terms mean. The sections that follow deal with a few more conceptual issues you should be aware of.

Variables

One of the fundamental concepts associated with any scripting or programming language is that of variables. Variables are nothing more than containers for data. Throughout the life of a program, variables are used to store information such as a user's name, the date, the time, as well as a wide range of other bits of information that need to be tracked.

Variables are dynamic in that the content they hold can change over time. For example, you could use a variable to keep track of a score in a computer game. As the user kills more beasties or solves more problems, the variable keeps track of such information. At the end of the experience, the score can then be retrieved and presented to the user. You could also dynamically display the score as the user progresses through the game. This would be accomplished by creating a text field that shared the variable's name.

Using Variables

In most programming and scripting languages there are many rules associated with the use of variables. The three main concerns in Flash are the variable's name, the scope of the variable, and the type of data contained in the variable. The following acknowledge the critical things to know.

- *Variable names:* All characters in a variable's name must be a letter, number, underscore (_), or dollar sign ($). Thus, you cannot use other symbol characters, such as an asterisk (*) or a slash (/), in a variable's name.

- *Data types:* In many programming languages you must specify the type of data contained in the variable before you can use it. Fortunately in Flash you do not need to worry about multiple types of strings or numerals, or other data contained in a variable. Flash determines this the moment you assign data to a variable.

- *Scope:* Scope refers to the length of time a variable is active or accessible. Local variables are normally active only for a brief period, serving as temporary storage, and are typically used in a function or object script. When the object ceases to exist or the script is finished executing, the variable, too, is removed from memory. Global variables, on the other hand, are usually alive and active during the entire duration of a program, no matter what object initiated them, or when. Flash provides one other type of variable, called a timeline variable. You can define global, timeline, and local variables in Flash. Use the Flash Help menu to learn more about how each is defined.

Operators

At the heart of any code are operators. Depending on the data, and on the results you are trying to obtain, different operators are used.

Thus, there are specific operators that apply to numerical expressions only, and specific operators that apply to string expressions only. Flash provides general, comparison, logical, and bitwise operators. Again, I will refer you to the Flash Help file for detailed specifics on the available operators.

Conditionals

Being able to respond to certain conditions allows you to control the program flow. There two general types of flow control statements: conditionals and loops. In the Actions panel, these two are grouped under Statements | Conditionals/Loops.

In Flash, you can use the *if* or *switch* constructs to react to a specific condition in a program. With the *do...while/while* and *for/for...in* constructs you can create repeating segments. Conditional statements allow you to create sets of actions that may or may not execute, depending on the condition. Loops allow you to create sets of actions that repeat themselves with various settings, which in essence is a means of shortening ActionScript code segments.

TIMELINE CONTROL ACTIONS

Now that the cursory programming concepts are out of the way, let's begin looking at the some specific functions in Flash. There's no way we can deal with everything, but I want to make you aware of some basic code words you can likely figure out and start using right away. The sections that follow examine each grouping, beginning with the Timeline Control actions. The following sections examine the *gotoAndPlay()*, *gotoAndStop()*, *nextFrame()*, *nextScene()*, *play()*, *prevFrame()*, *prevScene()*, *stop()*, and *stopAllSounds()* functions.

gotoAndPlay() and gotoAndStop()

The most basic of the actions in Flash is the *goto* action. This action can be used to jump to frames, labels, or named anchors in the current scene or in another scene. An important note is that the *goto* action, when used alone, is limited to jumping to frames and scenes in the current movie.

To set up a *goto* action, select the action from the Actions toolbox list. The general form for this function is as follows.

```
gotoAndStop(framenumber);
gotoAndStop("framelabel");
```

Note that you can also add a second argument, which causes the playhead to jump to a frame number or label in another scene, as follows.

```
gotoAndStop (framenumber, "scenename", framenumber);
gotoAndStop ("framelabel", "scenename", "framelabel");
```

play() and stop()

The *play()* and *stop()* actions give you the ability to play or stop the movie at will. There may be times when you want to use these facilities for specific reasons in the main timeline. Additionally, you can direct these actions to specific movie clips within your main movie using either of the following forms:

```
path.instance_name.play();
```

or

```
path.instance_name.stop();
```

stopAllSounds()

As its name implies, the *stopAllSounds()* action does just that. As with other actions, you can use the *stopAllSounds()* action in combination with a target or the *with()* statement to turn off specific sounds associated with specific objects. The *stopAllSounds()* action is not a permanent setting; that is, it does not permanently turn off the sound in the movie. It stops only the sound or sounds currently playing. Any sounds initiated later in the movie begin playing normally.

BROWSER/NETWORK ACTIONS

Now that you have examined the basic timeline control actions, let's turn our attention to the browser and network actions. This set of actions is designed to work with external data in the form of URLs, other Flash movies, and data from a variety of sources.

getURL()

The *getURL()* action is probably one of the most frequently used actions. With it, you can load a document specified at a URL into the current browser window that contains the Flash movie. The general form for the *getURL()* function is as follows.

```
getURL(path, target, method);
```

The path argument specified in a *getURL()* can be a relative or absolute URL, as well as a URL in the form of a JavaScript statement or an e-mail statement. An absolute URL is one that contains the entire path and file name of the document to be loaded, such as the following.

```
http://www.tech.purdue.edu/cg/facstaff/jlmohler/
```

Relative URLs, on the other hand, are statements that define a new document based on the placement of the current document on a web server. Most often, specifying relative URLs provides a shorthand method of defining a new document to be loaded. Relative statements entered as the path can include various things, as shown in table 14-1.

Table 14-1: Relative URL Entries for the getURL() Action

URL	Meaning
myfile.html	That *myfile.html* resides in the same directory or folder that contains the currently loaded document.
./myfile.html	That *myfile.html* resides in the parent folder of the folder in which the currently loaded document resides. In other words, *myfile.html* is one step backward in the directory structure.
../../myfile.html	That *myfile.html* resides two steps back in the directory structure.
/mystuff/myfile.html	That *myfile.html* resides in a folder named *mystuff*, which is set up as a relative directory on the server.

In addition to using URLs, you may also specify an e-mail address as something to "get." This allows the Flash movie to open the user's default mail program with a new message to the location specified. To create a mail link in Flash, assign the path to *mailto:* followed by an e-mail address. For example, if an e-mail to *jlmohler@purdue.edu* is desired, the URL would be *mailto: jlmohler@purdue.edu.*

In addition to the path argument, the *getURL()* function allows you to use HTML window naming (the target argument). This argument is used for targeting specific windows, usually when HTML frames are used. For example, if you had a frames page that had a window named Content, using code such as the following you could specifically target the Content window as the window to load the URL into.

```
getURL("http://www.excite.com", "Content");
```

In addition, Flash provides the following four default HTML target names.

- *_self* opens the URL in the current window or frame.

- *_blank* opens the URL in a new browser window in front of the currently open window.

- *_parent* opens the URL in the parent of the current window. For example, in a frames document that contains two frames the main document is the parent of both subframes.

- *_top* opens the URL in the topmost document. This is useful in situations in which a frames document has many subframes or has nested frames.

loadMovie() and unloadMovie()

The *loadMovie()* function allows you to load one movie into another movie. Similar to the layering capability of Cascading Style Sheets (CSS) and Dynamic HTML (DHTML), as well as the "movie in a window" (MIAW) capability of Director, the *loadMovie()* action can display several movies at once, each of which is layered over another and is identified by a level number.

When you use the *loadMovie()* method, the movie doing the loading defines the stage size, background color, and frame rate of all movies. The primary movie is identified as *_level0* in the hierarchy of movies. Subsequent movies loaded by the primary movie using the *loadMovie()* action can be placed on specific layers, such as *_level1*, *_level2*, and so on. As it relates to layering, *_level0* is the background level (or layer), with subsequent level or layer numbers proceeding forward.

If you use the *loadMovie()* and *unloadMovie()* actions, you should design all movies with the same stage size, background color, and frame rate. The primary movie will override settings in movies lower in the hierarchy anyway.

DON'T
GO THERE

If you use multilevel movies, the first instance of the *loadMovie()* action will likely exist in a frame action of the primary movie. Subsequent use of the *loadMovie()* action may be used in either object or frame actions. Loading a movie into a level that already has a movie in it replaces the original movie. For example, if *_level3* has a movie named *zapper* loaded into it, loading a movie named *zapper2* into *_level3* replaces the original movie *zapper*.

After selecting the *loadMovie()* action, you are required to supply a URL argument for the movie, a location for the loaded movie, and parameters for how existing variables are to be passed to the new movie. Thus, *loadMovie()* takes the following general form.

```
loadMovie(url, level, method);
```

Similar to the *getURL()* action, the entered URL may be relative or absolute. However, the entered URL must be representative of the file structure that exists during authoring and that will exist during playback. You may find it easier to test with all of your movies in the same directory, and then modify the URL entries for placement on a server.

Setting up a basic load and unload scenario in Flash is relatively easy, as long as you know the rules. Two of the first questions that should come to mind are "How are the stages of the two movies aligned?" and "What is, and where is, the registration point?"

Stage Attributes and Frame Rate

In general, the main movie, which loads the other movies, is paramount when it comes to several of the settings at playback. The main movie defines the stage size, background color, and frame rate that will be used for all movies. Therefore, when the movies you load have different stage sizes, background colors, or frame rates, the main movie will override these settings.

Concerning registration, the upper left-hand corner becomes the registration point of all movies, even if they are not all the same size. If a movie with a smaller stage size is loaded into a movie with a larger stage size, the upper left-hand corner point in both movies serves as the registration point, and the smaller movie will fit within the larger. If the reverse is true (that is, a larger movie loaded into a smaller movie), the loaded movie will be cropped to the size of the smaller. Thus, it is easiest to design all movies with the same stage size, to avoid registration problems.

loadVariables() and loadVariablesNum()

The *loadVariables();* method allows you to load data from a text file, or from text generated by a technology such as PHP, ASP, or CGI. The data being imported must be URL encoded. The Macromedia Help file can be used as a reference for using these two methods.

fscommand()

As mentioned previously, using the *getURL()* action as a means of calling a JavaScript function (or using any other web technology) is not the preferred method. In general, you can use the *fscommand()* action to send a message to whatever program is hosting or running the Flash Player. Thus, the *fscommand()* action is the action you should use when you want to call a JavaScript or VBScript function from Flash. *fscommand()* is the code equivalent of "FlashScript Command," and it can actually be used to communicate to several things, including the Flash player.

MOVIE CLIP CONTROL

The following sections provide an overview of the movie clip control actions. These include clip duplication, property modification, and draggable clips.

duplicateMovieClip() and removeMovieClip()

The *duplicateMovieClip();* method allows you to make duplicate copies of movie clips on the stage. The *removeMovieClip();* method allows you to remove copied clips. These methods are particularly useful for, among other uses, drag-and-drop types of games, for which a duplicate copy of an object may be needed. The general form for the *duplicateMovieClip()* function is as follows.

```
duplicateMovieClip(target, name, depth);
```

Within this function, you must define the target movie clip you wish to copy (target), the new name for the copied instance (name), and the depth (level) for the new object.

When a new instance is generated using *duplicateMovieClip()*, the depth of the object becomes important. The simple way of thinking about this is that the copied instance is layered above the original within the parent layer and movie. The instances become part of the parent movie. If the parent movie is unloaded, the instances will also be unloaded. Because the *duplicateMovieClip()* and *removeMovieClip()* methods are based on an instance name, only movie clip symbols may be duplicated.

setProperty()

As you know, properties are the attributes of objects. Objects in your movie, as well as the movie itself, have properties that can be tested and set during playback. The *setProperty()* method expects you to provide the name of the object instance to modify, what property you want to change, and the new value for the property.

Remember that two types of properties exist in Flash: global properties (which apply to the entire movie) and local (or movie clip) properties, which apply to movie clip instances currently on the stage. The following properties are settable.

- *_alpha* allows the transparency (opaqueness) of an object to be changed. The value is entered as a percentage, with 0 being fully transparent and 100 being fully opaque.

- *_focusrect* is a binary value determining whether the focus rectangle of buttons is displayed.

- *_height* is the height of the referenced object in pixels.

- *_name* is the name of the symbol instance on the stage.

- *_quality* is a string value specifying one of the following concerning display quality: LOW, MEDIUM, HIGH, or BEST.

- *_rotation* sets the rotation of a movie clip. The value is entered in degrees.

- *_soundbuftime* determines the size of the buffer used for sound clips.

- *_visible* is a binary value indicating whether the movie clip is visible. A visibility of 0 hides the object, and a visibility of 1 shows the object.

- *_width* is the width of the referenced object in pixels.

- *_x* changes the X position of a movie clip relative to the parent movie or movie clip.

- *_xscale* pertains to the X scaling of a movie clip. A value of 1 indicates no scaling.

- *_y* modifies the Y position of a movie clip relative to the parent movie or movie clip.

- *_yscale* relates to the Y scaling of a movie clip. A value of 1 indicates no scaling.

In addition to the settable properties associated with your movies, there are several properties that can be tested but not set. These properties apply only to the *getProperty();* method and conditional statements such as *if.* They include the following.

- *_currentframe* indicates the current frame of the movie.

- *_droptarget* indicates the target path of an object beneath an object that is being dragged. This permits the developer to determine intersections between two movie clips for such things as drag-and-drop games or exercises.

- *_framesloaded* can be used to determine if a frame has been loaded.

- *_target* identifies the name of a movie clip instance.

- *_totalframes* reveals the total number of frames in the movie.

- *_url* contains the URL location from which the movie was loaded.

- *_xmouse* is the *x* location of the cursor.

- *_ymouse* is the *y* location of the cursor.

startDrag(), stopDrag(), and updateAfterEvent()

The *startDrag()* and *stopDrag()* methods allow you to create entities within your movie that can be manipulated with the mouse. The *startDrag()* method is used to start the drag operation and the *stopDrag()* method is used to cease it. Note that once a drag is initiated it will continue until a *stopDrag()* or another *startdrag()* method is encountered. Note also that two dragging operations cannot occur at the same time. If a drag is initiated while one is already underway, the new drag will override the old. The general form for the startDrag() function is as follows.

```
startDrag(target, lock, l, t, r, b);
```

The *startDrag()* method requires a target object to drag, defined by the target argument. This can be defined using a standard target path or using an expression. The last four arguments allow you to define a constraining rectangle for the object. The coordinates for the rectangle are based on the parent movie's stage coordinates, and can be absolutely or relatively defined. Thus, *l* stands for left, *t* for top, *r* for right, and *b* for bottom.

The *lock* argument determines where the movie clip appears in relation to the user's mouse. If *false* is used for the *lock* argument, the point of the movie clip the mouse was over when clicked is the registration point between the mouse and the movie clip. If *true* is used for the *lock* argument, the center of the movie clip will follow the mouse position.

One of the properties mentioned earlier directly relates to the *startDrag()* and *stopDrag()* methods. The *_droptarget* property is constantly updated while a drag operation is taking place. By checking the *_droptarget* property immediately following a *stopDrag()*, you could determine if the released item intersected another movie clip on the stage. Use the *_droptarget* property to create drag-and-drop games and similar interactive components.

SUMMARY

In this chapter you have taken your first step into understanding the breadth and depth of coding in Flash. Indeed, there is much more that you can learn by scouring and collecting other resources fully devoted to ActionScripting. From this chapter you should be able to at least know what is possible—to some degree—as it relates to coding in Flash.

in review

1. What are the two primary things you need to know to be able code in ActionScript?

2. What are events? What are event handlers?

3. What are the three objects you can attach code to in Flash? When might you choose to use each?

4. How do you go about assigning code to an object in Flash? What tool do you use to do it?

5. What are some examples of events that buttons can respond to?

6. Frames don't have multiple events that they can respond to. Why?

7. What do the curly brackets and semicolons mean in ActionScript?

8. What is dot syntax and what is it used for? Must you worry about case sensitivity in Flash?

9. What are variables? What are conditional statements? What are operators?

10. Name some general things Flash allows you to do with ActionScript functions? For example, what do the timeline control actions do? What do the network and browser actions do? What do the movie clip control actions do? How could you use these in your movies?

↗ EXPLORING ON YOUR OWN

1. Try setting up your own movie using the simple timeline control actions to make the playhead jump to different locations as well as pause and play.

2. Take a look on the Web for resources you can use to further your knowledge in the area of working with ActionScript.

3. Try you hand at creating a prototype interactive interface for a portfolio or other information device.

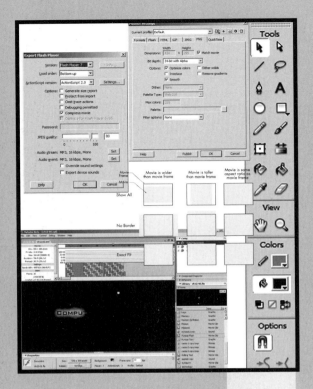

publishing your movies

5

charting your course

Throughout this book you have learned how to do a lot of things. Thus, we come to this final chapter where we will deal with several issues related to publishing your movies. You will find that Flash actually gives you several publishing options, and several tools for testing your movies. Most of the time, you will likely be putting your stuff on the Web—so we will predominantly focus on getting your movies on the Web. However, there may be times when you want your Flash content to run apart from the Web, and so that too will be covered in this chapter. Let's finish up with this important topic.

 goals

In this chapter you will:

- Learn methods for testing your movies in Flash

- Discover the four methods for distributing movies, including how you can specifically develop for each mode of delivery

- Learn to convert an SWF file into an executable file called a projector

- Find out about the Publish feature and how it can be used to automate the integration process

DELIVERING YOUR FLASH FILES

Flash files can be distributed to your audience in one of four ways. Flash files can be distributed as follows.

- An SWF file to be played back in the standalone Flash player, apart from the Web

- An SWF file to be played back in the browser

- A projector file that does not require the Flash player or the Flash application for playback

- A QuickTime file

Using the Flash Player for Delivery

The first method for distributing Flash files is to provide your audience members with web-ready SWF files. These SWF files can be played back on the user's computer either in the standalone Flash player or in the browser's player (as a result of a plug-in or ActiveX component). Thus, one of the assumptions you make when providing SWF files is that the audience has the Flash player in one form or another.

This method of distributing Flash movies is generally used for viewing movies apart from the Web, although the SWF file could very well be integrated into a web page as well. For example, you can show your Flash files to a colleague or friend in the SWF format as long as the user has the Flash player. Conceptually, this is the same idea behind Microsoft's PowerPoint viewer. The viewer allows you to open and play the file, but you cannot edit it.

NOTE: The Flash player for both the PC and Mac platform are located on the software installation CD-ROM and should be installed when you install Flash. Additionally, you can freely distribute the Flash player with your movies, much like the PowerPoint presentation player can be freely distributed with your PowerPoint files.

Creating Projector Files

If you are unsure whether or not your audience has the Flash player (and you don't want to have to worry about it), open a Flash file into the Flash player and create a projector file. This is probably the best technique if you are going to be distributing your movies via CD-ROM or other media and are not sure if the person you are giving it to has the player.

Making an SWF file into a projector converts the file into an executable application that can be run on any computer (of the same platform), regardless of whether the user has the Flash player. When you convert an SWF file to a projector, the Flash player adds the appropriate code to the file so that it can "play itself." The file will increase in size slightly when you convert it to a projector. But again, this method is predominantly used to distribute movies apart from the Web, so you have more flexibility in regard to file size.

Projectors created via the Flash player are not cross-platform capable. Thus, a projector created on the PC cannot be run on a Mac, and vice versa. However, Flash's Publish command will allow you to create projectors for both platforms simultaneously, but you must tell the software that you want it to do this.

Using QuickTime for Delivery

Another means of delivery that can be used on the Web or on CD-ROM media is made possible by QuickTime 4 or higher. If you have QuickTime 4 installed, you can generate QuickTime 4 files from Flash. If you have QuickTime 5 installed, you can generate QuickTime 5 files, and so on. QuickTime is one the most far-reaching software technologies that exists. It is installed on millions of computers and helps cross the great divide between Macs and PCs as it relates to the delivery of multimedia assets.

The latest versions of QuickTime (4 and 5) allow for Flash data to be integrated directly within it. Realize that the QuickTime format is much more than a format for digital video. It includes a wide range of data and support for over 30 file formats, not least of which are Flash movies. Think of QuickTime as more of a general "container." Flash elements can be intermixed with digital video data, virtual reality components (QTVR), and several other types of assets. For more information concerning the specifics of QuickTime 4 or 5, see Apple's web site (*http://www.apple.com*).

Within the application, Flash provides the ability to save directly to Apple's QuickTime 4 or 5 formats. The Publish command allows you to generate QuickTime files quickly and easily while you are also generating the other files required for publishing your Flash files. Although this book does not delve into great detail on the use of QuickTime, it is important that you understand the breadth of QuickTime and how it can help you in your development ventures. Just as Flash SWF files are integrated into web pages, so too can QuickTime movies.

As discussed in Macromedia's literature, all of the interactivity of the Flash file should be retained in the resulting QuickTime file. However, if you decide to use the QuickTime distribution option, make sure you test early and often. Also, it goes without saying that QuickTime versions of Flash files may work better on the Macintosh than on a PC, since that is where QuickTime started.

The Standard Approach: Web Delivery

The final means for distributing your movie, and the most common, is via a web page. To do this, you generate an SWF file and then include a reference to it using HTML code. Although the HTML tags for including Flash files are different and can be complex, the process is similar to creating references to graphic images within a web page. To write the required HTML code, you can use the Publish utility that automates the HTML coding process, or you can write the code by hand, using an ASCII-based text editor. Both of these methods are covered later in this chapter.

Once the HTML code has been written, the referenced SWF file will play directly within the browser, assuming the user has the Flash plug-in. When writing the appropriate HTML, you have several options concerning visual placement, formatting of the Flash elements on the web page, and so on. The HTML attributes and tags associated with this are reviewed later in this chapter.

GETTING AN SWF OUT OF FLASH

Once you have a completed movie and are ready to prepare it for the Web, use the File | Export Movie option to generate a web-ready SWF file. When using this option, you are first required to provide a name for the file. On the PC, the *.swf* extension is automatically applied to the file. On the Mac, you should get in the habit of adding the *.swf* extension to the end of the file. Once the file is named, the Export Flash Player dialog box is presented, as shown in figure 15-1. The optional settings are described in the sections that follow. Once the desired settings are established, click on OK to generate the SWF file.

As shown in figure 15-1, you see several options within the dialog box. Let's examine those that are the most important.

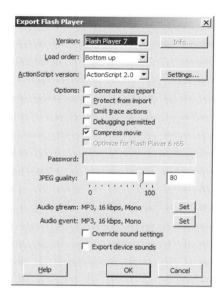

figure | 15-1

The Export Flash Player dialog box presents the optional settings that affect the generated SWF file.

- *Version:* This menu allows you to export movies as older-version Flash files. This feature is particularly useful for exporting Flash movies for use in other programs, such as Director and Authorware. When you select an older version, features supported in newer versions of Flash are disabled.

- *Load Order:* This controls how the content of the file is loaded. Selecting the Bottom Up option will cause layers further down in the layering order (farthest back in the screen order) to be displayed first. The Top Down option does the opposite. Use the Load Order option to set which layers will be rendered first over slower connections.

- *Generate Size Report:* If you select the Generate Size Report option, Flash automatically generates a text file that provides details about the size of each frame and the elements that occur within the movie.

● *Protect from Import:* This controls whether the file is protected or not. When an SWF is protected, it cannot be loaded back into Flash for editing. If this option is left unchecked, the generated SWF can be imported into Flash and made to yield its graphical and structural components (something you don't typically want).

● *Compress Movie:* Flash MX 2004 gives you a choice of whether you want to compress your SWF file content or not. The compression this option refers to is the compression of the vector elements in the file. Compression of raster and sound components is controlled by the JPEG Quality, Audio Stream, and Audio Event options, discussed later in the chapter. Select this option if you are delivering the file over the Web. If you are distributing your movie on a CD or other media (where file size is not as important), deselect this option.

● *Image Compression:* The JPEG Quality slider and field control the amount of JPEG compression applied to bitmap images. If no images are included in the file, the setting has no effect. Lower settings yield smaller file sizes and poorer visual results. Generally, it is best to experiment with various settings to get the best results, because compressibility and data loss with JPEG depends on the similarity of colors in the image.

● *Audio Compression:* The Set buttons can be used to modify the audio compression, even if the sound is stored in the FLA file at a higher sampling rate. This allows for flexibility as you generate SWF files. You can test various rates to compare file size to audio quality.

CONVERTING AN SWF TO A PROJECTOR FILE

Once you have an SWF file, you can quickly and easily convert the file to a projector using the Flash player. To convert the SWF file to a projector, perform the following steps.

1. Open the SWF file into the Flash player.

2. In the Flash player, use the File | Create Projector menu option.

3. Name the file and click on OK. The generated projector (executable application) can now be ported to any computer that has the same operating system for playback.

One thing I should acknowledge about this technique for creating projectors is that you can only create a projector for the platform you are currently working on. Later in this chapter I will mention how you can generate a Mac projector on a PC (and vice versa) using the Publish command.

CROSS-PLATFORM ISSUES

Before we move on, realize that the SWF file format is intended to be platform independent. For example, you should be able to play SWF files generated on the PC in the Macintosh Flash player, with few, if any, problems. Keep in mind that fonts, bitmaps, and sounds should play back and display normally because all of these elements are actually stored within the SWF format. Using "sneaker-net" (floppy disks or other media) as well as the Web, you can port an SWF file to any platform and play it back, as long as a player exists on that platform.

Now, native Flash FLA files are also platform independent. However, fonts assigned on the opposing platform can cause problems (because the fonts don't reside inside the FLA file). Rather, they are a part of the computer's operating system. Thus, the traditional problem of the unavailability of a font on one platform or the other still exists when porting FLA files cross-platform. This is the same problem you have to deal with when doing traditional print publication development.

For example, if you design an FLA file with a particular font on the PC and take the file to a Mac to continue editing, the specific font must also reside on the Mac. If not, Flash will tell you that the font is not available. Consequently, your text will be substituted with some other font of the system's choosing.

However, even if the font used does reside on the other platform, you will likely still have some editing to do. Although a particular Mac and PC font may be the same (even if they visually appear the same at first glance), often the size, kerning, letter spacing, and other type attributes will vary. You will almost always have some editing to do when you go cross-platform, so make sure you budget some time for it. For this reason, it is usually best to do all development on one platform or the other.

Publishing with Flash

The File | Publish command provides a quick means of getting your movies into a web page without having to do HTML coding by hand. With little if any knowledge of HTML code, you can set all of the options required to get your Flash movies up and running visually using Flash. You can also generate a range of other files that may be needed. Let's begin by looking at the settings that control how files are published out of Flash.

Publish Settings

Setting up the parameters for publishing your files is done using the File | Publish Settings command. You determine the media elements you want to generate and the characteristics of those media elements by selecting checkboxes and other controls. Realize that the settings established under File | Publish affect files generated by not only the Publish command but the Export Movie, Test Movie, and Test Scene commands.

Formats Tab

When you select the Publish Settings menu option, the dialog box in figure 15-2 is presented. In the Formats tab, you select the types of files you want to output via Publish. There is a correlation between the tabs shown at the top of the dialog box and the checkboxes you have selected. For example, if QuickTime (MOV) is not checked in the Formats tab, the QuickTime tab does not appear.

figure | 15-2 |

The Formats tab is used to indicate the elements to be published.

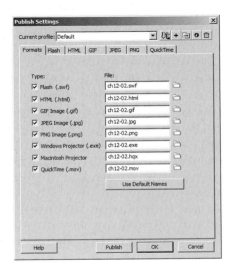

As shown in figure 15-2, note that the name of the media elements shown in the grayed fields to the right of the items is the same as the name of the current FLA file. Additionally, the files are output to the same directory as the currently open FLA file.

You can change the default names by deselecting the *Use default names* button. Then, enter a name for the asset being generated. Just be aware of the names you use so that you do not accidentally overwrite existing files. Remember: even on the Macintosh, use file extensions. If you don't you mistakenly overwrite a file you didn't intend on overwriting.

Flash Tab

The content of the Flash tab, shown in figure 15-3, should look familiar, because it is essentially the same as that shown in the Export Movie dialog box. The settings established in the Publish Settings are used as the defaults for the Export Movie, Test Movie, Test Scene, and Publish commands, as I mentioned earlier. Use the elements displayed in the Flash tab to set the default properties of the generated SWF file.

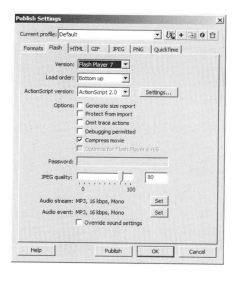

figure | 15-3

The Flash tab resembles the Export Movie dialog box, in which you establish the properties of the exported SWF file.

HTML Tab

The HTML tab, shown in figure 15-4, provides the controls necessary to define how the Flash file will be integrated into an HTML page. The Template drop-down provides several default "template" schemes that can be used to quickly assign the most commonly scripted elements. You can use any of the default templates or create your own.

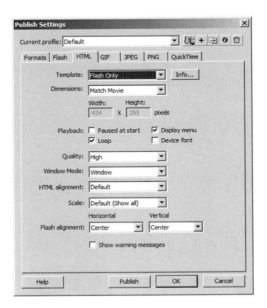

Let's quickly review the important settings in this tab.

- *Dimensions:* This is used to define the width and height of your Flash movie. When pixels are specified in the Dimensions drop-down, the element is inserted at a fixed size. If the browser display is smaller than the fixed size, scrolling will be necessary.

- *Playback:* The Playback checkboxes provide several controls over the movie's playback conditions.

- *Quality:* This setting allows you to modify the visual quality of the movie as it plays back (similar to the View | Preview Mode settings in the Flash application).

- *Window Mode:* One of the common questions asked is "How do you make the background of a Flash movie transparent so that the background color of the web page shows through it?" This is what the Window Mode feature is all about. Window Mode provides the following three options.

— *Window:* This plays the movie "normally" and provides the fastest animation performance.

— *Opaque Windowless:* Allows you to fluidly move elements behind Flash movies (using CSS or other technologies) without the moving objects showing.

— *Transparent Windowless:* Allows the elements behind the Flash movie to show through the blank areas of the movie.

figure | **15-5**

- *HTML Alignment:* This controls the alignment of other elements on the page in relation to the Flash element. Valid options for the Alignment drop-down include LEFT, RIGHT, TOP, and BOTTOM.

If the movie is not the same aspect ratio as the defined HEIGHT and WIDTH parameters (dimensions), a scale setting may be necessary.

- *Scale:* This controls how the Flash movie will fit into the area allotted within the Dimensions drop-down. The default is Show All. Figure 15-5 shows the results of the various settings on a movie that is wide and a movie that is tall.

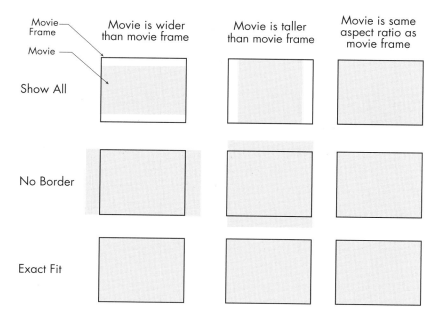

- *Flash Alignment:* These two drop-downs are used in conjunction with the Scale drop-down when percentages are used for the dimensions. Figure 15-6 shows the various results of the

Flash Alignment settings. In the HTML code, the single SALIGN attribute defines the alignment. Thus, if a movie is aligned left and top, the SALIGN attribute is set equal to LT. If the movie is aligned right and top, SALIGN is set equal to RT. The default when no SALIGN attribute is included is center horizontal and center vertical.

figure | 15-6 |

If the movie does not completely fill the defined area, the SALIGN attribute controls the place-ment of the movie.

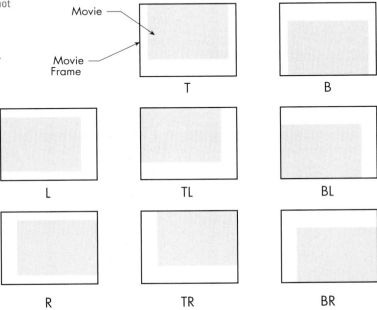

- *Show Warning Messages:* This is used to indicate any problems that may occur when the Publish command is executed.

GIF Tab

As you prepare your movies for web distribution, you always have to consider that there may be users that do not have the Flash plug-in. If so, they will see that ugly broken-link icon in place of your SWF file. For cases when the user cannot view Flash elements, the Publish utility allows you to generate a static GIF, JPEG, or PNG representation of the first frame of your movie, or an animated GIF.

If you selected the GIF image option in the Formats tab, the GIF tab is used to define the properties of the file that will be generat-ed, as shown in figure 15-7. As with the size of the embedded SWF file, you begin by defining the dimensions of the image. You then establish whether you want to use a Static or Animated GIF. If you select Animated, you can control the number of loops it plays by either selecting the Loop Continuously option or by entering a number of repetitions.

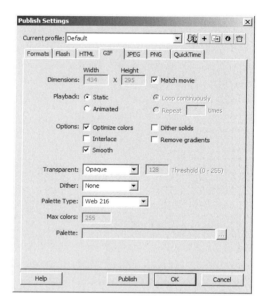

figure | 15-7

The GIF tab is used to define the type of GIF file that will be generated.

Other important options shown in figure 15-7 include the following specifications, which affect how the GIF file is generated, as well as how it is saved.

- *Optimize Colors* attempts to reduce the number of "odd colors" found in the image. By reducing outlier colors via averaging, the colors of the image can be more easily made to fit the 256-color restriction of the GIF file format.

- *Dither Solids* attempts to reduce colors by replacing solid colors with dithered complements as much as possible. This reduces the total number of colors required by the image.

- *Interlace* allows you to specify that the GIF file is written so that it can be progressively viewed during download. Progressive images give the perception that the file downloads from the Web more quickly. Interlacing images neither increases nor decreases file size significantly.

- Much like the Dither Solids checkbox, *Remove Gradients* attempts to replace gradients with dithered combinations of color to reduce the number of colors required by the image.

- *Smooth* antialiases vector elements before creating the GIF file.

- *Transparent* provides the ability to select a color or colors (using Threshold) that will be transparent. Keep in mind that GIF transparency is 1-bit, meaning that a pixel can only be 100-percent transparent or 100-percent opaque. The Transparent option sets the background of the image to 100-percent transparent. The Threshold option allows you to choose a number between 0 and 255. Any color in the image with luminosity falling below the number entered will be assigned as transparent.

- Because GIF files can only contain 256 colors, Flash must reduce the colors in the image. The *Dither* option makes the resulting color reduction less noticeable by dithering adjacent pixels. By default, no dithering occurs. The Ordered option presents a patterned replacement, whereas Diffusion presents a fractal or random replacement. Generally, Diffusion will provide the best results.

- When developing images for the Web, remember that some users may be limited to a 256-color display. When this is the case, the browser uses a default set of colors, called the Web (or browser-safe) palette, to display all images. Any color used by an image that is not in the Web palette is interpolated to the closest available color that is in the palette. This means that colors that do not exist in the palette will not display as you designed them. Use the *Palette Type* option to assign the palette to be used for the 256-color image. The *Web 216* option should be used if you are likely to encounter users browsing at 8 bits (256 colors). The Web 216 option is the palette of browser-safe colors and will force the generated GIF image to use only those colors.

- If you are not limited by your audience's display, you can use the *Adaptive* option, which generates a palette of colors from the colors needed in the image. The Web Snap Adaptive option yields colors that are a mix of those generated by Adaptive and those that exist in the Web (browser-safe) palette. The Custom option allows you to load Photoshop ACT (Swatch) files for use as the image's palette.

JPEG Tab

Within the JPEG tab, shown in figure 15-8, you set the dimensions for the image to be generated, as well as the quality of compression. Higher numbers equate to lower compression, larger file sizes, and more visually pleasing images. Lower numbers equate to higher compression, smaller files, and less pleasing images. The Progressive checkbox can be used to create an interlaced JPEG image. Much like the interlaced GIF, progressive JPEG images appear to download more quickly because they can be instantaneously read even though the entire image has not been downloaded.

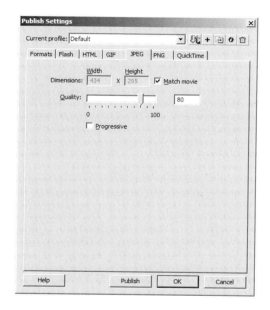

figure 15-8

The JPEG tab is used to define the parameters for the generated JPEG image.

PNG Tab

The Portable Network Graphics (PNG, pronounced "ping") format is a relatively new format to the Web. Developed as a response to developers wanting a patent-free format, it provides most of the capabilities of GIF and JPEG in one format. Again, it does not support multiple images (animation).

The PNG tab, shown in figure 15-9, contains most of the controls found in the GIF and JPEG tabs. The primary difference between PNG and JPEG images is that PNG's compression is a lossless scheme. This means that PNG's compression does not lose data and creates an exact replica of the original file when uncompressed.

figure | 15-9

PNG provides most of the features of GIF and JPEG, except for GIF's multiple image capability.

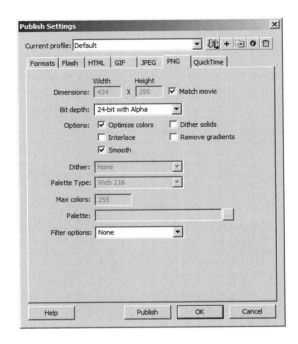

Different, too, are the color capabilities of the PNG format. PNG can contain 24-bit data or 8-bit data. Realistically, GIF is limited to 8-bit (256 colors), whereas JPEG is usually limited to near 24-bit data (16.7 million colors). Thus, PNG can do both, and you will find that the Bit Depth drop-down found in the PNG tab allows you to select either. The color options found at the bottom of the dialog box are enabled only when you select the 8-bit option from the Bit Depth drop-down menu.

QuickTime Tab

As shown in figure 15-10, the QuickTime tab provides control over several aspects of the resulting video clip. As with other tabs, Dimensions specifies the image size for the video clip. The Alpha drop-down permits you to define portions of the Flash movie as transparent. This is useful if you decide to composite generated QuickTime movies in other packages and technologies. The Layer drop-down lets you set the layer on which the SWF information will reside.

Although Flash uses its own compression techniques for audio, the Use QuickTime compression option allows you to choose from any one of the many QuickTime-accessible compressors that may be on your machine. Codecs (short for compressors/decompressors) such as Sorenson, QDesign, or Qualcomm can be chosen. If you are a digital video developer as well, you will find that the ability to use QuickTime's compressors may provide more flexibility and possibly better compression. The remaining checkboxes within the QuickTime tab, as follows, are standard elements you can control.

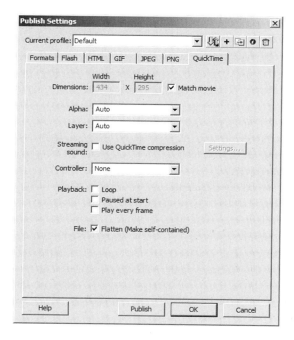

figure | 15-10

The QuickTime tab is used to define the parameters for the generated MOV file.

- Use the Controller drop-down to select the type of control you would like for the movie to display. Options include None (No Controller), Standard, and QTVR.

- Loop and *Paused at start* are self-explanatory.

- Use *Play every frame* to ensure that graphic components of the QuickTime clip are not dropped to attain synchronization.

- The File option allows you to flatten the generated movie. When working on the Macintosh, QuickTime movies can be made to store data outside the QuickTime movie. This increases playback performance. For movies to be cross-platform, however, make sure you use the Flatten checkbox.

USING THE PUBLISH COMMAND

Once you have established the Publish settings, selecting the File | Publish menu option generates the files you have selected, using the options you have set. The generated files will be created in the same directory as the Flash FLA file, with the names defined in the Formats tab of the Publish Settings dialog box. Again, remember that it is vital that you name your files with extensions.

DON'T GO THERE

As soon as you select the Publish menu option from either the File menu or the Publish Settings dialog box, the respective files are generated. There is no prompt asking if you are sure you want to publish. This is true even if a series of files with the same names already exists in the current directory. Be careful you do not over-write files you want to keep.

WRITING HTML

Although this section is not intended to be an extensive HTML indoctrination, knowing enough HTML to be able to integrate a Flash element is pretty straightforward. The two main tags used to integrate Flash movies in HTML are *<EMBED>* and *<OBJECT>*. The difference between these two may not be readily apparent. However, it boils down to what is used to support the Flash element in the browser (as far as software components are concerned) and which browser is being used. The difference between the *<EMBED>* tag and the *<OBJECT>* tag really centers on implementation. Both tags can also be used for media elements other than Flash.

Embed Versus Object

To successfully integrate a Flash movie into a page so that it will work on both Netscape and Internet Explorer requires the use of both the *<EMBED>* and the *<OBJECT>* tag. The *<EMBED>* tag forces the browser to use a plug-in to support the Flash element, whereas the *<OBJECT>* tag forces the browser to use an ActiveX control.

Thus, the *<EMBED>* tag provides the needed information for Netscape, which uses only plug-ins, and the *<OBJECT>* tag provides the necessary information for Internet Explorer, which uses

ActiveX components. Both tags are used simultaneously within one another so that regardless of browser only one of the two linked files is displayed in the page.

To integrate an SWF file into your web page, use the <OBJECT> and <EMBED> tags within the <BODY> section of the web page. Internet Explorer interprets the <OBJECT> information and ignores the <EMBED> information. Netscape ignores the <OBJECT> information and reads the <EMBED> information. Therefore, it does not matter which browser you are using; only one Flash element will be inserted into the browser. Additionally, depending on what is contained within the Flash file, you may use a variety of attributes within the tags, as discussed further in the next section. Code example 15-1 provides a basic implementation.

Code Example 15-1: Use of <EMBED> and <OBJECT> Tags to Integrate Flash Files in HTML

```
<HTML>
 <HEAD>
  <TITLE>A Simple Example</TITLE>
 </HEAD>
 <BODY>
  <CENTER>
  <OBJECT classid="clsid:D27CDB6E-AE6D-11cf-96B8-
444553540000" codebase="http://download.macromedia.com/
pub/shockwave/cabs/flash/swflash.cab#version=7,0,0,0"
WIDTH="250" HEIGHT="300" id="sim_reflection" ALIGN="">
   <PARAM NAME="movie" VALUE="sim_reflection.swf">
   <PARAM NAME="quality" VALUE="high">
   <PARAM NAME="bgcolor" VALUE="#FFFFFF">
<EMBED src="sim_reflection.swf" quality="high"
bgcolor="#FFFFFF" WIDTH="250" HEIGHT="300"
NAME="sim_reflection" ALIGN=""
TYPE="application/x-shockwave-flash"
PLUGINSPAGE="http://www.macromedia.com/go/
getflashplayer"></EMBED>
   </OBJECT>
   <NOEMBED>
    <IMG src="ch9-01.gif" width=250 height=300>
   </NOEMBED>
   </OBJECT>
 </BODY>
</HTML>
```

EMBED Attributes and Object Parameters

The previous section showed a simple implementation of the <OBJECT> and <EMBED> tags for Flash elements. Depending on the features your files use, you may need to add more or less optional parameters for your Flash files. Some of the optional settings apply to a particular browser only. Thus, some apply to <OBJECT> only or to <EMBED> only. Table 15-1 outlines the settings that can be used with both the <OBJECT> and <EMBED> tags. The various parameters and attributes of the <OBJECT> and <EMBED> tags are specified in HTML documents. The required parameters in the table are denoted with an asterisk (*). The remaining settings are optional, but they are frequently included.

Table 15-1: HTML-specified Parameters/Attributes of <OBJECT> and <EMBED> Tags

Function	Description
MOVIE* SRC*	Provides the URL for the Flash movie that is being included. Can include both relative and absolute references.
WIDTH* WIDTH*	Defines the width of the Flash movie window. Can be specified as a fixed pixel size or a percentage.
HEIGHT* HEIGHT*	Defines the height of the Flash movie window. Can be specified as a fixed pixel size or a percentage.
CLASSID*, CODEBASE* PLUGINSPAGE*	Provides the URL and information for acquiring the ActiveX component or plug-in. *CLASSID* is specified as a version number, *CODEBASE* and *PLUGINSPAGE* are defined as URLs.
ID NAME	Specifies a name for the element for scripting. Permits the object to be controlled via scripting.
N/A SWLIVECONNECT	Specifies whether Java should be loaded when the Flash player loads. A *TRUE* setting forces Java to load. *FALSE* prevents Java from loading. This is required for use of FS Commands and JavaScript.
N/A MAYSCRIPT	Identifies that the object may use scripting. *MAYSCRIPT="MAYSCRIPT"* is required to use JavaScript and FS Commands.
PLAY PLAY	Determines whether the movie plays automatically. *True* causes the movie to play after the first frame is loaded. *False* stops the movie at the first frame.
LOOP LOOP	Determines whether movie loops when it reaches the last frame. *True* causes the movie to loop. *False* causes the movie to stop on the last frame.
QUALITY QUALITY	Controls the display quality of the movie during playback. Options include Autohigh, Autolow, High, and Low (described earlier in this chapter). Best is an undocumented value that allows the Flash player to choose the quality based on performance at playback.
BGCOLOR BGCOLOR	Determines the background color of the movie. Note that if this attribute is used it will override the background color assigned in the movie. Six-digit hexadecimal values are entered, two values representing each of the RGB components.

Function	Description
SCALE SCALE	Determines how the movie resizes to fit the space allocated by the browser (area defined by *HEIGHT* and *WIDTH*). Can include *SHOWALL*, *NO BORDER*, and *EXACT FIT* (described earlier in this chapter).
SALIGN SALIGN	When the movie's aspect ratio does not match the area aspect ratio, this controls the placement of the movie within the area. Options include *T, B, L, R, TL, TR, BL*, and *BR* described earlier in this chapter.
BASE BASE	Defines a reference URL/address for relative URLs in a movie (similar to the *BASEREF HTML* attribute). The value is defined as a URL from which all other relative URLs are based.
MENU MENU	Defines what options appear in the context menu when the user right-clicks on a Flash movie in a web page. A value of *TRUE* displays all menu options, and a value of *FALSE* displays the About Flash 3.0 option only.
WMODE N/A	Provides additional features in Internet Explorer 4.0, including positioning, layering, and transparency. Options include *WINDOW, OPAQUE*, and *TRANSPARENT*. Window is the default wherein the movie simply plays in its window. *OPAQUE* allows objects to pass behind the opaque Flash movie. *TRANSPARENT* allows objects to pass behind a Flash movie whose background area is transparent.

STREAMING, TESTING, AND PLAYBACK

As mentioned earlier, Flash SWF files are a streaming file format. This means that the playback of files can begin before the file is completely downloaded. In reality, for the Flash player to play any frame all of the elements used in that frame (including vector shapes, bitmaps, and event sounds) must be downloaded.

Keep in mind that streaming is always limited by the slowest connection through which the downloaded data must travel. Often, the slowest connection is the user's computer. Network traffic or other variables can also affect this "link." Nevertheless, the speed of the end user's connection is what often dictates what is reasonably deliverable.

Thus, it is vitally important to closely examine the content of your movies to make sure that the end user sees what you see. Flash provides a couple of tools that make examining movies much easier, which are described in material to follow.

The perceived effectiveness of Flash's streaming capability during playback depends solely on the amount of data required to render each frame. For smooth playback, the size of the data for each frame should be as small as possible. This is performed through analysis and optimization.

Additionally, the amount of time required to download a series of frames should take no longer than the amount of time required for playing those frames. When it takes longer to download a series of frames than to play it back, noticeable pauses or gaps may appear to the user, and likely where you do not want them to occur. The goal in analysis and optimization is to reduce any lapses, or at least to control when those lapses occur.

Before you can control or prevent pauses in your presentation, first figure out where they might occur. The next two sections provide a look at the facilities within Flash that allow you to identify potential problems related to downloading and playback.

Flash Size Reports

One of the two most import features for creating efficient and effective movies is the Size Report option. When you export an SWF file from Flash, you have the option of generating an ASCII text file that provides valuable information about the file. Use Size Report to help you figure out where the bandwidth-intensive portions of your file are, as well as information concerning where some "fat" could be trimmed away.

Using the Size Report feature, you can easily troubleshoot and optimize your movies. By providing detailed information about your movie's media elements you can visually determine the trouble spots and attempt to deliver quality appropriate for the given circumstance.

Bandwidth Profiling

The Bandwidth profiler is the second tool that is quite valuable when you are preparing, testing, and optimizing your movies. A component of the Test Movie command, the Bandwidth profiler shows a graphic of the amount of data required for the movie over time, as shown in figure 15-11. To turn on the Bandwidth profiler, select Control | Test Movie to start the movie in test mode. Then select View | Bandwidth Profiler to view the profiler.

The most powerful feature of the Bandwidth profiler is the View | Simulate Download option. This option provides a means of getting a more accurate simulation of performance over the Web, because it takes into account the downloading of the file.

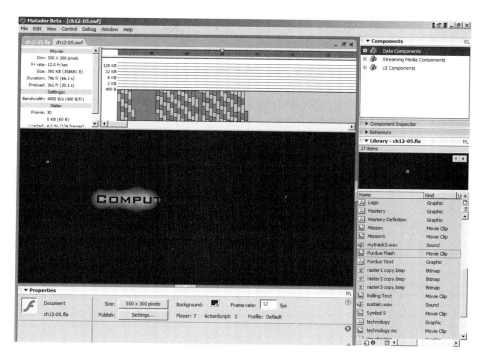

figure | 15-11 |

The Bandwidth profiler shows a chart representing the amount of data within each frame.

To use the View I Simulate Download option, select a data rate in the View I Download Settings submenu. Select Control I Rewind and then View I Simulate Download (or Ctrl + Enter) instead of Play. The file will begin to play automatically once enough of the file has been downloaded, which is represented by the green bar.

The Simulate Download option, when selected, reveals a green bar at the top of the timeline in the Bandwidth profiler. The bar represents how much data has been downloaded over time, using the connection setting in the View I Download Settings submenu. Once enough of the file has been downloaded to start playback, the playhead begins to play the file while the green bar continues to move. If the playhead reaches the end of the green bar, you know for sure that there will be problems (a pause in the presentation) when the user views it over the Web. This is probably the most effective means of testing, aside from uploading the files to a live server for testing.

OPTIMIZING YOUR FILES

A portion of this chapter has been devoted to finding problems in your movies. Features such as the Bandwidth profiler and Size Report are used to locate areas where optimization may be necessary (there are almost always places where you can trim fat out of your files). Nevertheless, you can do other things to optimize your files and reduce the data needed to play back your presentation.

In general, the heftiest items in your files will be bitmap images and sound files. Note that as you are constructing the vector elements in your file there are several additional things you can do to help reduce the overall file size. Although optimization of bitmaps and sound files will show the most dramatic effects on file size, optimizing even the vector elements is prudent. When dealing with web delivery, every little "bit" counts (no pun intended).

It is really never too early to start using the Test Movie, Bandwidth Profiler, and Size Report features. Often, most problem areas in a movie can be addressed much easier if they are caught early in the development. It is much more difficult to come back and try to optimize than it is to optimize during the process.

The sections that follow provide some guidelines for maximizing the outcome of optimization. These sections include general tips and tips for bitmaps, audio snippets, vector elements, and video.

General Tips

The following are tips for maximizing the effect of optimization overall.

● *Use shared libraries as much as possible.* Shared libraries can provide a significant file size savings because they allow you to share symbols across multiple files, including sound, bitmap, and font symbols.

● *Do not use or import too many fonts.* If you add a significant number of fonts to your files, you will find that your files grow very quickly.

Tips for Bitmaps

The following are tips for maximizing the effect of optimization regarding bitmap images.

● *First and foremost, use bitmap images sparingly.* The more bitmaps you add to a Flash file, even with JPEG compression, the larger the file size. Use bitmaps only if they are necessary. Use them for effects that cannot be easily achieved using vector components.

● *Import bitmap images at sizes that are as small as possible.* Size your bitmaps to the exact size needed before importing them into Flash, just as you would if you were creating bitmaps for the Web. Do not import more data than you need.

● *Reduce image quality as much as possible.* Unless complete image quality needs to be maintained, use JPEG compression in Flash. Because the JPEG compression algorithm discards a certain amount of data to attain smaller file sizes, JPEG compression should be used unless an exact representation of imported bitmap is needed in the presentation. Try various settings for the JPEG Quality to get the optimum size-to-quality ratio. Lossless should be used only if you must retain the exact visual quality and resolution of an image.

● *Avoid animating bitmaps at all costs.* Like most multimedia authoring programs, bitmap images do not scale or rotate very well because of the real-time processing that must occur on them. Each time you rotate or scale a bitmap in Flash, you can expect some type of slowing in the playback, because the bitmap must be processed and redrawn through each step of the animation.

● *Reduce computation (playback) time by turning off the Smoothing option for an image.* In the Bitmap Properties in the library, you can speed up the rendering of bitmaps to the screen by deselecting the Smoothing checkbox. Although this should not affect file size, it will increase playback speed, depending on the size of the bitmap image.

- *Watch the size report for data spikes that may be a result of bitmap images.* When you use the size report, you will be able to easily see where there are "larger-than-normal" data spikes. Focus on optimizing or reducing the amount of data required in these areas.

Tips for Audio Snippets

The following are tips for maximizing the effect of optimization regarding audio snippets.

- *Use the lowest sampling rate and bit depth required.* As mentioned in Chapter 8, the sampling rate, bit depth, and number of channels (mono versus stereo) can significantly impact the size of an audio clip, which is transferred to the Flash file. As with raster images, test various quality settings to find the optimal ratio of quality to file size.

- *Brevity is the key to efficient and effective sounds.* Even though Flash offers ADPCM and MP3 compression, the longer the clip, the larger the compressed file. Try to loop sounds as much as possible. Looping is often a feasible alternative to a large, long-playing sound clip.

- *Use the Size Report feature to locate spikes caused by sounds.* Event sounds do not play until they are loaded in their entirety. Thus, the size report of a movie often shows spikes before the playing of an event sound. Be cautious of bottlenecking caused by several event sounds (look at frame numbers near the location of keyframes that contain event sounds).

Tips for Vector Elements

The following are tips for maximizing the effect of optimization regarding vector elements.

- *Use symbols exclusively.* Anytime you have a set of repeating elements, even if they are only repeated once, they should be converted to a symbol. Grouped items, even though they act as a single unit, do not share the symbol's reusable nature. Copied groups add size to a file no matter how simple. Symbols should be used as frequently as possible.

● *Use Flash's Modify | Shape | Optimize command.* Imported elements from Adobe Illustrator and other packages can often bring with them much extraneous information that is not really needed. Make sure to at least attempt to use the Optimize feature of Flash on vector elements. Additionally, imported images can often be simplified by reducing the number of lines. Fills imported from other programs also frequently cause problems regarding file size. Inspect all of these options as you are working. Again, it is much easier to optimize an image the moment you import it, rather than waiting until it is animated and the movie is half completed.

● *Avoid using too many complex tweening operations at a time.* Although tweening does not necessarily affect file size, it does affect playback. The more complex tweens you have, particularly motion and shape tweens, the greater chance you will have of significantly slowing playback. Additionally, animating large areas can also be problematic. Be aware of how many effects you are accruing at any given point.

● *Avoid breaking apart large quantities of text or using too many curve modifications.* Breaking text apart converts outline text into individual fill components. When this is done on a large body of text, you may be instantaneously creating several hundred objects. Similarly, the Lines to Fills, Expand Shape, and Soften Edge commands (found in the Modify | Shape submenu) all increase the number of vector elements in your movies. If at all possible, leave text as editable outlines. Be mindful also of the number of curve effects you use. Line and arc components and curve effects can dramatically affect file size.

Tips for Video

The following are tips for working with video.

● *Know your audience's bandwidth.* Video is the largest consumer of bandwidth, much more so than bitmaps and audio. You should pay special attention to the attributes of your video clips and make sure it makes sense to deliver video to your audience. Choose an appropriate frame size and frame rate, based on the bandwidth available to your audience and the content you are trying to deliver.

- *Work with a clean source.* It is imperative that when working with video (or audio) you start with a clean source that has not already been lossy compressed. If you work with a second-rate capture, or content that has already been lossy compressed, you will end up with less than acceptable video in Flash.

- *Keep video clips simple.* Every frame in a video clip costs you something as far as file size is concerned. Do not waste data on complex transitions or lengthy blank pauses. Also keep in mind that the codec used in Flash is an interframe algorithm, meaning that while it will compress high-motion video it excels with clips that do not incorporate a lot of motion.

SUMMARY

This chapter examined the major issues concerning testing, integration, and distribution of your movies. Designing Flash movies is one thing; compiling and preparing them for delivery is another. To be a successful Flash developer you must know how to do both. As you have read, the Publish utility goes a long way toward getting Flash movies on the Web. Indeed, it is an ingenious tool that can do most of the basic coding. Yet, knowing the code is also important.

in review

1. What are the advantages and limitations of using the different methods of distribution?

2. When might you use each of the different distribution methods?

3. How do you create a web-ready SWF file?

4. How do you create a projector file?

5. Are SWF and FLA files platform independent?

6. Do you have to be worried about fonts when dealing with SWF files? With FLA files? Why or why not?

7. What is the difference between Publish and Export Movie?

8. Where do you set the preferences for the Publish feature? Do those settings only apply to the Publish command?

9. What is the size report feature and what can you use it for? What is the Bandwidth profiler and what can it be used for?

10. Name five different ways you can optimize content in your Flash movies.

➜ EXPLORING ON YOUR OWN

1. Try creating an SWF file using Export Movie and then play it back in the standalone Flash player.

2. Create a projector file from an SWF file.

3. Using the Publish feature, create a web page that includes a Flash movie of your choosing. Once you have created it, upload it to the Web and test it to see if it works.

index